BETTER THAN CHOCOLATE

Tasty Morsels of God's Goodness

DEBBY MAYNE & TRISH PERRY

BroadStreet
PUBLISHING

BroadStreet Publishing Group LLC
Racine, Wisconsin, USA
Broadstreetpublishing.com

BETTER THAN CHOCOLATE

© 2015 by Debby Mayne & Trish Perry

ISBN 978-1-4245-5073-9 (hardcover)
ISBN 978-1-4245-5074-6 (e-book)

Scripture quotations marked (NLT) are taken from the Holy Bible, New Living Translation, copyright © 1996, 2004, 2007. Used by permission of Tyndale House Publishers, Inc., Carol Stream, Illinois 60188. All rights reserved. Scripture quotations marked (NIV) are taken from the Holy Bible, New International Version®, NIV®. Copyright © 1973, 1978, 1984, 2011 by Biblica, Inc.™ Used by permission of Zondervan. All rights reserved worldwide. www.zondervan. com. The "NIV" and "New International Version" are trademarks registered in the United States Patent and Trademark Office by Biblica, Inc.™ Scripture quotations marked (NCV) are taken from the New Century Version®. Copyright © 2005 by Thomas Nelson. Used by permission. All rights reserved. Scripture quotations marked (AMP) are taken from the Amplified Bible, Copyright © 1954, 1958, 1962, 1964, 1965, 1987 by The Lockman Foundation. Used by permission. Scripture quotations marked (NASB) are taken from the New American Standard Bible®, Copyright © 1960, 1962, 1963, 1968, 1971, 1972, 1973, 1975, 1977, 1995 by The Lockman Foundation. Used by permission. www.Lockman.org. Scripture quotations marked (NRSV) are taken from the New Revised Standard Version Bible, copyright 1989, Division of Christian Education of the National Council of the Churches of Christ in the United States of America. Used by permission. All rights reserved. Scripture quotations marked (ESV) are from the ESV® Bible (The Holy Bible, English Standard Version®), copyright © 2001 by Crossway, a publishing ministry of Good News Publishers. Used by permission. All rights reserved. Scripture quotations marked (TLB) are taken from The Living Bible copyright © 1971. Used by permission of Tyndale House Publishers, Inc., Carol Stream, Illinois 60188. All rights reserved. Scripture quotations marked (TPT) are taken from The Passion Translation® of the Holy Bible. Copyright © 2014, 2015 by BroadStreet Publishing. All rights reserved.

Design by Chris Garborg | www.garborgdesign.com
Editorial services provided by Vicki Kuyper and Michelle Winger.

Cover and interior art © BigStock / mart_m

Printed in China.

15   16   17   18   19   20   21   7   6   5   4   3   2   1

The Lord is always good
And ready to receive you.
He's so loving that it will amaze you;
So kind that it will astound you!

PSALM 100:5 TPT

INTRODUCTION

Being busy is a way of life for most women, but it's essential to take time and immerse our thoughts in what's really important: God's Word. His message is often the only thing we have to cling to when things get rough.

My comfort in my suffering is this: Your promise preserves my life.
    PSALM 119:50 NIV

And when everything is going well, we need to remember where the blessings originated.

Rejoice in the Lord always. I will say it again: Rejoice!
PHILIPPIANS 4:4 NIV

As you read *Better than Chocolate: Tasty Morsels of God's Goodness*, reflect on how each verse relates to you and your life. We all have to deal with the same ups, downs, and everything in between. And like you, we know that the Lord is with us every step of the way, and his goodness never wavers.

Your sisters in Christ,
Debby and Trish

JANUARY

So celebrate the goodness of God!

He shows this kindness to everyone who is his!

Go ahead—shout for joy,

all you upright ones who want to please him!

PSALM 32:11 TPT

A NEW SONG

He put a new song in my mouth, a song of praise to our God. Many will see and fear, and put their trust in the LORD.
PSALM 40:3 ESV

Some of us have what could be considered go-to hymns or songs of praise that we draw on when we have a moment. A tune we can belt out and just love on the Lord! As we start a new year and make goals we want to achieve, a worthy goal would be to decide on at least one song we can draw on that immediately draws us into God's presence. Let it become our official "soundtrack" of thanks and praise for the coming year. It's a wonderful way to honor God and focus on him.

Lord God, I thank you for another year of life. I thank you for my challenges and my blessings. And I thank you for songs of praise made available for me to open my heart and worship you. I give this year to you.

WHAT NEW SONG HAS HE GIVEN YOU LATELY? SING IT WITHOUT HOLDING BACK!

WHERE IT ALL STARTS

The King will reply, "Truly I tell you, whatever you did for one of the least of these brothers and sisters of mine, you did for me."
MATTHEW 25:40 NIV

Some people in our lives are gourmet truffles. Others are the chocolates we choose to leave in the box. For one reason or another, they don't suit our taste. But we're all made in God's image, even those who happen to rub us the wrong way. When it comes to loving those who have hurt us or who we'd simply rather ignore, we may need to get creative in finding ways we can be kind.

We can begin by looking for traces of God's image within them. Even the smallest of gifts we can give—a smile, a compliment, a moment of our time to listen to what they have to say (even if we disagree!)—is not only a gift to them, but to Jesus. If people were chocolates, he'd choose every one in the box.

Lord, it is with your grace that I'm able to do anything, including being kind to others. Lead me to where I need to be and continue to remind me that everything good comes from you.

HAVE YOU EVER HAD A DIFFICULT TIME BEING KIND TO SOMEONE WHO ISN'T A TRUFFLE? BE ENCOURAGED BY GOD'S PLEASURE IN THAT SMALL ACT OF KINDNESS.

IT'S ALL NEW

*I will give you a new heart and put a new spirit in you;
I will remove from you your heart of stone and give you
a heart of flesh.*

EZEKIEL 36:26 NIV

No doubt we've all heard that we are new creations in Christ.
We might look the same physically, but there has been major
overhauling going on otherwise. There is no way to truly
embrace Christ's gift of forgiveness and salvation and not
notice a change of heart. We may not have even known our
hearts were stony before, but with the Holy Spirit's compassion
within us, we see mankind with more kindness.

*Thank you, Lord, for the indwelling of the Holy Spirit. I pray
you will continue to make me a kinder yet stronger Christian
every day. Please guide me and keep me from a hardness of
heart toward those who need you. I am determined to reflect
your love this year.*

HAVE YOU INCLUDED THE LORD IN YOUR GOALS THIS
YEAR? HE WANTS TO BE INVOLVED IN YOUR LIFE.

FREE FROM TROUBLE

The righteous person faces many troubles,
but the LORD comes to the rescue each time.
    PSALM 34:19 NLT

Just because we lead a good life, it doesn't mean it will be free from trouble. Everyone has problems on this earth—even our Savior. He was misunderstood, persecuted and executed. But then came the resurrection, which changed the course of history and our lives along with it.

When we're in the midst of trouble, we need to remember there will be a "resurrection" for us somewhere along the way. God will rescue us from the chaos we find ourselves in, if not in this world, then in the next. Whatever you face today, God is near. He knows what you're facing. And you never have to face it alone. God's rescue operation is underway.

Heavenly Father, thank you for your promise to deliver us. I know that I can take you at your word—that I'll be triumphant over all afflictions on this earth.

HOW ARE YOUR TROUBLES AFFECTING YOUR WALK WITH JESUS? ASK HIM TO DELIVER YOU, AND REST IN THE SHELTER OF HIS EMBRACE.

OUR PURPOSE

We are God's masterpiece. He has created us anew in Christ Jesus, so we can do the good things he planned for us long ago.

EPHESIANS 2:10 NLT

When we embrace Jesus as our Savior, God fashions us anew, freely forgiven for our sins and failings. Even though we did nothing to deserve such grace and acceptance, we do have work to do as his new creations. God has a purpose in mind for each of us. And for the rest of our lives as his children, we strive to determine and complete the work he sets out before us.

Heavenly Father, your amazing love for me could never be fully repaid. But I want to please you forever. Please guide me in recognizing the work you prepared for me to do. Please give me the strength, courage, stamina, and grace to think of you and represent you well in all the work I do.

WITH WHAT WORK HAS GOD BLESSED YOUR LIFE? SHOW HIM HOW THANKFUL YOU ARE BY DOING YOUR VERY BEST.

COMMAND OF THE HEART

"A new commandment I give to you, that you love one another: just as I have loved you, you also are to love one another. By this all people will know that you are my disciples, if you have love for one another."
JOHN 13:34-35 ESV

The Lord has commanded us to love one another, and he has absolutely no exclusions in this decree. When we think about how he loves all of us and provides his goodness, in spite of the fact that we've done nothing to deserve it, we should see ourselves as brothers and sisters in Christ. We are family, tied together by a Father's love.

When other people see us working side-by-side in spite of differences in our personalities, opinions, backgrounds and church theology, it will stand out. That's because this kind of love isn't natural. It's supernatural. With God's help, we can learn to love like him—one unique individual at a time.

Lord, thank you for your love and the reminder that I need to follow your lead in loving others. I pray that I can show love to my neighbors, my coworkers, and others I come into contact with throughout the day.

HOW CAN YOU SHOW LOVE TO OTHERS? REMEMBER HOW MUCH GOD LOVES YOU, AND REFLECT THAT LOVE TO THOSE AROUND YOU.

IN HIS WAY?

Abraham waited patiently, and he received what God had promised.
HEBREWS 6:15 NLT

Most of us have heard the adage about not praying for patience because of the way God may teach it to us. But patience is truly a virtue that will bless our lives abundantly. It doesn't come naturally to us—even Abraham got it wrong— but when we strive to wait on the Lord's will, we can relax in the knowledge that we aren't standing in God's way.

Lord God, only you know my true needs. I want to walk in faith and know the difference between my needs and my desires. Sometimes I struggle to know if a decision feels right because it bears your blessing or because I just want it that much. Please help me to recognize the difference, Lord. Help me to wait on you.

WHAT IS TESTING YOUR PATIENCE TODAY?
GIVE IT TO GOD!

PRIVILEGE OF FRIENDSHIP

When Jesus saw their faith, he said, "Friend, your sins are forgiven."
   LUKE 5:20 NIV

We all need friends—people we can do things with, talk to when we need a listening ear, laugh with during good times, and cry with when bad things happen. The most amazing friend we can have is Jesus. He knows us better than anyone else ever will. He shares our joys and our sadness, always providing celebration or comfort during times of need.

Lord, thank you so much for being my friend. You have been there for me during the good times and the bad. I pray that I am able to share your love with others by being a good friend to them.

WHEN WAS THE LAST TIME YOU TURNED TO A FRIEND FOR COMFORT OR LAUGHTER? KNOW THAT YOU CAN ALWAYS TURN TO GOD IN YOUR TIME OF NEED.

EVERLASTING JOY

Our mouths were filled with laughter,
our tongues with songs of joy.
Then it was said among the nations,
"The Lord has done great things for them."
The Lord has done great things for us,
and we are filled with joy.
      PSALM 126:2-3 NIV

There can be no doubt that laughter is a gift from God. It opens our hearts, it connects us to each other emotionally, and it lifts us up when life is not perfect. The Lord truly has done great things for us, and the enrichment we feel when we are joyful should linger behind everything else we experience.

Lord Jesus, my true joy comes from the knowledge that you chose me, you love me, you forgive me, and you gave your all—your very life—for me. That's how much you love me and how graphically you demonstrated your love. No matter what else life brings me, how can I not feel joy when I consider all of that? Please help me to return to that thought when my circumstances cause me to wander from it.

HOW DOES THE LORD GIVE YOU JOY TODAY? THINK OF ALL THE BLESSINGS HE HAS GIVEN YOU—THAT IS SOMETHING TO SMILE ABOUT.

BRAND-SPANKING NEW

Therefore, if anyone is in Christ, he is a new creation;
old things have passed away; behold, all things have
become new.
    2 CORINTHIANS 5:17 NKJV

All of us have a past, and many of us might not be proud of some of the things we have done. The good news from the Lord is that as soon as we declare our faith in him, he erases our past and gives us a new life. In a way, it's a come-as-you-are party with Jesus as the ultimate host. Even though our past sins are forgiven, and God sees as a new creation, we may still have to live with the earthly consequences of our actions. But they do not define. We're forgiven, once and for all. And we're free to make choices today that prove we're not the same person we were yesterday.

Dear Jesus, thank you for taking me as I am and giving me
a clean slate. I pray for your wisdom and strength to change
what needs to be changed and to keep me immersed in your
holy Word.

HOW HAS GOD CHANGED YOU? DWELL ON THAT TODAY
INSTEAD OF ON THE MISTAKES OF THE PAST.

ALWAYS THERE, LOVING US

For the LORD your God is a merciful God; he will not abandon you or destroy you.

DEUTERONOMY 4:31 NLT

How many of us, deep down inside, harbor the fear that we will lose God's love and protection because of our sins? Logically we *know* the reality of God's promise of eternal life and acceptance as his children. But sometimes, when we've fallen short yet again, we might struggle to believe in our hearts that our sin isn't going to cause him to turn away. We need to remember that thoughts like that do *not* come from our heavenly Father.

Lord God, thank you for your unconditional love. Please help me to remember you offered salvation to me knowing I would continue to sin. When I feel I've let you down, please remind me you will never do the same to me.

CAN YOU EMBRACE THAT HE LOVES YOU TODAY, NO MATTER WHAT?

INSEPARABLE

I am convinced that neither death nor life, neither angels nor demons, neither the present nor the future, nor any powers, neither height nor depth, nor anything else in all creation, will be able to separate us from the love of God that is Christ Jesus our Lord.

ROMANS 8:38-39 NIV

There is absolutely nothing that can separate us from God. He is stronger than any other power in this universe, including all of the angels and demons that vie for our time and attention. People may pull away from us, but Christ is stuck to us faster than melted chocolate on the finest silk. We couldn't get rid of him even if we wanted to.

Our relationship with God is so sweet, we can't help but cling to him with all our might. Even so, if something in this life threatens to try and loosen our grip on him, he will never, ever lose his hold on us.

Lord, I am blessed that you have claimed me as your own. Your love is beyond anything that can be measured in depth or height, and I am eternally grateful. Thank you for never letting me down.

HAVE YOU EVER HAD A FRIEND WHO LET YOU DOWN? HOW DID THAT MAKE YOU FEEL? DO YOU KNOW, WITHOUT A DOUBT, THAT GOD WILL NEVER DISAPPOINT YOU?

GRACEFUL GIVING

God is able to make all grace abound to you,
so that always having all sufficiency in everything,
you may have an abundance for every good deed.
2 CORINTHIANS 9:8 NASB

When we freely give of our time, gifts, and money in service to God, he grants us amazing grace. Sometimes it can be frightening to give of ourselves and our precious resources, but when we hold back, we lose out on so much. We interfere with God's blessings on us, and we miss the joy felt when sharing God's gifts with others. We must fight against the self-love that keeps us from giving as God intends.

Dear God, you bless my life in so many ways. I pray you will keep my mind open to how (and how much) I should give in service to you and your saints. I know you return the blessings abundantly and in ways I don't always recognize. Help me to remember that, always.

ARE YOU COMFORTABLE WITH HOW MUCH OF YOURSELF AND YOUR RESOURCES YOU GIVE TO GOD? GOD DELIGHTS IN YOUR GIFTS!

BLESSED COMPANIONSHIP

The LORD God said, "It is not good for the man to be alone. I will make a helper who is just right for him."
GENESIS 2:18 NLT

God's love is so amazing that he provided a companion and helper for the man he created. He continues to do this by bringing others into our lives—husbands, friends, and even coworkers who need companionship. We are to gratefully accept this gift and feel blessed with the goodness he continues to shower upon us in marriage and in friendship. We weren't created to be alone. Let's reach out to others and be open in allowing them to reach out to us. After all, it's the way we were designed.

Father, thank you for the people you have brought into my life. I pray that I am the best companion and helper that I can possibly be. Allow me to share your love and goodness with the people you have blessed me with.

HOW HAVE YOU BEEN A HELPER AND COMPANION TO YOUR LOVED ONES? SHARE MORE OF GOD'S LOVE WITH THEM TODAY!

THE THIRD PERSON

I will ask the Father and he will give you another Counselor to be with you forever.

JOHN 14:16 NIV

Many people equate the Holy Spirit with one's conscience, and that's understandable when you consider that both trigger our sense of right and wrong. But the Holy Spirit is so much more. The Holy Spirit is a gift reserved only for those who believe in Christ. He is our comforter, our counselor, who strengthens us in weakness, guides us, intercedes for us, and eases our pain and worry.

Heavenly Father, Lord Jesus, and Holy Spirit, I thank you for the overflow of blessings you gave to me when I accepted Jesus as my Lord and Savior. Whenever I feel overwhelmed, lost, or lonely, please remind me of the power, love, and comfort you shower upon me every day. Help me to remember that I am yours and you are mine.

HOW CAN OUR COUNSELOR HELP YOU TODAY?
HE IS ALWAYS READY TO ANSWER WHEN YOU CALL.

VICTORY

Do not gloat over me, my enemies! For though I fall, I will rise again. Though I sit in darkness, the LORD will be my light.
    MICAH 7:8 NLT

Even the best life is filled with difficulty, pain, and sadness. It happens. But those who trust in the Lord have the gift of his light shining through the storm. On your dark days, look for those little rays of God's light shining through. An unexpected call from a friend, the beauty of a flower in bloom, a good cup of coffee (and morsel of chocolate!) enjoyed in a quiet moment, the smile of someone you love…thank God for even the smallest of blessings.

Gratitude is like a ray of sunshine, brightening the path that stretches ahead of you today. Take a moment to say "thanks" and then keep moving forward, one step of faith at a time.

Lord, you are fully aware that I have experienced pain and suffering. But I know that you will always be by my side, providing comfort and assurance of eternal life with you. Without you, there is no hope. With you, the worst enemy can be defeated.

WHAT COMFORT DO YOU TURN TO WHEN YOU FEEL BEATEN DOWN? GOD WANTS TO BE YOUR TRUE SOURCE OF COMFORT.

MIRACLES FOR TODAY

Jesus performed many other signs in the presence of his disciples, which are not recorded in this book. But these are written that you may believe that Jesus is the Messiah, the Son of God, and that by believing you may have life in his name.

JOHN 20:30-31 NIV

Some of us found our belief in Christ because of a miracle in our lives or in the life of someone we love. Jesus's miraculous works didn't stop when he went to the cross. He still lives, and if we pay attention, we'll continue to see his miracles all around us: an unlikely healing, the birth of a child, the salvation of a long-lost soul, or a simple answered prayer. With his miracles, Jesus constantly reminds us that he is among us.

Precious Lord Jesus, I thank you for the miracle of each new day you give. May I never take for granted the miracles you work all around me, and may I marvel at every blessing, as if you were standing right before me, saying, "Look! This is happening because of me. You have life because of me. Believe!"

WHAT MIRACLE HAVE YOU RECENTLY EXPERIENCED? THANK GOD FOR HIS GOODNESS!

COME CLOSER

Come near to God and he will come near to you. Wash your hands, you sinners, and purify your hearts, you double-minded.
JAMES 4:8 NIV

What keeps you from drawing close to God? Sometimes, we tell ourselves we just don't have the time, when the truth is we feel as though we're not good enough to draw near to him. Perhaps we've done something we're ashamed of. Perhaps, we simply feel unworthy of his love. Whatever is keeping us away is a much bigger obstacle to us than it is to God. If we draw close to him—humbly, honestly, daily—he will open our eyes to what we need to change to help make us more like him.

Do we need to apologize? Forgive? Break a bad habit? Mend a relationship? It's our job to act on what we know we should do. But ultimately, it's his job to cleanse and purify us from the inside out. Only he can make our fallen hearts as white as snow.

Lord, thank you for accepting me the way I am, but refusing to allow me to stay that way. Show me what I need to change in my life and give me the strength to act on it.

HOW DO YOU DRAW NEAR TO GOD? IS THERE ANYTHING STANDING IN YOUR WAY? WHAT'S KEEPING YOU FROM MOVING IT OUT OF THE WAY?

SINGING OUR PRAISES

Give to the LORD the glory he deserves! Bring your offering and come into his presence. Worship the LORD in all his holy splendor.

1 CHRONICLES 16:29 NLT

For many believers, "worship" refers to singing God's praises. Singing is an absolute joy for a lot of us, but it's not the only way to praise God. While worshiping God is something we can do silently, privately, or out loud with our church body, the exhortation above is for us to focus on the Lord and his splendor when we worship. Our focus is more important than where or how we worship.

Heavenly Father, the gift of song and the ability to use music to praise you enables many of us to express the passion of our faith in ways we can't otherwise do. Thank you for accepting our worship, however we choose to do it.

WHAT WORSHIP SONG COMES TO MIND FOR YOU TODAY? SING IT BOLDLY! PONDER THE WORDS IN YOUR HEART. HE IS WORTHY OF ALL YOUR PRAISE.

UTTER JOY

"I have told you these things so that you will be filled with my joy. Yes, your joy will overflow!"
JOHN 15:11 NLT

The joy of the Lord is available to all of his followers even during the most difficult times of our lives. We can be suffering from illness, dealing with financial hardships, or worrying about anything that isn't what we want in our lives. True peace comes from knowing Jesus—the deliverer of genuine joy and goodness.

If you're having trouble finding that joy and peace, spend a few quiet moments with God. Ask him to bring to mind all you have to be grateful for today. Thank him for each and every blessing he brings to mind. There's joy in counting our blessings—and drawing close to our Savior.

Heavenly Father, in spite of all the trials I experience in life, you have been faithful to me. Your provisions are greater than anything worldly that may drag me down. I pray that my worries will fade as I turn to you for comfort.

HAVE YOU LOST YOUR JOY IN LIFE? ASK GOD TO HELP YOU FIND IT. HE KNOWS JUST WHERE IT IS.

DISCIPLES OF LIGHT

"You are the light of the world. A city set on a hill cannot be hidden."
MATTHEW 5:14 ESV

During his Sermon on the Mount, Jesus encouraged and exhorted his disciples so they would successfully spread his love and message everywhere. We're not just followers of the Lord, we're also his disciples, whether we realize it or not. Our behaviors teach the people around us. We need to remember to be his light in a world where many people are seeking a way out of the darkness.

Dear God, I love the light you bring into my life. I want to honor your gift by showing that light to everyone who is hurting, or has questions, or who just doesn't know how amazing you are. I seek your help with this every day.

HOW WILL YOU REFLECT GOD'S LIGHT TODAY? BE ENCOURAGED TO SHINE BRIGHTLY FOR HIM!

ALWAYS THERE

What is mankind that you are mindful of them,
human beings that you care for them?
PSALM 8:4 NIV

God is always watching over us, always aware of everything we do, always caring. There is nothing we can do to change that. He is fully aware of every sin we commit, whether physically, emotionally, or in our thoughts. He's also aware of every act of love and sacrifice we do in the shadow of anonymity. Even if we can't fully understand the depth of his love and care, or the reasons behind it all, the Bible assures us over and over again that it is steadfast

Our great God is mindful of our seemingly small lives. Even the goodness of chocolate can't hold a candle to the goodness of a gift like that!

Lord, thank you for being there every minute of every day.
I know that your plan for me is bigger than anything I can
imagine.

HAVE YOU EVER HAD TIMES WHEN YOU WONDERED IF GOD WAS THERE? REST ASSURED THAT HE WAS. HE IS MINDFUL OF YOU.

WORKING FOR HIM

Whatever you do, work at it with all your heart, as working for the Lord, not for men.
   COLOSSIANS 3:23 NIV

We don't all have dream jobs. Sometimes the only way we can get ourselves motivated for the workday is by making note of our next day off! Sometimes we feel underpaid, overworked, and unappreciated. But God loves our work ethic. Whenever the job seems too rough, we need to remember we're serving the Lord. He's the one we're working for.

Dear God, you know how I crave to do my dream job and forego the day job, but I thank you that I even have a job. I pray for those who are struggling to find employment. The work I do, I do for you.

CAN YOU TAKE A MOMENT TO THANK GOD FOR THE WORK HE HAS GIVEN YOU?

WELL MADE

Thank you for making me so wonderfully complex!
Your workmanship is marvelous--how well I know it.
PSALM 139:14 TPT

We are designed by the Master Creator whose work is always good. The Lord sees us as beautiful, regardless of how much makeup we have on, whether we're having a bad hair day, whether we've gained or lost weight, whether we're wearing the latest fashion or a threadbare hand-me-down. The same way an artist loves his creation, proudly showing it off to those around him, God wants to show us off to the world.

One masterpiece can't be compared with another. We each have our own unique beauty, inside and out, which the world would be incomplete without. When you look in the mirror today, try and view yourself as the work of art created by God's own hand. What beauty can you find staring back at you?

Thank you, Lord, for crafting me so well. I pray that I live each day in appreciation of your creation.

HAVE YOU EVER LOOKED IN THE MIRROR AND WISHED YOU COULD CHANGE SOMETHING ABOUT YOURSELF? THANK GOD FOR WHAT YOU SEE INSTEAD!

THE KINDNESS OF STRANGERS

Do not forget to entertain strangers, for by so doing some people have entertained angels without knowing it.
HEBREWS 13:2 NIV

It's amazing to consider that God might actually place angels in our midst to give us help when we need it. We should always bear that in mind when strangers come to our aid or even when they need our help. Where it is safe and possible, we should interact with strangers who may need a blessing or who might be trying to bless us. We never know exactly how God may choose to come to our aid.

Dear Lord, I would consider it an honor if you ever allowed one of your angels to assist me. Whether I meet angels or strangers, please help me to appreciate kindness when it's extended to me and to show that kindness in return.

DO YOU REMEMBER A TIME YOUR HELP MAY HAVE COME FROM AN ANGEL? LOOK AT PEOPLE DIFFERENTLY TODAY. FIND WAYS TO BLESS THEM.

Remember this—a farmer who plants only a few seeds will get a small crop. But the one who plants generously will get a generous crop.
2 CORINTHIANS 9:6 NLT

The Lord makes it clear that we are to be generous, and then he heaps all sorts of blessings on us. In other words, when you give, you are not subtracting from what you have. You're growing a more fruitful crop. Not all of these blessings will come in a form we expect. Some may be spiritual. Others may be relational. We may make a new friend, realize that satisfaction has replaced discontent in our heart, or receive an unexpected gift that fills a desperate need.

You never know what kind of fruit you'll harvest when you plant seeds of generosity. God's fruit of blessing comes in endless varieties.

Lord, thank you for all the wonderful blessings you have provided my family. I pray that I am able to show your love by being generous to others.

HOW HAVE YOU BLESSED OTHERS LATELY? BE ENCOURAGED TO SOW INTO THOSE AROUND YOU.

IMPERFECT VESSELS

*The pot he was shaping from the clay
was marred in his hands;
so the potter formed it into another pot,
shaping it as seemed best to him.*

JEREMIAH 18:4 NIV

At times we might see failure in our lives. But we don't see those moments the way God does. We strive to be the people we think we should be, accomplishing what we think God wants, and sometimes we seem flawed in our efforts. That isn't a problem for God. He has reshaping in mind for us. We simply need to submit ourselves to his remolding. It's all part of becoming the vessels he planned us to be.

Father, I know you want me to work on myself, trying to mirror Jesus and trying to honor the gifts you have given me. When I get it wrong, Lord, please help me to relax into your loving hands and allow you to redirect my efforts and my life.

CAN YOU LOOK BACK ON A TIME GOD REDIRECTED YOU AFTER A FAILURE? DOESN'T IT FEEL GOOD TO KNOW THAT HE DOESN'T THROW YOU AWAY WHEN YOU MESS UP? HE MAKES SOMETHING BEAUTIFUL INSTEAD.

WIN THE PRIZE

I press on to reach the end of the race and receive the heavenly prize for which God, through Christ Jesus, is calling us.
PHILIPPIANS 3:14 NLT

Life is often a challenge, and it's not always easy to press on. It's like the person running a race with a stone in her shoe… or worse. But God calls us to keep going because our prize is living in heaven with him forever. Nothing can be better than that!

Dear heavenly Father, sometimes I complain about how difficult life is, but I know that you have prepared my ultimate prize for continuing on. May I constantly be reminded that living with you forever is my goal.

HAVE YOU EVER HAD CHALLENGES IN LIFE THAT MADE YOU WANT TO DROP TO THE GROUND AND WEEP? HOW DID YOU HANDLE THEM? LET THE ETERNAL PROMISES THAT AWAIT YOU HELP YOU TO PRESS ON!

AN ETERNAL PERSPECTIVE

After you have suffered a little while, the God of all grace, who has called you to his eternal glory in Christ, will himself restore, confirm, strengthen, and establish you.
1 PETER 5:10 ESV

It's difficult to consider enduring long-term suffering as "a little while." Surely Peter is talking in eternal terms! When we're in the midst of a trial, there's only one way we can possibly consider eternity and gain perseverance from that perspective: through God's grace. And there's only one way we can lay ourselves open to God's grace: humility. We need to come to him, and be honest in our neediness.

Heavenly Father, I know you are my protector and my source of all grace. In times of suffering, I humbly kneel before you and ask for strength and steadfastness. I ask for relief from my trials, Lord, because I know you are able to do anything and everything if it is your will. I pray for restoration in your precious name.

DO YOU TURN TO HIM IN TIMES OF TROUBLE? HE HAS GRACE FOR YOUR EVERY NEED, AND HE WILL GIVE YOU STRENGTH THROUGH YOUR SUFFERING.

LOVE IS GRAND

Three things will last forever--faith, hope, and love--and the greatest of these is love.
    1 CORINTHIANS 13:13 NLT

We all know that God is mighty and powerful, but it's important to remember that he is also love. It is through this love that he has admonished our sin and provided shelter and comfort as we come to know him through his Son. As we approach others and give witness of our faith, we need to include the element of love.

First and foremost, God gave his son because he "so loved the world." Every individual we meet is part of that world, someone God loves and wants to draw closer to himself and closer to becoming the person he created him or her to be.

Thank you, God, for loving me enough to send your Son and sacrificing him out of your amazing mercy and grace. I pray that I am able to extend your love to others as I share my faith.

HOW CAN YOU ADD THE ELEMENT OF LOVE TO YOUR WITNESS?

WAKE UP!

As for me, I shall behold your face in righteousness;
when I awake, I shall be satisfied with your likeness.
PSALM 17:15 ESV

The Psalmist was most likely speaking here of his awakening after death. But isn't it a source of joy when we awaken each day to know that the Lord is right there with us? He has given us a new day, and he is ready to bless us and guide us if we will pay attention. The best resource we have for seeking his face is his holy Word. The deeper we delve into the Bible, the better we will "see" him. What motivation!

Dearest Lord, I want to see you. I want to be aware of your presence the moment I awaken each day. I pray that you will bless me with that awareness. Help me to stay motivated to read your Word and draw ever closer to you. I want to truly understand who you are.

DOES THE IDEA OF SEEING GOD EXCITE YOU? SPEND SOME TIME IN HIS PRESENCE TODAY AND THANK HIM FOR THE GIFT OF HIS WORD.

FEBRUARY

You anoint me with the fragrance
of your Holy Spirit;
You give me all I can drink of you
until my heart overflows.
So why would I fear the future?
For I'm being pursued only
by your goodness and unfailing love.

PSALM 23:5-6 TPT

BOUNDLESS LOVE

This is my prayer: that your love may abound more and more in knowledge and depth of insight, so that you may be able to discern what is best and may be pure and blameless for the day of Christ.

PHILIPPIANS 1:9-10 NIV

It's so easy to look at something shiny and assume that it's good. However, the Lord warns us to be discerning in what we embrace. Our time and resources are limited. There are good things, better things, and God's best. When we need to make a decision about how to spend our time, our talents, our resources, or even our heart, let's first ask God for wisdom. If we're unsure of which way to go, it's okay to sit with indecision for a while and wait for God's lead.

If you're still uncertain, make the best decision you can using common sense, the counsel of respected friends, and God's Word as your guide. Once you've made your decision, throw your love and energy into following it. Embrace what you believe to be God's will with open arms.

Dear Lord Jesus, thank you for the deepest love of all through Christ. Allow me the ability to discern and know the difference between your will and my own personal desires that may not be pleasing to you.

HOW DO YOU KNOW THAT SOMETHING IS TRULY GOOD? LOOK AROUND YOU TODAY AND RECOGNIZE THE TRULY GOOD THINGS—THOSE THAT ARE FROM THE LORD.

ETERNAL FLAME

Never be lacking in zeal, but keep your spiritual fervor, serving the Lord.
    ROMANS 12:11 NIV

Nothing reignites our zeal for Christ like meeting a passionate new believer. That fervor and wide-eyed amazement at the gift of Christ—the relationship that has been available all along—is infectious. Sometimes the passage of time leads to our going through the motions of serving the Lord without allowing the flame to truly burn within our hearts.

Lord Jesus, when I consider the joy that filled my heart on that day I recognized you as my Savior, I sometimes wonder how I could ever let that joy diminish in the slightest. Please remind me daily about the unfathomable, awe-inspiring love you set aside just for me. Help me burn with the desire to thank you by living my life as you designed it.

HOW ARE YOU KEEPING YOUR ZEAL FOR THE LORD ALIVE? FEEL THE FIRE LIKE A BRAND-NEW BELIEVER AS YOU SEEK GOD'S DIRECTION IN YOUR DAY.

THE BEST LOVE EVER

The LORD appeared to us in the past, saying:
"I have loved you with an everlasting love;
I have drawn you with unfailing kindness.
    JEREMIAH 31:3 NIV

Have you ever used the term, "falling in love"? That's an interesting way of phrasing a feeling that is supposed to be good and wonderful. Think about it: falling typically involves pain. God's love for us cannot be described as *falling*, because his love is strong, kind, and soothing. Think about the love you've experienced for another person and multiply that by infinity. That's how much God loves you.

Thank you, God, for loving me as much as you do. Although I don't deserve your everlasting love, I am grateful for it.

HAVE YOU EVER THOUGHT ABOUT THE VASTNESS OF GOD'S LOVE? WHAT WORDS WOULD YOU USE TO DESCRIBE IT? HIS LOVE REALLY IS THE BEST LOVE YOU WILL EVER EXPERIENCE.

RELIABLE LOVE

Jesus Christ is the same yesterday and today and forever.

HEBREWS 13:8 NIV

Not only is Jesus the same, regardless of our circumstances, he has always been the same, regardless of his own circumstances. We might struggle to remember he is showering us with his love when life is less than sweet, but we know in our hearts it's true. How often do we consider that he was showering us with his love, even when *his* life here on earth was difficult and rife with sacrifice? His love never faltered then, and it never falters now.

Dearest Lord Jesus, thank you for your consistency in my life. Thank you for the consistency you demonstrated while you walked the earth. Your love is all that matters, and my life would be nothing without you. Please help me to remember on those days when I'm just not feeling loveable or loving that you have me in your heart.

WHERE DO YOU SEE THE LOVE OF JESUS IN YOUR LIFE TODAY? SIT FOR A MOMENT AND ENJOY THE UNCHANGING LOVE OF JESUS.

HEAVENLY DELIGHT

"Those who wish to boast should boast in this alone: that they truly know me and understand that I am the LORD who demonstrates unfailing love and who brings justice and righteousness to the earth, and that I delight in these things."

JEREMIAH 9:24 NLT

God our Creator is delighted with his creation. He loves us as a parent does, and he is happy to celebrate all of our joys and triumphs, especially when we follow in his holy footsteps by taking a stand against evil and injustice. This doesn't mean holding up a sign denouncing others. It means drawing those who are far away from God closer to him by allowing God's love to flow through us into their lives.

A word of welcome, a helping hand, the gift of our time or resources…we're surrounded by opportunities to reach out to others in Jesus' name. When people see Jesus at work in us and through us, there's no room for boasting about our "sacrifice." We know full well we could never love those we struggle to understand or accept on our own. It's God's love at work, not our own.

Dear Lord Jesus, I am grateful to be one of your children. May I stay in your favor and grace for the rest of my life.

HAVE YOU EXPERIENCED THE JOY OF DELIGHTING IN YOUR CHILDREN OR SOMEONE YOU LOVE? KNOW THAT THIS DOESN'T EVEN BEGIN TO COMPARE WITH THE DELIGHT THAT GOD TAKES IN YOU.

WORTHY ADMIRATION

Whatever is true, whatever is noble, whatever is right, whatever is pure, whatever is lovely, whatever is admirable—if anything is excellent or praiseworthy—think about such things.
PHILIPPIANS 4:8 NIV

Military heroes, movie stars, teachers, politicians, religious leaders, musical celebrities, parents, sports figures, children, rebels, friends, survivors—the people we choose to admire may form a wide and varied group. And who we admire says a lot about us and our values. What, exactly, do we admire about the people on our personal list?

Dear Jesus, you are the most admirable person to have ever walked the earth, and no one else will ever earn the admiration you deserve. Please help me to hold in esteem only the personal qualities you want your children to adopt. Help me to demonstrate and truly embrace those qualities myself. I want to be an admirable, inspirational reflection of you.

WHO MERITS YOUR ADMIRATION TODAY? HOPEFULLY, JESUS IS AT THE TOP OF YOUR LIST.

FEELING LOVED

Therefore, as God's chosen people, holy and dearly loved, clothe yourselves with compassion, kindness, humility, gentleness and patience.
COLOSSIANS 3:12 NIV

Many of us enjoy going shopping and getting a new outfit. However, there is one outfit that money can't buy, and it's the one the Lord has called us to wear. Clothing ourselves with compassion, kindness, humility, gentleness, and patience will make us sparkle as we go through our daily lives, reflecting God's goodness.

But we can't just grab these out of our closet and pull them on every morning before we run out the door. These are woven of heavenly fabric, a couture design courtesy of God's Spirit. The more we spend time "working out" with the Lord (reading the Bible, applying what we learn, and connecting with God through prayer), the better they fit and more comfortable they'll be. In time, they'll feel so natural we may forget we have them on. But those we interact with certainly won't.

Heavenly Father, I know that what pleases you cannot be bought at a mall for any price. I pray that I am able to show the compassion, kindness, humility, gentleness, and patience that will shine your light so others can see you in me.

DO YOU EVER FIND IT DIFFICULT TO SHOW ALL OF THE TRAITS LISTED IN THIS VERSE? REST ASSURED THAT WHEN GOD ASKS SOMETHING OF US, HE IS ABLE TO HELP US CARRY IT OUT.

HE'S THE ONE

My daughter, don't be afraid. I will do for you all you ask. All my fellow townsmen know that you are a woman of noble character.
RUTH 3:11 NIV

Some Bible commentators see the story of Ruth—who placed herself in a position of submission and trust before Boaz—as a symbol of how we are to approach Christ. For some of us, that sense of submission and trust was nurtured by Christian mentors who shared their salvation stories and taught us about Christ's love as depicted in the Scriptures. For others, submission and trust didn't come until we exhausted all other means of "salvation" from the confusion and heartbreak of the world. Either way, once we lay at his feet, we know what true salvation is all about.

Dear Jesus, I willingly and passionately accept your love and your gift of salvation. Thank you for the way you showed me the truth and continue to do so. May I help others to see the life you have to offer.

WHO CAN YOU THANK FOR YOUR INTRODUCTION TO JESUS? PRAY TODAY ABOUT WHO YOU CAN BLESS WITH THE STORY OF SALVATION THROUGH JESUS.

FIRST AND LAST LOVE

I have this against you, that you have abandoned the love you had at first.
REVELATION 2:4 ESV

Do you remember the first time you fell in love? Do you recall how excited you felt anytime that "someone special" was near? You'd go out of your way to catch even a glimpse of that person. Do you feel that way about God? Or over time has your relationship come to feel less like love and more like duty? If so, it's time to rekindle the flames.

It's tough spending time with someone you can't see, hear, or touch in the same way you do with others you love. But think back to when you first caught a glimpse of who God was and the depth of his love for you. Start there. Tell God how knowing him has changed your life. Reminisce. Share your heart. The more you realize you miss him, the more you'll long to regain, and re-grow, that "first love."

I love you, Jesus. You have not only shown me the most impactful, selfless love possible, you are the first to ever love me. I pray for the passion and excitement of loving you back.

DO YOU REMEMBER THE FIRST TIME YOU FELL IN LOVE? HOW DOES IT COMPARE TO YOUR LOVE FOR GOD RIGHT NOW?

FREEDOM FROM RESTRICTIONS

God's law was given so that all people could see how sinful they were. But as people sinned more and more, God's wonderful grace became more abundant.
ROMANS 5:20 NLT

Many unbelievers say they don't want to embrace Christ because of all the restrictions of the faith. Far from it! We have so much freedom, especially compared to the Hebrews of Old Testament times who were burdened with many laws. Our freedom should not be treated lightly, not only because infringements lead to negative consequences, but because we represent an awesome God who paid such a great price to give us the freedom we now enjoy.

Dear Lord, thank you for setting me free from the consequences of my sin. I welcome your gentle prodding when I slip off the proper path, and I thank you for your grace that is always abundant.

DO YOU FEEL FREEDOM IN THE SALVATION JESUS HAS GIVEN YOU? TRUST THAT GOD'S GRACE IS ALWAYS ENOUGH FOR YOU.

PERFECT LOVE

Love is patient, love is kind. It does not envy, it does not boast, it is not proud. It does not dishonor others, it is not self-seeking, it is not easily angered, it keeps no record of wrongs.

1 CORINTHIANS 13:4-5 NIV

As believers in Christ, we're called to show our love to others. This verse tells us the way we're supposed to do it. As difficult as it is, God showed us this perfect love and mirroring what he did honors him. As we are kind to others, our hearts and minds should move away from ourselves and focus on the subject of our love. That's the opposite of what the world around us tells us to do. We're told that if someone doesn't meet our needs or make us happy, then we should simply move on. We deserve more!

But love isn't earned. It's a gift. The more we choose to think about what we can give, instead of what we can get, the more Christ-like our love will be. And, believe it or not, the more love we'll experience in our own lives.

Lord, thank you for showing me your perfect love. May I take your example to give others patience, kindness, humility, and honor.

IS SHOWING GOD'S PERFECT LOVE TO OTHERS SOMETHING YOU COULD DO BETTER? THANK JESUS FOR HIS EXAMPLE OF PERFECT LOVE TOWARD YOU.

ALWAYS ATTENTIVE

This is love, that we walk according to His commandments. This is the commandment, just as you have heard from the beginning, that you should walk in it.
  2 JOHN 1:6 NASB

Most of us seek God's will when we face challenges in life. We want to discover which way he wants us to turn. But even when we don't have that kind of motivation, we still need to seek his will. We should still strive for obedience when life is relatively calm. We're wise to pray for the ability to live obediently in love in every way we can. That effort will lead us down the path he chose for us.

Lord, I definitely turn to you first when something troubles me; that comes naturally. But when life feels smooth and I am able to smile about everything in my day, I don't ever want to forget to turn to you. I know I always need you. Thank you for the relatively easy times in life. Thank you that even then you're awaiting my attention. Please help me to remember that.

DO YOU TURN TO GOD IN BOTH GOOD AND TROUBLING TIMES? TURN TO HIM TODAY NO MATTER WHAT IS HAPPENING, AND FEEL HIS SMILE AS YOU DO.

LOVE SERVICE

You, my brothers and sisters were called to be free. But do not use your freedom to indulge the flesh; rather, serve one another humbly in love.

GALATIANS 5:13 NIV

Freedom sounds great. But freedom comes with boundaries. We're free to drive a car. But we have to get a license beforehand and obey traffic laws or that freedom could lead to disaster. The same is true with the freedom that comes with following God. His grace frees us from condemnation when we sin. But instead of using that freedom to sin more (and lean more heavily on his grace), wouldn't it make more sense to love more instead?

One way to love is to serve. With God's help, we're free to serve everyone, even those we may not personally deem "worthy." We're free to serve in any situation, even if there's no promise of receiving anything in return. Let's use the free-will God's given us wisely. How will you exercise your freedom to love and serve today?

Lord, thank you for providing for my needs. I know that everything I have is from you, and you want me to help others with all you have given. May I do this in the spirit of humility and love as you have done for me.

HOW CAN YOU SERVE OTHERS WITHOUT MAKING THEM FEEL INDEBTED TO YOU? IT MIGHT HELP TO REMEMBER HOW JESUS SERVED HIS DISCIPLES—WITH UNCONDITIONAL LOVE.

THEY'RE PLAYING OUR SONG

You are my hiding place; you protect me from trouble.
You surround me with songs of victory.
PSALM 32:7 NLT

Even if we are not in a place of trouble or heartbreak, nothing brings tears to our eyes and warmth to our hearts like songs about how Jesus loves and delivers us. The Bible speaks of songs in heaven, and perhaps we're feeling a hint of heaven when songs about him touch us that way.

Dear Jesus, thank you so much for music and for gifting us with the ability to express a fraction of the joy we feel for having you as our Savior. Please keep songs about you close to my heart and running through my mind all day. It's one of my favorite ways of giving thanks.

WHAT'S YOUR FAVORITE SONG ABOUT HOW HE DELIVERED YOU? KEEP THAT SONG RUNNING THROUGH YOUR HEAD TODAY AND THANK THE LORD FOR HIS DELIVERANCE.

SINCERE LOVE

Love must be sincere. Hate what is evil; cling to what is good. Be devoted to one another in love. Honor one another above yourselves. Never be lacking in zeal, but keep your spiritual fervor, serving the Lord.
ROMANS 12:9-11 NIV

We have been called to show true love as God loves us. He doesn't want us to put on a show of appearing to care, only to go about our business after barely listening to someone else's words or acting as though we care—when we couldn't care less.

When someone speaks to us today, let's look them in the eye and really listen. Let's refuse to spend the time formulating a clever response, mentally planning our grocery list or looking for an escape. When it's our turn to speak, let's choose our words carefully. We don't need to simply fill space with the sound of our own voice. Let's consider every conversation a God-given appointment, an opportunity to sincerely share our love, as well as our words.

Dear Jesus, you have called me to show your love by being sincere in how I love others. I want to continue to be fervent in my faith and in worshiping you.

HAVE YOU EVER EXPERIENCED SOMEONE'S INSINCERE LOVE AND CARING? MAKE IT A POINT TODAY NOT TO DO THE SAME TO SOMEONE ELSE.

AWAITING A STAR

I see him, but not now; I behold him, but not near. A star will come out of Jacob; a scepter will rise out of Israel.
NUMBERS 24:17 NIV

If we ever need a lesson in patience, this verse provides it. The prophecy of a star coming out of Jacob was first fulfilled by King David, nearly 400 years after the verse was written. Then the prophecy was truly fulfilled by Jesus more than a thousand years later. We don't know how long we will have to wait for him to return, but we should live as if he could come back at any moment. We should also live as if every moment is an opportunity to contribute to his kingdom.

Lord Jesus, I eagerly await your return, and I ask that you help me to serve you by example. Please use me every day. Show me opportunities and bless me with the wisdom to act on them for you.

DO YOU LIVE YOUR DAY AS IF HE COULD RETURN AT ANY MOMENT? TAKE THIS OPPORTUNITY TO DO SOMETHING LASTING FOR HIS KINGDOM.

FOREVER KIND OF LOVE

For the LORD is good.
His unfailing love continues forever,
and his faithfulness continues to each generation.
    PSALM 100:5 NLT

Always is a very long time; yet God promises his love will last forever. He loved our ancestors from the past, and he'll love our children and grandchildren just as much. Isn't it reassuring to know that he will always love us? God has such a great capacity to love that it's hard to fathom. But we are assured by his promises that it will always be there. How can I express my thanks to him today for a gift as priceless as this?

I am eternally thankful for your forever kind of love, Lord,
and I pray that my eyes will remain open to your goodness.

HOW DO YOU COMPARE YOUR LOVE FOR YOUR FAMILY TO GOD'S LOVE FOR YOU? TAKE SOME TIME TODAY TO PRAY FOR THOSE YOU LOVE. ASK THE FATHER TO SHOW THEM HIS UNENDING LOVE IN A TANGIBLE WAY TODAY.

FLOWERS AMONG THORNS

I am a rose of Sharon, a lily of the valleys.
Like a lily among thorns
is my darling among the maidens.
SONG OF SONGS 2:1-2 NIV

Song of Songs has a lot of flowery language in it, and these two verses especially so. Solomon's bride is overjoyed and confident of her beauty (signified by the rose) and her purity (signified by the lily) because of the love showered on her by her groom. This is how we should feel in Jesus' love for us. Thanks to him, we are pure and beautiful in God's sight.

Thank you, Jesus, for loving me so much and covering my sins so I can present myself to God, unblemished, beautiful, and pure. Because of you, I can approach God with confidence of his love and acceptance. You have made all the difference in my life here on earth and, more importantly, in my eternal life.

HOW DO YOU FEEL, KNOWING YOU ARE A ROSE AND A LILY? REFLECT ON THE LOVE JESUS HAS FOR YOU AND KNOW HOW BEAUTIFUL YOU ARE TO HIM.

WALKING IN LOVE

Be imitators of God, as beloved children. And walk in love, as Christ loved us and gave himself up for us, a fragrant offering and sacrifice to God.
EPHESIANS 5:1-2 ESV

We humans are great imitators. We like to wear the styles celebrities wear, sprinkle our conversations with the most current catchphrases, pick up the latest "must have" gadget and adapt our mannerisms to those of the crowd we happen to be hanging out with. If imitation truly is the sincerest form of flattery, we are lavishing praise on those around us with what we do and say.

But how closely do we imitate God? He's someone who is actually worthy of our praise—and our imitation. What is one way you can follow in his imitation-worthy footsteps today?

I am grateful, Lord, for the blessing of your goodness and love. I pray that others will see you through me.

IS THERE ANYTHING THAT HOLDS YOU BACK FROM SHOWING GOD'S LOVE TO OTHERS? WHEN YOU KNOW HOW MUCH GOD LOVES YOU, YOU CAN LOVE OTHERS WITHOUT RESTRICTION.

KEEPING HEARTS SOFT

I will give you a new heart and put a new spirit in you; I will remove from you your heart of stone and give you a heart of flesh. And I will put my spirit in you and move you to follow my decrees and be careful to keep my laws.
EZEKIEL 36:26-27 NIV

God promised his people he would soften their hearts, enabling them to absorb and accept his guidance and his will. That acceptance leads to greater understanding and an even greater willingness to follow him, including keeping his laws. It's a cycle we would all do well to follow.

Dear God, please keep my heart soft and open to your will and teaching. If I ever start to stray and let my heart start hardening, please draw me back. I don't ever want to find I'm too stubborn to listen to you. I don't want to miss a thing you have to offer!

DO YOU CONSCIOUSLY SOFTEN YOUR HEART EACH DAY? LOOK AROUND YOU TODAY AND GAIN THE LORD'S HEART FOR THE SITUATIONS AND PEOPLE IN YOUR WORLD.

DEEPEST LOVE

We know how much God loves us, and we have put our trust in his love. God is love, and all who live in love live in God, and God lives in them.

1 JOHN 4:16 NLT

We talk about love a lot when we talk about God. Or, at least, we should. That's because the Bible does exactly the same thing. Our personal experience with love may be different than the love God extends to us. Our love may be based more on emotion, here today and gone tomorrow. But God's love isn't an emotion he feels. It isn't even what he does. Love is who he is. And that love lives in us. What a gift and a responsibility!

God and his love can change our lives, our relationships, our priorities, and our future destiny in almost indescribable ways. That's a love we can trust, no matter what comes our way.

Lord, thank you for loving me so deeply. You have provided a shining example of how you want me to love others.

WHAT DO YOU EXPECT FROM THE DEEPEST KIND OF LOVE? SIT AND ENJOY THE DEPTH OF GOD'S LOVE FOR A MOMENT TODAY.

RADIANCE

When Moses came down from Mount Sinai with the two tablets of the Testimony in his hands, he was not aware that his face was radiant because he had spoken with the LORD.
    EXODUS 34:29 NIV

Is it any wonder that Moses returned from his sacred meeting with God with radiance all over his face? His appearance actually frightened those who saw him it was so out of the ordinary. While we don't want to frighten people, wouldn't it be wonderful if our faces reflected the radiance of God's presence? If nothing else, our behavior and demeanor should radiate his influence. That can happen if we truly open our hearts to him when we pray.

Lord, I want to show the radiance of your love in my everyday life. Please help me focus on you when I pray and absorb the joy and peace you offer all believers. I know there will be no hiding your blessings if I always put you first in my thoughts.

DOES YOUR FACE EVER REFLECT HIS RADIANCE? PUT HIM IN THE FOREFRONT OF YOUR MIND, AND WATCH HIS LOVE SHINE THROUGH YOU TO OTHERS.

FIRST LOVE

We love each other because he loved us first.
    1 JOHN 4:19 NLT

Why do we love others? Because we're attracted to them? Because we're related to them? Because they love us? The Bible tells us it's because God loved us first. He's the one who's shown us what love is all about. Often the love we share with others is a pale reflection of the love God's shared with us. But that's a start!

Consider those you love—or are trying hard to love—as an empty pitcher. Ask God how you can help fill them up to overflowing with his good gifts. Prayer is the perfect start. When you pray for someone you're reaching out to them with love—even if they're halfway around the world. The more you pray for those you love, the more God will open your eyes to their needs, their wounds, their beauty, and their irreplaceable value in this world. And the more deeply your love for them will grow.

Thank you, Lord God, for loving me and for showing me how to love. Help me to increase that love and share it with others so that they may see you.

WHAT DIFFERENT TYPES OF LOVE HAVE YOU HAD IN YOUR LIFE? GOD'S LOVE FOR YOU IS GREATER THAN ANY LOVE ANYONE ELSE CAN OFFER. BELIEVE IN HIS LOVE FOR YOU TODAY.

NOTHING HIDDEN

O LORD, you have searched me and you know me.
PSALM 139:1 NIV

Whether we realize it or not, no matter how comfortable we are with our friends, co-workers, and even our loved ones, we all have thoughts and feelings we keep to ourselves. But they're not kept *totally* to ourselves. God knows more about us than we realize; he knows our fears, our motives, and our true hopes. When we consider this, along with the fact that he accepts us regardless, can we even *try* to fathom his love?

Heavenly Lord, thank you that you have always known what my thoughts and actions would be throughout life, and yet you sent your precious Son to me. Please help me to reflect on the unconditional love and protection you bring to my life every day.

WHAT THOUGHTS OR FEELINGS WILL YOU TURN OVER TO GOD TODAY? RECOGNIZE THAT HE ALREADY KNOWS WHAT YOU ARE THINKING AND FEELING, AND HE STILL DELIGHTS IN HEARING YOU TELL HIM!

FACING THE TRUTH

If anyone acknowledges that Jesus is the Son of God, God lives in them and they in God. And so we know and rely on the love God has for us. God is love. Whoever lives in love lives in God, and God in them.

1 JOHN 4:15-16 NIV

To "acknowledge" means to accept or admit the existence of truth. Have we done that with Jesus? Accepting him means more than inviting him into our lives and asking forgiveness for our sins. It means we accept he's the Son of God, the one who died in our place—our Savior. Do you believe you need saving? Really?

Most of us consider ourselves "pretty good" when it comes to comparing ourselves with the world. We aren't murderers or thieves…or are we? In the Sermon on the Mount, Jesus tells us that our thoughts condemn us as well as our actions. Have we ever wished someone would take a flying leap—so to speak? Have we ever wished what someone else owned belonged to us? Even if we look good on the outside, our hearts reveals how desperately we need a Savior. Let's acknowledge what's true: we need Jesus, just like everyone else.

I love you, Lord—and need you. I pray that I may be comforted by the goodness of your love.

HOW HAVE YOU RELIED ON GOD'S LOVE LATELY? THANK HIM FOR THE GIFT OF BEING ABLE TO LIVE IN THE KNOWLEDGE OF HIS LOVE.

ANYTHING YOU WANT

I will do what you have asked. I will give you a wise and discerning heart, so that there will never have been anyone like you, nor will there ever be.

1 KINGS 3:12 NIV

When Solomon had the chance to request *anything* of God, he asked for wisdom and discernment. God was so pleased, he granted that and all the good things Solomon hadn't requested. That's how much the Lord treasures wisdom and discernment. He wants us to ask for and seek those qualities even today.

Dear God, it can be so simple to lean on my own understanding, which I know can be colored by emotion or the influences around me. I need to come to you first, not last. I know how important a discerning heart can be in living the life you planned for me, and I know the only wisdom that really matters is that which you give me. Please help me start each day seeking your wisdom in all choices and actions. Help me vividly see the difference between right and wrong.

WILL YOU START YOUR DAY BLESSED WITH HIS WISDOM AND DISCERNMENT? HE WILL GLADLY GIVE IT IF YOU ASK!

ENCOURAGEMENT

Christ died for us so that, whether we are dead or alive when he returns, we can live with him forever. So encourage each other and build each other up, just as you are already doing.

1 THESSALONIANS 5:10-11 NLT

Everyone needs encouragement from time to time. It's easy to feel lonely and isolated, particularly when we go through troubling times. In God's goodness, he has provided communities of believers through the church, and he calls us to be there for each other. Sharing our burdens as well as our joys makes life so much easier and sweeter.

Who could use a word of encouragement today in your life? Send an email, make a phone call, or work up the courage to speak encouraging words aloud anytime you feel God's nudge in that direction.

I am grateful for the people you have put in my life, Lord. I pray that I can be an encourager to others so they don't have to carry the load of life alone.

HOW CAN YOU ENCOURAGE SOMEONE TODAY? LOOK FOR WAYS YOU CAN BUILD UP THE COMMUNITY OF BELIEVERS GOD HAS PLACED IN YOUR LIFE.

WELL WORTH THE WAIT

When a woman is giving birth, she has sorrow because her hour has come, but when she has delivered the baby, she no longer remembers the anguish, for joy that a human being has been born into the world.
JOHN 16:21 ESV

Considering how painful childbirth is, it's a wonder women go through it again and again, isn't it? Well, not really. Children are immediately amazing. They are a powerful reward for the months of waiting and discomfort and the hours of pain endured to get them here. If only we saw that with all of God's ultimate blessings. Jesus used today's analogy to give hope to his disciples before he left them. No matter what we encounter in life, when Christ returns, we will have even more joy awaiting us than a mother feels for her children. That's pretty hard to grasp, but it's true.

Precious Jesus, please help me to have the same patience and strength in awaiting the rewards you have planned for me as a mother has for the arrival of her child.

IS THERE SOMETHING GOD IS ASKING YOU TO WAIT FOR? TO SUFFER FOR? BE ENCOURAGED THAT THE REWARD THAT FOLLOWS YOUR OBEDIENCE IS WELL WORTH IT.

TRUE VALUE

"Are not two sparrows sold for a penny? Yet not one of them will fall to the ground outside your Father's care. And even the very hairs of your head are all numbered. So don't be afraid; you are worth more than many sparrows."

MATTHEW 10:29-31 NIV

In this world where we constantly seek to attain more, it's easy to forget our true value. Regardless of our worldly wealth, God values who we truly are without all the trappings of money, big houses, cool cars, and designer clothes. We are his children. Even earthly parents, whose love is imperfect, treasure their children more than anything they own or any accomplishment they achieve—they value them so much they would sacrifice their own lives to save them. A mother wouldn't run into a burning house to save a worthless old toaster. But she would go back to save her child.

The enormity of God's sacrifice reflects the value we hold in his eyes. It reveals a Father's love.

Dear Jesus, thank you for loving me for who I am rather than what I have. There will always be someone richer in worldly wealth, but nothing is richer than faith in you. My true security comes from you and nothing else.

DO YOU KNOW THAT GOD PLACES A HIGH VALUE ON YOUR LIFE? HE DOESN'T CARE HOW MUCH YOU HAVE OR DON'T HAVE. HE JUST WANTS YOU.

MARCH

Lord, it is clear to me now that how we live

will dictate how you deal with us.

Good people will taste your goodness, Lord.

And to those who are loyal to you,

you love to prove that you are loyal and true.

PSALM 18:25 TPT

NOT MY FIGHT

This is what the LORD says: "Do not be afraid! Don't be discouraged by this mighty army, for the battle is not yours, but God's."
2 CHRONICLES 20:15 NLT

We may feel that the battles we face today are minor compared to the actual battles fought during Old Testament days. But they're our battles, nonetheless, and they can cause fear and discouragement. The Lord wants to impress upon us that we should turn our fear and discouragement over to him. No matter how minor our battles seem, they are still his to fight.

Lord, I know my life is full of blessings not experienced during Biblical times, and I thank you for that. I know my struggles are also quite different from those faced by your people many years ago, or even by many of your people today. I want to accept your assurance that my battles—no matter how small by comparison—are your concern. Please help me to feel relief in knowing you have my struggles in hand.

WHAT BATTLE DOES GOD WANT YOU TO TURN OVER TO HIM TODAY? LET HIM TAKE IT AND FIGHT FOR YOU. LET HIM BE YOUR STRENGTH.

SWEETNESS OF GOD'S GOODNESS

*Every good gift and every perfect gift is from above,
and comes down from the Father of lights, with whom
there is no variation or shadow of turning.*
  JAMES 1:17 NKJV

We use the word "good" like we do the word "love."
Without a lot of thought. We say chocolate is "good." Sure,
it tastes good. (To most people!) Yes, it can be good for us.
(If we munch a couple of squares of dark chocolate, instead
of finishing off the whole carton of chocolate-fudge-cookie
dough-crunch ice cream on our own.)

Unlike chocolate, God's goodness has no qualifiers that follow
it. It's good through-and-through, forever and always. From
the first taste to the last, God's goodness is sweet.

*Thank you, Heavenly Father, for all your goodness. You have
blessed me with the sweetness of knowing that I'll have
eternal peace in your kingdom.*

HAVE YOU EVER THOUGHT SOMETHING WAS BAD BUT IT
WOUND UP BEING GOOD IN THE LONG RUN? GOD DOES
NOT CHANGE. HE IS ALWAYS GOOD, AND HE ALWAYS
WANTS WHAT IS BEST FOR YOU.

THE FIRST STEP

Cast your cares on the LORD and he will sustain you;
he will never let the righteous fall.

PSALM 55:22 NIV

Because we all hope to make the best of our lives, sometimes we enthusiastically dive into projects, try to resolve problems, or make major decisions before going to God for guidance. Then, if anything goes awry, we realize we need to seek his help. If we can catch ourselves in that, if we can open each day asking the Lord for his leading in all of the day's events and decisions, we might just avoid going astray in the first place!

Precious Father, thank you for your love and for your plan
for my life. I want to live as you want, and I want to use the
gifts and resources you've given me in wise and productive
ways. Please help me to remember to seek you first, before
beginning a project, making a decision, or even starting my
day.

HAVE YOU SOUGHT HIS GUIDANCE TODAY? BEFORE YOU DO ANYTHING ELSE, SUBMIT THE REST OF YOUR DAY TO THE LORD AND TRUST HIM TO LEAD YOU.

DRAW NEAR AND HEAL

The LORD is good to all;
He has compassion on all he has made.
   PSALM 145:9 NIV

The world we live in isn't always good. People use their free will to do evil, hurtful things. Earthquakes and tornadoes leave disaster in their wake. Cancer attacks the bodies of those we love. But God's compassion is there in the midst of it all. Even when we feel life isn't good, God still is.

Those words can sound empty when our world feels like it's falling apart. But how we feel doesn't always reflect reality. God still cares. He hasn't turned his back on us. He weeps with us. He longs for the day when we'll be with him in heaven and our tears will be a thing of the past. But for now, he calls us to simply draw near. He is there with us, a calm within the storm. Together we can move forward, one small step toward healing at a time.

God, I thank you for your boundless love and goodness
regardless of what's going on around us. I pray that you
will show me the way to embrace your blessings and resist
anything you don't want for me.

HAVE YOU EVER FELT GOD'S PULL WHEN YOU'VE TRIED TO PUSH HIM AWAY? HIS COMPASSION WILL CONTINUE TO DRAW YOU TO HIM. HE WON'T GIVE UP ON YOU.

SPIRITUAL STABILITY

We will no longer be immature like children. We won't be tossed and blown about by every wind of new teaching. We will not be influenced when people try to trick us with lies so clever they sound like the truth.
EPHESIANS 4:14 NLT

The world is full of clever people who can be very persuasive. Because we are emotional beings, at times our judgment may be swayed by sentiment or artful arguments. This may not matter when choosing which brand of peanut butter to buy, but for important issues our spiritual maturity must be honed and strong. It must be based on the guidance God gives us in his Word.

Heavenly Father, I thank you for the guidance always inherent in your Word. Please remind me to seek your truth and weigh all of my important decisions against that, rather than against the arguments and temptations of mankind.

HAVE YOU WEIGHED RECENT DECISIONS AGAINST HIS WORD? ASK HIM TO GIVE YOU A WISE, DISCERNING HEART AND TRUST THAT HE WILL DO IT.

NOW I LAY ME DOWN TO SLEEP

In peace I will lie down and sleep,
for you alone, LORD, make me dwell in safety.
   PSALM 4:8 NIV

Sleep doesn't always come easy. The cares of today, commitments of tomorrow, sick kids, leaky faucets, bad dreams, and good old insomnia can rob us of what our bodies need—a good night's sleep. When that happens, there's someone we can spend time with—and it's not late night talk show hosts, the shopping channel, or a carton of ice cream. It's God himself. Talk to him. Tell him what's on your mind and heart. Bring every tired thought to his throne. Picture putting it into his open, waiting hands. He doesn't mind if you fall asleep in the middle of your conversation. And if sleep still eludes you, his peace will hold you, offering your weary mind a safe place to rest every worry and care.

Heavenly Father, I'm grateful to have you watching over me as I lie down each night. I pray that my worries will fade as I focus on you and your watchful eye.

DO YOU EVER HAVE TROUBLE SLEEPING? TAKE YOUR CONCERNS TO THE LORD, AND ASK HIM FOR HIS PEACE TO RULE YOUR HEART AND MIND.

HIS MYSTERIOUS WAYS

"For My thoughts are not your thoughts, Nor are your ways My ways," declares the Lord.

ISAIAH 55:8 NASB

We've probably all heard this verse. It's easy enough to grasp that the Lord was advising his people not to lean on their own understanding because his thoughts and plans are absolutely impossible for us to fully grasp. It's especially difficult to accept this when bad things happen to us or to our loved ones. At such times, we must commit to accepting that God's will for us is good, and *somehow* these rough times will lead us there.

Lord God, you alone know why everything happens as it does. You know our struggles and pains. I trust that you have our good in mind in all that we experience—even in sorrow. Help me to find strength and endurance in that knowledge.

CAN YOU GIVE YOUR THOUGHTS AND WAYS OVER TO THE LORD? YOU CAN TRUST IN HIS GOODNESS. BELIEVE THAT TODAY.

IMPATIENTLY WAITING ON THE LORD

Wait patiently for the LORD. Be brave and courageous.
Yes, wait patiently for the LORD.
　　PSALM 27:14 NLT

Most of us have learned to wait in line for things, but that doesn't mean we like it. We may shift from foot to foot, roll our eyes, groan and grumble, or become abrupt with others when we have to wait too long. God is fully aware of our thoughts and feelings, including the fact that we don't enjoy waiting for anything—including his blessings. When we get antsy, let's take a look backward. Instead of focusing on what hasn't come our way yet, let's focus on what God's already brought us through. His timing is perfect. Even when our patience is not.

Lord, thank you for your understanding and mercy in my impatience. I pray that you will teach me to wait graciously for your blessings that you will bring when you see fit.

HOW DO YOU FEEL ABOUT HAVING TO WAIT? GOD IS FULL OF PATIENCE. ASK HIM TO GIVE YOU A MEASURE OF HIS PATIENCE AND WATCH WHAT IT DOES FOR YOU.

SHARING YOUR BREAD

Cast your bread upon the waters, for you will find it after many days.
ECCLESIASTES 11:1 ESV

There are a number of ways we can be generous. We can give of our physical blessings, contributing to those in need. One never knows when that kindness might be repaid. But we can also be generous with sharing our Lord even if the recipient seems completely unreceptive. Again, we never know how that seed might one day spring up to a godly harvest.

Give me wisdom and courage, Lord, to share my abundant wealth with others, both physical comfort and spiritual hope. If I can take those steps, I know you will use my efforts in ways that will bring glory to your kingdom. Thank you for allowing me to participate in that glory!

YOU HAVE SO MUCH TO GIVE. HOW WILL YOU SPREAD YOUR WEALTH TODAY?

GOODNESS OF GRACE

From his abundance we have all received one gracious blessing after another.
JOHN 1:16 NLT

In spite of our imperfections, God provides a never-ending supply of grace. He wants us to walk in step with him, so he gives us every opportunity to do that. There are so many times in life when we would love to have a do-over, but we can't. Fortunately, God gives his children one chance after another. When we count our blessings, let's take time to include his grace. It's a gift we need, and receive, each and every day.

Dear God, I can't thank you enough for your continued faithfulness and for providing grace to those who love you. Have mercy on me, and give me the heart to give the same grace to others.

HAVE YOU EVER MADE A MISTAKE AND WISHED YOU HAD A DO-OVER? DO YOU GIVE GRACE TO OTHERS WHO MAKE MISTAKES? GRACE WILL BE GIVEN TO YOU AS YOU CONTINUE TO EXTEND IT TO OTHERS.

THE NEW WORLD

The creation was subjected to futility, not willingly, but because of Him who subjected it, in hope that the creation itself also will be set free from its slavery to corruption into the freedom of the glory of the children of God.

ROMANS 8:20-21 NASB

It seems unlikely that the world we live in today, with earthquakes and floods and erupting volcanoes, is the same world we would have experienced had Eden never been sullied. And while conservation is important, our world does suffer from decay and loss. But when Christ returns and brings restoration to the earth, our world will be perfect again. Creation will be free of blemish, and so will we!

Heavenly Father, I want to do my part to respect and preserve this beautiful world you have given us. I am amazed at the glory you show across the globe in your creation. I can't imagine what the new earth will be like upon your return! Thank you for your promises.

WHAT DO YOU LOVE THE MOST ABOUT THE WORLD GOD CREATED? TAKE SOME TIME TO REFLECT ON THE AMAZING CREATOR AND HIS GLORIOUS WORK.

EVERYTHING IS BEAUTIFUL

He has made everything beautiful in its time. Also He has put eternity in their hearts, except that no one can find out the work that God does from beginning to end.
ECCLESIASTES 3:11 NKJV

Most of us do whatever we can to look good before we leave the house. We spend time applying makeup, brushing our hair, dressing in something that we think looks nice, and standing in front of the mirror for one last look. One thing we often forget to do is check out what's going on inside our hearts. God is constantly at work in us, transforming us to be more like his Son. No wonder we become more beautiful as time goes by. Not all beauty can be seen in the mirror. But rest assured, a beautiful heart is visible to God, as well as each and every person we meet.

I am so honored, Lord, that you see me as beautiful in the true sense of the word. Although I spend time trying to look good on the outside, your everlasting love is all I really need to have true inside beauty.

HOW MUCH TIME DO YOU SPEND GETTING READY BEFORE YOU LEAVE YOUR HOUSE? INCLUDING PRAYER IN YOUR MORNING ROUTINE IS A GREAT WAY TO BEAUTIFY YOURSELF FROM THE INSIDE OUT.

UNTO MY PATH

The way of the righteous is like the first gleam of dawn, which shines ever brighter until the full light of day.

PROVERBS 4:18 NLT

When we first open our eyes in the morning, we usually squint at the light and briefly struggle to get used to it. As the day wears on (if it is a gloriously sunny day), we feel our spirits uplifted, we know where to go, and nothing is hidden in darkness. The same is true when we first behold the light of God's Word: it's new, something we may not be used to, but the more we walk in it, the more life makes sense.

Lord God, I thank you so much for opening my eyes to your Word and constantly bringing new light into my life. I ask that you consistently remind me to turn to the light of your Word in times of darkness and in times of light.

ARE YOU WORKING AT MAKING HIS WORD MORE FAMILIAR? AS YOU DO, YOU WILL FIND ITS LIGHT LIFTING YOUR SPIRITS AND ILLUMINATING YOUR WAY.

AN ATTITUDE OF GRATITUDE

I have learned in whatever situation I am to be content.
PHILIPPIANS 4:11 ESV

Have you ever wished you had something that belongs to someone else? It could be their house, their paycheck, their job, or their car. Have you ever complained because something doesn't seem fair? The easiest way to foster discontent in our lives is to measure what we have against the lives of those around us. This is like comparing one piece of chocolate to another. Which is better? It depends. Do we prefer dark or light? Creams or chews? We may look at someone else's life and think it suits our taste just right. But we have no idea what it's really like.

Everything we have is a gift from God. There will always be those who have more—and those who have less. Let's shift our prayers from asking God for things to thanking him for what we have. The more grateful we are the more content we'll be.

I pray that I will learn to be satisfied and content with what I have, Lord. Please deliver me from the dissatisfaction that pulls my eyes and my heart away from you.

DO YOU FIND YOURSELF LETTING ENVY GET THE BETTER OF YOU? PUT AN END TO IT BY THANKING THE LORD FOR EVERYTHING HE HAS BLESSED YOU WITH.

INDIVIDUAL TEMPLES

In him the whole building is joined together and rises to become a holy temple in the Lord. And in him you too are being built together to become a dwelling in which God lives by his Spirit.
EPHESIANS 2:21-22 NIV

What a beautiful image Paul creates in these verses. We know that as members of the church body, we are a part of God's holy temple. The more we seek unity, the stronger our temple will be. But on a personal level, our individual bodies and souls are dwellings for God, whose Spirit lives in us. Like the church body, we are being built into strong temples when we seek to be united with God.

Lord God, thank you for my fellow Christians and my everlasting bond with them. Thank you, too, for loving me so much that you desire to live within my heart and soul. I love that because of you I am being built stronger in spirit. Thank you for promising to always dwell in me.

HOW HAS GOD BEEN BUILDING YOU LATELY? STRENGTHEN YOUR TEMPLE BY SEEKING UNITY WITH OTHER BELIEVERS.

ONLY ONE WAY

Jesus said to him, "I am the way, and the truth, and the life; no one comes to the Father but through Me."
JOHN 14:6 NASB

Jesus has made it clear that there are no other paths to God but through him. Having faith that Jesus is our Savior is the only thing that leads us to our ultimate destiny. That makes our life choices easy, doesn't it? He has simplified the way we get to heaven. We don't have a list of feats to accomplish to attain righteousness. Although he is pleased when we do good works out of love for him, the actions we perform are not necessary for salvation. He has already paved our way with his monumental sacrifice.

Lord, thank you for providing a path that all may follow to live with you for eternity. I am grateful that I don't have to perform any difficult tasks to know that I am loved by you.

DOES IT MAKE YOU HAPPY TO DO THINGS FOR OTHERS? ALTHOUGH IT IS GOOD TO SERVE OTHERS, REMEMBER THAT YOU ARE SAVED ONLY THROUGH YOUR BELIEF IN CHRIST'S WORK ON THE CROSS.

JOYFUL DANCING

You have turned my mourning into joyful dancing.
You have taken away my clothes of mourning
and clothed me with joy,
that I might sing praises to you and not be silent.
O Lord my God, I will give you thanks forever!
    PSALM 30:11-12 NLT

Some of us came to our acceptance of Christ through a crisis, when we didn't know where else to turn. There is something so liberating about knowing and accepting that God is in total control no matter how hard we try to make it otherwise. While life can still involve sadness, there is an inner dancing of joy when we give total control to the Lord.

Jesus, I thank you so much that you put the right words in the right person's mouth when I needed to hear them, leading me to you. I thank you that you are in control of every aspect of my life, and all I want to do is attempt to deserve what I don't deserve—your grace.

CAN YOU GIVE TOTAL CONTROL OF YOUR LIFE TO GOD? THERE IS INCREDIBLE JOY WAITING FOR YOU IF YOU TRUST HIM WITH EVERYTHING.

SEEING GOD

No one has ever seen God. But if we love each other, God lives in us, and his love is brought to full expression in us.

1 JOHN 4:12 NLT

All of us have heard the expression, "Seeing is believing." And if some people can't see God with their eyes, they don't believe. However, God is seen in other ways, including in love between his followers. When a friend listens to our sorrows and offers comforting words, we see God's love. When a stranger smiles at us in passing, it can brighten an otherwise dreary day. That's God's love. He gives us tasty morsels of his goodness in ways greater than anything we can see with our eyes.

Lord, although I can't see you with my eyes, I see you in so many ways that remind me you are ever-present. I pray that others can see you through me.

HOW HAVE YOU SEEN GOD? MAKE IT A GOAL TO SHOW SOMEONE GOD'S LOVE THROUGH YOUR ACTIONS TODAY.

HE STANDS AT THE DOOR

I have not spoken in secret,
from somewhere in a land of darkness;
I have not said to Jacob's descendants,
"Seek me in vain."
I, the LORD, speak the truth;
I declare what is right.
ISAIAH 45:19 NIV

We probably all know people who claim they've tried the Christian faith and it just didn't work. That's heartbreaking, especially when you consider how open Jesus is. When we truly seek Christ with a humble heart, he walks right in. When people say Christianity didn't work, what they're really saying is that they didn't want it to work. They just aren't at a point of submission yet.

Jesus, I know you are abundantly patient with us, and I'm so glad you waited for me to figure out that I needed you. I know it breaks your heart, too, when your children haven't reached the point of submission necessary to give their lives to you. I pray they will eventually be sufficiently humble and open to you.

WHO COMES TO MIND WHEN YOU CONSIDER THIS? PRAY GOD'S MERCY AND REVELATION OVER THEM TODAY.

SING PRAISES

*I will give to the L*ORD *the thanks due to his righteousness,
and I will sing praise to the name of the L*ORD,
the Most High.
    PSALM 7:17 ESV

The Lord hears our voices when we sing his praises, and he doesn't even care if we're tone deaf and sing off key. He's listening to the melody of love that's playing in our hearts. After all, worship is just another way of saying "I love you" to the Lord.

We can worship God through song, through acts of service, through sacrificial giving or times of prayer. Anything we do that honors him, that proclaims how great he is and how thankful we are for his presence in our lives, is a form of worship. Let's not wait until Sunday to offer a gift of worship to the one who is worthy of more than we can ever give.

Lord, I sing your praises out of gratitude for your goodness. May I lay aside my worries that my voice may not be worthy of your song and let everyone around me know how wonderful you are.

DO YOU LET OTHERS HEAR YOU SING THE LORD'S PRAISES? IF YOU CAN'T SING—SHOUT! THE LORD IS WORTHY OF YOUR PRAISE.

FAITH AND MIRACLES

You yourselves have seen what I did to Egypt, and how I carried you on eagles' wings and brought you to myself.
EXODUS 19:4 NIV

When God's people were in distress, he worked amazing miracles on their behalf and brought them to freedom. Although we don't always experience miracles that alter our circumstances, God never wants us to forget what he can do for us. He wants us to have faith in the good he can work in our lives. If everything always worked out as *we deem*, miracles wouldn't really be miracles, and we would have no need to exercise faith. Clearly, faith is important to God.

Heavenly Father, no matter how much I trust in your plan, I often catch myself pulling back and trying to force my will on situations. Even though I mean well, please help me to remember you are in control. Help me to accept whatever your plan is in every circumstance.

ARE YOU ABLE TO PUT YOUR FAITH IN HIM FOR EVERYTHING TODAY? YOU CAN LET GO OF YOUR HOLD. HE IS TRUSTWORTHY.

LAUGH AND LEAN

Rejoice with those who rejoice;
mourn with those who mourn.
ROMANS 12:15 NIV

The Lord wants us to celebrate—and yes, mourn—with those around us. This shows his desire for us to be deeply involved in the lives of others. When we rejoice together in God's goodness, and weep together over the sorrows of living in a broken world, we mirror God's relationship with us. We connect with one another on a deep, emotionally honest, heart-to-heart level. As we do, our care for each other grows right along with our empathy. This is an extremely vulnerable place to be.

When we join in the celebrations and sorrows of others, true relationship invites us to be as transparent with them as they've been with us. That means allowing others to see us at our best and worst—and lean on them when when we're in need. Who knows? They may be God's answer to our own heartfelt prayer.

I am grateful for you reaching out to me when I have something to celebrate or mourn, oh Lord. I pray that I can extend this to others you have put in my path. Allow me to do so with compassion, joy, and empathy.

DO YOU KNOW SOMEONE WHO NEEDS A FRIEND TO CELEBRATE WITH OR TO LEAN ON DURING A DIFFICULT TIME? REACH OUT TODAY AND SHOW GOD'S CARE.

BLESSED INHERITANCE

*From everlasting to everlasting the LORD's love
is with those who fear him,
and his righteousness with their children's children—
with those who keep his covenant and remember to
obey his precepts.*

PSALM 103:17 NIV

Most of us have heard the warning of Exodus 20:5, about the sins of the father bringing punishment to the children, but today's verse emphasizes what God *wants* for us. If we strive for righteousness on a daily basis, the Lord will bless us *and* our children. What a legacy to pass on to our sons and daughters!

Lord, thank you for your cautions and for your promises. I want to follow your guidance always, and I lean on you for discernment and obedience. Please help me to live a righteous day today, for my sake and for the sake of my children and their children. May my example supplement the guidance you offer them. Thank you for your everlasting love and patience.

HOW WILL YOU MODEL RIGHTEOUSNESS FOR YOUR CHILDREN TODAY? THINK ABOUT THE LEGACY YOU CAN LEAVE THEM WHEN YOU WALK IN THE WAY OF THE LORD.

BEST FRIEND EVER

Give all your worries and cares to God,
for he cares about you.
1 PETER 5:7 NLT

Do you have any close friends who will listen to everything that concerns you? Jesus is that kind of confidant and friend. Sure, it's wonderful to share our heart with our circle of friends. But first, why not share our deepest concerns with the one who can actually do something about them?

No worry, fear, complaint, regret or request is too small to be placed in Jesus' hands. As a matter of fact, if we turn to God first and get the heaviness we're feeling out in the open, we may find we spend less time grumbling with our friends and more time simply enjoying their company.

Thank you, Lord Jesus, for being the best friend a person could possibly have. I know that I'm blessed to have you available every hour of every day and night, listening to whatever I have on my mind, no matter how great or small it is.

DO YOU HAVE A BEST FRIEND WHO IS ALWAYS THERE FOR YOU? THANK THE LORD THAT HE HAS PLACED THAT FRIEND IN YOUR LIFE.

JEWELS IN OUR CROWNS

Children's children are a crown to the aged,
and parents are the pride of their children.
PROVERBS 17:6 NIV

One of the greatest joys in life is enjoying grandchildren. It's a different kind of love in some ways, different from what we feel for our own children. By the time we have grandchildren, our own children have become friends we love more than anyone else in the world. And then, these delightful little gifts from God bring freshness into our lives. If God's plan for us has not included children or grandchildren, we can still demonstrate his loving kindness toward the little ones and experience that crown of today's verse.

Lord, thank you for my children and grandchildren. May I always behave in a way that honors you and enables my children to be proud of me. Let me be a good role model for them and for every child I meet.

HOW DO YOU REPRESENT CHRIST TO THE CHILDREN IN YOUR LIFE? ENJOY THE ENERGY OF THEIR WIGGLY BODIES, THE CONTENTMENT OF THEIR SLEEPING FACES, AND THE JOY IN THEIR SMILES.

TASTY AND SWEET

Oh, taste and see that the LORD is good!
Blessed is the man who takes refuge in him!
    PSALM 34:8 ESV

Isn't it interesting that this verse mentions two different senses in the first line? Both of these senses are closely linked. When we look at a beautifully handcrafted truffle in the window of a fancy chocolatier, our mouth begins to water. But we need to do more than look at it from afar to enjoy it. We need to take action—and bite right in! Or, if we have more self-control, we can savor it slowly, allowing it to melt on our tongue.

In the same way, it isn't enough to see God's hand at work in the world. We need to join our hand in his and get involved in what he's doing. Then we'll truly begin to taste the goodness of God, to take its sweetness into our lives, so it can delight and nourish our soul.

Lord, I am grateful for the sweetness of your embrace. I know that as long as I take refuge in you, I will experience the monumental joy of peace on earth and eternal salvation that only faith in you can bring.

HOW CAN YOU SEE SOMETHING FROM TASTING IT? GOD IS GOOD. BE BLESSED AS YOU TASTE AND SEE THAT TODAY.

BECAUSE THE BIBLE TELLS ME SO

Fix these words of mine in your hearts and minds; tie them as symbols on your hands and bind them on your foreheads.

DEUTERONOMY 11:18 NIV

It's impressive how much Scripture most pastors have memorized and are able to retrieve at the appropriate moment. While we may not have as much of the Bible in our minds as pastors do, it is wise to remember verses that will help us when needed. The effort is so worth it when God is ready to remind us of his promises, exhortations, and guidance.

Lord, thank you so much for speaking to us through your Word. Please help me put forth the effort to memorize verses you want me to have near my heart. I ask for your guidance in selecting which verses to study. Never let me take your Word for granted.

WHAT IS ONE OF YOUR FAVORITE VERSES? RECITE IT NOW AND PONDER IT AS YOU GO ABOUT YOUR DAY.

WALKING BY FAITH

Thomas answered him, "My Lord and my God!"
Jesus said to him, "Have you believed because you
have seen me? Blessed are those who have not seen
and yet have believed."
JOHN 20:28-29 ESV

Suppose a trusted friend told you she'd bought you a box of chocolates. Instead of taking her word for it, you refused to believe her claim until you not only had the box in your hands, but a chocolate in your mouth.

Thomas was that kind of guy. Other disciples had told him Jesus had risen from the dead, but Thomas refused to believe because he hadn't seen Jesus with his own eyes. Like Thomas, before he witnessed the risen Christ firsthand, we haven't seen Jesus. But we can choose to place our trust in the eyewitness accounts in the Bible, in the testimony of those we know who've experienced God's presence and power, and in the whisper of God's Spirit. Or not. It's our choice. But it's a choice with eternal consequences—a choice God promises to bless when we risk walking by faith, instead of sight.

Dear God, thank you for sending your Son to wash away my sins. I believe in his resurrection and the fact that the price has already been paid for my entry into heaven.

WHAT DOES IT TAKE FOR YOU TO BELIEVE? LEAVE YOUR DOUBTS BEHIND AND FULLY TRUST IN OUR RISEN SAVIOR!

RESURRECTIONS

Jesus said to her, "I am the resurrection and the life. He who believes in me will live, even though he dies, and whoever lives and believes in me will never die. Do you believe this?"

JOHN 11:25-26 NIV

After he spoke these words to Martha, Jesus resurrected Lazarus from the grave. Not only did he foreshadow his own resurrection, he foreshadowed ours. This is the power of Christ's resurrection. If we are his, we are his eternally. His earthly death returned him to eternal bliss with his Heavenly Father, as will ours.

Lord, sometimes I lose track of the eternal picture. The matters of the day overwhelm me and cloud my vision of your amazing plan. Thank you for drawing me back to the greatest aspect of life on earth—each day brings me closer and closer to seeing you face-to-face, forever.

ARE YOU EXCITED ABOUT THE ETERNAL PICTURE? TAKE STRENGTH IN KNOWING THAT GOD'S PLAN IS GOOD AND HIS PROMISES ARE TRUE.

NOTHING IS IMPOSSIBLE

Jesus looked at them intently and said, "Humanly speaking, it is impossible. But not with God. Everything is possible with God."

MARK 10:27 NLT

God can do anything. We can't. It's as simple as that. But if we inspect this verse a little bit closer, we understand the condition that makes it not quite so simple. Some of us want to ask God for what we want because we know he can get it for us. But there's one stipulation. Is it God's will for us—or simply our own desire? Sometimes it's hard to tell them apart, especially when we long for something very deeply. We can pray for anything, including the impossible. But then we need to let go of how we expect God to answer our prayer. After all, his ways and his will are not always clear to us. But they're always in line with his love.

Thank you, Jesus, for knowing what is right for me. You are perfect and holy, which is why I need to stop trying to make demands and remember you are in control.

HAVE YOU PRAYED FOR SOMETHING YOU THOUGHT YOU SHOULD HAVE, BUT IT DIDN'T HAPPEN? MAYBE IT WASN'T RIGHT FOR YOU AT THAT TIME. GIVE YOUR DESIRES TO THE LORD AND SEE WHAT HE DOES WITH THEM.

FREE FLIGHT

"Look at the birds of the air, for they neither sow nor reap nor gather into barns; yet your heavenly Father feeds them. Are you not of more value than they? Which of you by worrying can add one cubit to his stature?"
MATTHEW 6:26-27 NKJV

How often do we find ourselves building a dense fog of worry without stopping to consider that God's plans for us are already in place? And his plans are for our good. We see the birds of the air flying through life, fully present in the day, stopping not to worry but simply to rest. When we cast off worry, our hearts fly, too.

Lord, thank you for how you value me. Help me to value every hour of my life as a gift from you. I don't want to waste a single hour regretting the past or dreading the future. When you pull me from my fog of worry, I see only you and your love.

WHAT WORRY WILL YOU SURRENDER TO THE LORD TODAY? FEEL THE LIGHTNESS IN YOUR STEP WHEN YOU GIVE YOUR LOAD OF WORRY TO HIM.

APRIL

Every field is watered with the abundance of rain—
showers soaking the earth and softening its clods,
causing seeds to sprout throughout the land.
You crown the earth with its yearly harvest,
the fruits of your goodness.

PSALM 65:10-11 TPT

NO FOOL

The way of a fool is right in his own eyes,
but a wise man listens to advice.
PROVERBS 12:15 ESV

Sometimes we find ourselves in circumstances that don't allow for a lot of time to make a decision—a possible accident needs to be prevented, someone suddenly needs comfort, immediate danger prompts us to change our circumstances. But whenever possible, we need to seek the advice of wise people God puts in our path before we take action. That may be the very reason he introduced us to them.

Lord, thank you for the wisdom and the advisors you have placed in my life. I pray you will bless me with discernment to know when you are speaking through someone I know. I want to make the choices that fit with your plans for me.

WHO IS GOD USING TO ADVISE YOU? ASK GOD TO GIVE YOU DISCERNMENT IN CHOOSING WISE COUNSELORS.

TRUTH BE TOLD

"When the Spirit of truth comes, he will guide you into all truth. He will not speak on his own but will tell you what he has heard. He will tell you about the future."
JOHN 16:13 NLT

In the Old Testament, God's Spirit came to specific people like Samson or Saul—and then the Spirit left. For various reasons, the wisdom, truth, power, and presence of God's Spirit simply picked up and moved out. That same Spirit came to indwell Jesus' followers at Pentecost—and lives in us today.

Unlike Samson and Saul, we don't have to worry about God's Spirit disappearing one day. When we invite God into our lives, his Spirit makes a permanent home in our heart. If we ignore him, or choose to go our own way instead of the way God is leading us, his voice may be hard to hear. But that doesn't mean he's gone. It means we've pulled back from God. If we want to hear his truth more clearly, we need to refocus on God and draw close to him once more.

Dear Father in heaven, thank you for sending your Son to guide us to your truth. I pray for the strength to continue holding your hand as I journey through life.

DO YOU PRAY FOR THE LORD'S WILL TO BE DONE RATHER THAN YOUR OWN WILL? BELIEVE IN HIS GOODNESS AND TRUST THAT HIS WILL IS SO MUCH BETTER!

TAKING GOD AT HIS WORD

The Lord then said to Noah, "Go into the ark, you and your whole family, because I have found you righteous in this generation."

GENESIS 7:1 NIV

When God issued this command to Noah, others ridiculed him for building the ark. However, after the rains came, all those naysayers probably wished they'd paid closer attention to him. Although God isn't asking any of us to build an ark, he still makes clear what he wants from us through his Word. It may not make sense to those around us, or even to us, at times.

Take purity. God commands us to reserve sexual intimacy for marriage. Modern culture says that's a nice ideal, but unrealistic and unnecessary. We trust God knows best. We don't have to understand all of the "whys" behind God's Word to know what he wants us to do—and then do it. We can save ourselves from a flood of trouble by simply taking him at his Word.

Heavenly Father, I am grateful for your sacrifice and clarity in your Word. I pray for your continued mercy as I study it and live my life to please you.

HAVE YOU EVER BEEN RIDICULED BY OTHERS FOR FOLLOWING YOUR FAITH? TAKE HEART IN THE DELIGHT THAT GOD HAS IN YOUR OBEDIENCE.

THY WILL BE DONE

The LORD answered Moses, "Is the LORD's arm too short? You will now see whether or not what I say will come true for you."
NUMBERS 11:23 NIV

No doubt we all have petitions we put before God when we pray. We may have broad requests, like asking for the ability to represent Christ well. Or we may have specific requests, like asking that we arrive at an appointment on time despite the traffic. Sometimes we hesitate to make the big requests—the ones that defy earthly logic. Healing a loved one suffering from a fatal disease. Undoing the damage done by a mistake we've made. Bringing a hard-core atheist to salvation. Do we think the Lord's arm is too short to accomplish *anything* that falls within his will?

Lord God, you parted the Red Sea, you raised Lazarus from the dead, you freed a man in chains from prison, and you even made a donkey speak on your behalf! Please help me to remember that I can come to you with all of my prayers and know that everything will unfold according to your loving will.

WHAT LOGIC-DEFYING PRAYER DO YOU HAVE FOR GOD TODAY? PRAY BELIEVING THAT HIS ARM IS NOT TOO SHORT TO MOVE ON YOUR BEHALF.

QUIETING THE STORM

*When Jesus woke up, he rebuked the wind and said
to the waves, "Silence! Be still!" Suddenly the wind
stopped, and there was a great calm.*
MARK 4:39 NLT

How many times have you had storms in your life—when bad
or even frightening things seemed to swirl out of control? As
Jesus admonished the wind and ordered the waves to calm
down, he can do the same for us.

The wind and waves of our lives can come in many forms:
rocky relationships, a deluge of unexpected debt, a fog of
doubt or depression, storm clouds of chronic illness. God may
not immediately part the clouds of our circumstances, but he
will ride the storm out by our side. By clinging to prayer and
God's promises, we can find a place of peace and hope even
when the winds around us continue to howl. Call to him now.
There's no storm loud enough to drown out your cries—or
fierce enough to hold back God's comfort.

*Jesus, I know that life is filled with a mix of good times and
bad. May I remember to pray for your mighty hand of comfort
during the difficult periods and accept your will.*

WHO DO YOU TURN TO DURING THE STORMY TIMES OF
YOUR LIFE? TRUST IN GOD'S GOODNESS AND GRACE TO
GET YOU THROUGH THOSE TIMES.

JUST THE MESSENGERS

"He himself was not the light; he came only as a witness to the light."
JOHN 1:8 NIV

John the Baptist never set out to have followers. He set out to lead others to follow Christ. Every once in a while we hear of the moral downfall of a renowned pastor, or the shady dealings of a famous church's board of elders. Or maybe we'll get close enough to our own church staff to learn things we don't like. None of those people are Jesus, and we must always be sure to keep the focus of our faith on Christ, not on people. Christ will never falter. He'll never let us down.

Thank you, Jesus, for being the one perfect person in my life. As I learn from pastors and famous Christian leaders, please help me to remember that no person's mistakes will alter your consistent love and promise. Help me to listen to the teachings of Christian leaders but always turn to you and your Word for the absolute truth.

IS YOUR FAITH BASED SOLELY ON JESUS AND HIS WORD? BELIEVE THE BEST ABOUT OTHERS, BUT DON'T EXPECT THEM TO BE JESUS. GIVE THEM GRACE JUST AS YOU HAVE RECEIVED IT.

BEAUTIFUL YOU

The King will greatly desire your beauty;
Because He is your Lord, worship Him.
   PSALM 45:11 NKJV

There are no bad hair days in God's kingdom. We're always beautiful in his eyes. How about our own? Can we see our own beauty or are we distracted by what we consider flaws in our physical appearance?

Instead of using the mirror to assess our beauty, let's look into God's eyes. How does he see us? What beauty does he find? Love, growth, humility, generosity, compassion—traits such as these add more to a woman's natural beauty than having the "perfect" figure or full-bodied hair. What do you think God finds most beautiful about you?

I am honored and grateful, God, for your ability to see my inner beauty. I pray that I can stop tearing myself down when my outer appearance isn't perfect. In your goodness, you have created only that which is lovely.

WHAT DID YOU SEE THE LAST TIME YOU LOOKED IN THE MIRROR? THE LORD SEES YOUR HEART, AND HE THINKS YOU ARE BEAUTIFUL. LET THAT SETTLE OVER YOU TODAY.

CLEAN FOREVER

Cleanse me with hyssop, and I will be clean:
wash me, and I will be whiter than snow.
PSALM 51:7 NIV

Just as our homes need constant cleaning (no matter how hard we work at it), our souls need constant cleaning as well. Certainly, we are to strive always to live Godly, clean lives, and it's vital to be vigilant about keeping dirt from creeping in. But when we ask Jesus to wash us whiter than snow, he does it. Our souls are safe and clean, thanks to his sacrifice and love. We should take greater joy in that than in any other aspect of our lives.

Thank you, Jesus, for washing my soul whiter than snow. I know I owe my eternal life to you. I ask that you help me to always embrace the joy of knowing I can't lose that cleanliness; you'll never take it away, not even because of my many imperfections.

CAN YOU REJOICE TODAY, KNOWING YOU WILL ALWAYS BE CLEAN IN GOD'S EYES? FEEL THE INNER WASHING OF HIS LOVE AS YOU SPEND TIME IN HIS PRESENCE TODAY.

CONSTANT STRENGTH

My health may fail, and my spirit may grow weak, but
God remains the strength of my heart; he is mine forever.
PSALM 73:26 NLT

Life is difficult, particularly when we don't feel good. Whether we're sick with a cold or have a more serious ailment, it's easy to wallow in our discomfort and feel sorry for ourselves. Jesus doesn't make light of our suffering. He knows all about pain firsthand. When we need strength, we need to cut ourselves some slack, take care of ourselves, and allow ourselves time to heal. But when we've done all we can, one thing remains: draw close to Jesus' side, our fellow-sufferer and almighty Savior.

I may not always feel great or be on top of my game, Lord,
but knowing you are always there for me gives me comfort.
Thank you for your strength and love that remind me that my
infirmity is temporary.

WHERE DO YOU FIND STRENGTH WHEN YOU'RE SICK? ASK THE LORD FOR EVERYTHING YOU NEED TO GET THROUGH THE DAY. HE IS FAITHFUL, AND HE IS GOOD.

PRAYER PARTNER

The Spirit helps us in our weakness. For we do not know what to pray for as we ought, but the Spirit himself intercedes for us with groanings too deep for words.
ROMANS 8:26 ESV

Sometimes life gets so complicated we don't even know what to pray for. We simply can't tell which steps Jesus wants us to take next on the path before us. Such indecision weakens our endurance and enthusiasm, but the confusion is only on our part. The Holy Spirit understands our situation and steps in for us in a way only possible for him. We might feel impotent, but even in that weakness, our prayers are strong. Have patience! Help is coming.

Holy Spirit, you are so close to me that you understand my every thought, fear, and uncertainty. You know my hopes and desires, and you love me unconditionally. Help me to trust in your ability to intercede for me when I've run out of words or ideas. I love you.

DO YOU NEED TO SEEK THE HOLY SPIRIT'S HELP TODAY? HE IS NOT FAR FROM YOU, AND HE IS DELIGHTED TO SHOW YOU THE WAY.

UNDER THE MAGNIFYING GLASS

Search me, O God, and know my heart;
test me and know my anxious thoughts.
Point out anything in me that offends you,
and lead me along the path of everlasting life.
    PSALM 139:23-24 NLT

It's difficult to have anyone take a magnifying glass and look at our lives, but this verse is doing just that. What a beautiful thing—to know that God has the power to turn things around for us. It's true, he knows our sins. But he's atoned for each and every one.

We no longer need to fear that our anxious thoughts or careless actions will lead to abandonment or punishment. When we feel God using our conscience or the words of others to hold a magnifying glass over areas in our lives that need to change, we can be sure it's done out of love and concern, not condemnation. Instead of fearing God sees us as we really are, let's rejoice that he knows us so well—and continues to love us so deeply.

Lord Jesus, I know that your magnifying glass is constantly looking at me, inspecting my heart. Thank you for providing me with a path toward everlasting life with you.

WHAT DOES GOD SEE WHEN HE LOOKS AT YOUR HEART? DON'T SQUIRM UNDER HIS GAZE. REST CONFIDENTLY IN THE WORK THAT JESUS HAS DONE FOR YOU.

BOASTING IN GOD

In God we have boasted continually,
and we will give thanks to your name forever.
    PSALM 44:8 ESV

Is anything as heart-stirring as witnessing God's answer
to prayer, especially when his answer is exactly what we
requested? We all remember times we desperately needed his
hand to intervene, and it did. When that happens, he deserves
public acknowledgment. If we're ever going to boast, that's
the proper time, and it can be done in a gentle, appreciative
way. We never know who is listening.

I realize, Lord God, that I will not always experience the answers
I seek when I pray. And I know to be thankful always for your
answers. But for those miraculous times when you've answered
my prayer as I requested, please help me to remember to
rejoice publicly. Help me to do so in a way that serves as an
inviting witness to the grace you offer your children.

DO THOSE AROUND YOU KNOW WHEN GOD ANSWERS
YOUR PRAYERS? SHARE YOUR ANSWERED PRAYERS WITH
THEM—BRAG ABOUT THE GOODNESS OF YOUR GOD!

HEAVENLY MANNA

Give us today our daily bread.
    MATTHEW 6:11 NIV

So many times we say the Lord's Prayer without thinking about each sentence—each word. This part of our petition is powerful because it exposes our true need for God's provision. We need sustenance—food and water—each and every day. When we ask God to provide for our daily needs, we know he's fully aware of what they are. Our prayer is a reminder for us, not him, of the blessings we receive each day that we so easily take for granted.

Lord, thank you for providing me with everything I need. Never let me forget that everything good comes from you.

DO YOU THINK ABOUT HOW YOUR DAILY NEEDS ARE MET? TAKE SOME TIME THANKING THE LORD FOR YOUR DAILY BREAD AND THE MANY OTHER BLESSINGS HE HAS GIVEN YOU.

ALWAYS WATCHING OVER YOU

*My help comes from the L*ORD*,*
who made heaven and earth!
He will not let you stumble;
the one who watches over you will not slumber.
PSALM 121:2-3 NLT

We've all experienced something at some point in our lives that caused us to lose sleep over worrying for our safety or the safety of our loved ones. Yes, we do live in a fallen, sinful world, but the Lord made heaven and earth, and he can surely protect us. He asks us to trust him in that. When fear plagues our rest, we need to remember these calming words. He never slumbers, so we can!

Thank you, God, for promising to protect me and those I love.
When my heart starts racing because of some fear I develop at
night, please remind me to turn that fear over to you. Please
take my focus off what frightens me and place it on your
promises, so I can relax and rest well.

ARE YOU ABLE TO TURN YOUR FEARS OVER TO HIM AS HE ASKS? GIVE YOUR WORRIES TO THE LORD AND ASK HIM FOR A GOOD NIGHT'S REST. ASK HIM TO QUIET YOUR HEART AND YOUR MIND AS YOU TRUST IN HIS GOODNESS.

TOTAL TRUST

O my people, trust in him at all times.
Pour out your heart to him, for God is our refuge.
    PSALM 62:8 NLT

So many times we hear people say, "Trust me," yet that often comes from someone who isn't trustworthy. The only one we can put our total trust in is God because he is 100 percent trustworthy. No matter who we are or what we do, his Word is always true. He provides for our needs and comforts us through pain, showing his goodness to us every minute of every day.

We may not always be aware of all the ways he's continually providing refuge in our lives. But if we voice our gratitude for his trustworthiness in prayer, we may catch a glimpse of how he's at work behind the scenes in our lives.

I trust you, oh Lord, with everything in my life. Thank you for your abundant provisions, constantly reminding me of your goodness.

DO YOU PUT YOUR TOTAL TRUST IN GOD? WHEN HE TELLS YOU TO TRUST HIM, YOU REALLY CAN.

THE LIGHTER SIDE OF THE PLAN

A time to weep and a time to laugh,
a time to mourn and a time to dance.
ECCLESIASTES 3:4 NIV

Laughter is such a wonderful gift from God. It relieves stress, it joins people together, and it helps us to humble ourselves and admit our weaknesses in a less vulnerable way. God made a point of condoning laughter. When we consider the glorious future we have in store, how can we not be upbeat and full of joy? Yes, every person's life includes time to weep and mourn, but God encourages us to laugh and dance as well. That is part of his design.

Heavenly Father, some of my favorite times in life involve laughter. I thank you so much for putting humor into our lives. Help me, please, to never take myself so seriously that I fail to recognize times to laugh or dance.

CAN YOU REMEMBER THE LAST TIME YOU REALLY LAUGHED? ASK GOD TO GIVE YOU JOY THAT WELLS UP TO OVERFLOWING.

YOU ARE A TREASURE

Since you are precious and honored in my sight,
and because I love you,
I will give people in exchange for you,
nations in exchange for your life.
ISAIAH 43:4 NIV

What do we treasure? Those family heirlooms that have been passed down through generations? The artwork of our children, drawn with the clumsy fingers of a growing toddler? The wedding ring with which we pledged our love? Photos of family and friends we hold close to our heart?

Losing any of our personal treasures due to fire, flood, theft or our own negligence can cause our hearts to break. Things like this can never be replaced. Neither can we. Jesus treasures each one of us so much that he was willing to trade his life for ours to keep us by his side throughout eternity. Once we've found Jesus, he makes certain we will never be lost.

Thank you for calling me precious and making me feel special,
Lord Jesus. Show me the way to honor you, and never let me
forget to be joyful and grateful as I do.

CAN YOU SEE HOW GOD HAS MADE YOU SPECIAL? THERE IS NO ONE ELSE LIKE YOU IN ALL OF CREATION. REFLECT ON THAT TODAY AND BE GRATEFUL FOR IT.

ATTENTION TO THE VINE

"Already you are clean because of the word that I have spoken to you. Abide in me, and I in you. As the branch cannot bear fruit by itself, unless it abides in the vine, neither can you, unless you abide in me."

JOHN 15:3-4 ESV

Jesus assures us that although God (the vineyard keeper) may occasionally prune us to keep us spiritually healthy, we are already clean. Jesus has declared us branches on the vine. He won't turn from us, and we are cautioned not to turn from him either. He wants us to exemplify him and his glorious qualities. We can't do that if we stop focusing on him.

Dear Jesus, thank you for grafting me into the vine and promising to never let me go. I know I represent you best when I think of you more. It's an honor to be enlisted to demonstrate your love, strength, and grace to others. Please remind me of that when I start to turn away. My life is always cleaner when I hold on to you.

HOW WILL YOU KEEP YOUR FOCUS ON HIM TODAY? SPEND TIME PONDERING HIS GLORIOUS QUALITIES— THAT'S A GREAT PLACE TO START!

FAMILY TIES

See how very much our Father loves us, for he calls us his children, and that is what we are! But the people who belong to this world don't recognize that we are God's children because they don't know him.

1 JOHN 3:1 NLT

Families share a special kind of bond. Even if they're not biologically related, over time they pick up each other's habits, mannerisms, and speech patterns. When we spend time with our heavenly Father, we pick up a few of his traits as well. What a blessing!

Those who don't know God yet may not recognize our "family" resemblance right away. But hopefully, the longer we walk in our Father's loving footsteps, the more people will begin to notice that there's something different about us—something that can only be described as traces of God's peace, joy and grace. Our family ties with our Father are just another way he's improving our lives, as well as the lives of those with whom we cross paths.

Dear Father, thank you for your amazing love, regardless of where I am and what I do. May I never take my relationship with you for granted. Help me to share your goodness and holiness with others.

HAVE YOU EVER SACRIFICED FOR SOMEONE YOU LOVE? GOD'S SACRIFICE GOES SO FAR BEYOND THAT YOU CAN'T HELP BUT BE THANKFUL FOR HIS GOODNESS!

SHINING LIGHT IN THE DARKNESS

*Do not be yoked together with unbelievers. For what
do righteousness and wickedness have in common?
Or what fellowship can light have with darkness?*

    2 CORINTHIANS 6:14 NIV

This is a tough verse for many of us, either because we are
personally married to unbelievers or our loved ones are.
In some cases, marriage came before the awareness and
acceptance of Christ. This can be an even more difficult
struggle because sometimes the unbeliever feels duped. The
only hope in such circumstances is total devotion to Christ's
miraculous power and his ability to make himself attractive
through our own behavior.

*Lord Jesus, thank you for my salvation. Please help me and
my fellow believers to avoid judgmental or superior attitudes
toward unbelievers whether they're in my family or in the
families of dear friends. Please show your abundant grace
toward them. Please show them unconditional love through me.*

WHO COMES TO MIND WHEN YOU THINK OF THIS VERSE?
PRAY FOR THOSE YOU KNOW WHO ARE IN THESE DIFFICULT
SITUATIONS. PRAY FOR THE SALVATION OF THE UNBELIEVERS
IN YOUR LIFE. NOTHING IS IMPOSSIBLE FOR GOD.

HOLY OBEDIENCE

You must live as God's obedient children. Don't slip back into your old ways of living to satisfy your own desires. You didn't know any better then. But now you must be holy in everything you do, just as God who chose you is holy. For the Scriptures say, "You must be holy because I am holy."

1 PETER 1:14-16 NLT

When Peter speaks of holiness, he's telling us to be different from the rest of the world. The word "holy" means "set apart." It's much easier to give in and fit in, but doing so pulls us away from God who's perfectly holy in every way.

Sometimes, following in God's holiness means physically setting ourselves apart from what's going on around us. We may have to walk out of a movie if we realize the onscreen images are ones we don't want replaying in our head. Or we may have to excuse ourselves from a conversation when it shifts from sharing the latest news to spreading the juiciest gossip. When we feel God's nudge, let's budge—and set ourselves apart in the name of holiness.

Heavenly Father, I know the temptations of the world, and I confess that I have fallen into common thinking. I pray that I can be more like you and attempt to be more holy in my thinking.

ARE YOU TEMPTED TO FIT IN WITH THE WORLD? DON'T OPPOSE GOD'S HOLINESS TODAY. HE WILL GIVE YOU THE STRENGTH TO REMAIN IN HIS HOLINESS.

TRUMPET CALL

It will happen in a moment, in the blink of an eye, when the last trumpet is blown. For when the trumpet sounds, those who have died will be raised to live forever. And we who are living will also be transformed.
1 CORINTHIANS 15:52 NLT

We all change in many ways as we go through our childhood, teen years, adult years, and elder years. Our bodies change, our opinions and attitudes change, and our view of the future—our perspective—changes. But the most amazing change is yet to come. When Christ returns to establish his kingdom on earth, we will become new, imperishable, and completely eternal.

Dear Jesus, I get so excited when I consider the day you will return to draw us to eternity with you. As I go through life and its many stages, I can't begin to fathom what it will be like to have an eternal body to match my eternal soul. I can never thank you enough for making me a part of your kingdom. Please help me to remember this gift when I get hung up on my earthly body, which will change in the twinkling of an eye.

HOW DOES THIS PERSPECTIVE HELP YOU TODAY? DWELL ON THE PROMISE OF YOUR ETERNAL BODY AND LET THE CONCERNS OF YOUR EARTHLY BODY FADE IN COMPARISON.

POWER UP

"You will receive power when the Holy Spirit comes on you; and you will be my witnesses in Jerusalem, and in all Judea and Samaria, and to the ends of the earth."
ACTS 1:8

God wants us to share his message with others, which can make many of us feel uncomfortable. We know it's the right thing to do, but the fear of rejection can paralyze us and keep us from doing what we are called to do. Just remember that he has empowered us, and as long as we speak the truth, we have nothing to worry about. God, in his goodness, is on our side.

Lord, I pray that I can overcome the fear of rejection as I encounter opportunities to talk about you. I know that you have promised to give me the power to witness to others, and I want to honor you and do your will.

HOW DO YOU FEEL ABOUT SHARING YOUR FAITH WITH OTHERS? TRUST THAT GOD WILL GIVE YOU THE RIGHT WORDS AT THE RIGHT TIME. IF HE WANTS YOU TO SHARE, AND HE DOES, HE WILL ALSO GIVE YOU THE STRENGTH TO DO IT!

WORKING AND THRIVING

Whoever trusts in his riches will fall,
but the righteous will flourish like a green leaf.
  PROVERBS 11:28 ESV

God tells us he loves a hard worker. So it is good for us to strive for success, and there is nothing wrong with earning a very good wage and saving wisely for the future. Financial success is a wonderful thing and doesn't have to be anyone's spiritual downfall, but God does ask us to keep everything in perspective. If we focus so heavily on money that we neglect our connection with and need for God, we will fall. If we focus on him, we will thrive, regardless of our financial situation.

Dear God, thank you so much for the finances you have blessed me with, even if sometimes I may struggle. I know if I keep working hard and keep focusing on you, it will all be okay. Sometimes finances might not work out on paper, but they work out because your will decrees it. No matter what I have or don't have, my blessings depend upon you.

ARE YOU TRUSTING IN YOUR RICHES OR IN GOD'S WILL? SUBMIT YOUR FINANCES TO THE LORD AND BE FAITHFUL WITH WHAT HE HAS GIVEN YOU.

SPEAK OUT

"Go and make disciples of all the nations, baptizing them in the name of the Father and the Son and the Holy Spirit. Teach these new disciples to obey all the commands I have given you. And be sure of this: I am with you always, even to the end of the age."
  MATTHEW 28:19-20 NLT

Have you ever been shy about sharing your faith, particularly when you aren't sure where the other people in the conversation are spiritually? God tells us in this verse that he is by our side as we witness to others. We don't have to hammer anyone over the head with God's message. After all, the heart of God's message is love.

We can share that love by listening, asking questions or even reaching out a helping hand. Words work too, as long as love, grace, and humility work together with truth. All we need to do is share how we've seen God at work in our lives. That's what a witness does: simply tells others what he or she has seen and heard.

I pray, dear Jesus, that I will shed my fear of sharing your message in my everyday life. You have promised to be there beside me, and with your presence, I am strong.

DOES FEAR KEEP YOU FROM PRESENTING THE GOSPEL TO OTHERS? ASK GOD FOR COURAGE AND FOR CREATIVE WAYS TO SHARE HIS LOVE WITH THOSE AROUND YOU.

EYES ON YOUR OWN WORK

Commit your way to the LORD,
Trust also in Him,
And He shall bring it to pass.
He shall bring forth your righteousness as the light,
And your justice as the noonday.

PSALM 37: 5-6 NKJV

Today's verse is nestled between several verses counseling us not to have our eyes on the successes of others with envy or with disappointment that someone's ill-gotten success so far outweighs our efforts. That feeling of injustice is something many of us may have experienced, but God counsels us to keep our eyes on him and to remain patient and humble because in that way we allow his righteousness to shine.

Dear Lord, it can be difficult at times when I look at the success of others if I know that success came dishonestly. Please help me to commit every day to you and to keep my eyes focused on the path you set out before me, knowing if I am humble, patient, and obedient, far better things are in my future. Thank you for your constant blessings.

IS THERE SOMEONE WHOSE SUCCESS YOU NEED TO LET GO? CHOOSE INSTEAD TO FOCUS ON WHAT THE LORD HAS BLESSED YOU WITH.

LOVE TRANSFORMATION

I trust in your unfailing love;
my heart rejoices in your salvation.
I will sing the LORD's praise,
for he has been good to me.
    PSALM 13:5-6 NIV

How has God been good to you? At times, it's easy to forget. We thank God for the big things, like forgiving our sins and assuring us of eternal life. But it's the little everyday gifts we often overlook: the beauty of a wildflower at our feet, the bounty of food in our pantry, a job that pays the bills, a body that's in good health, our children's laughter, or an unexpected call from someone we love. God's hand holds them all.

Today, take time to notice the little things. Thank God for each one. The more often you do, the more signs of his goodness you'll notice in the days to come.

Lord, thank you so much for your love that is unconditional and so immense I can't fathom its depth. I pray your gift of love will transform my life and allow me to shine your light for others to see.

HOW HAS GOD'S LOVE AFFECTED YOU IN YOUR EVERYDAY LIFE? BASK IN THE GLOW OF HIS LOVE AS YOU SPEND TIME WITH HIM TODAY.

ALWAYS FORGIVEN

I the LORD do not change. So you, O descendants of Jacob, are not destroyed.
MALACHI 3:6 NIV

Even those of us who are saved sometimes shudder at something we've done, or said, or even thought. We wonder if this is the sin that will cause God to turn away—maybe not for eternity, but long enough to teach us a lesson. At such times it's important to remember the moment when we humbly admitted we were hopeless sinners in need of a Savior. Sin is sin. We were no less tarnished before salvation than we are now, and Jesus forgave us and saved us. We will always need our Savior. And he will always answer our prayers for forgiveness.

Lord Jesus, please forgive me—again—for making a bad decision. For sinning again. Help me to behave as you want me to. Thank you for saving me forever from my sinful nature and its eternal consequences. Thank you for never leaving me.

IS THERE SOMETHING YOU NEED TO ASK GOD'S FORGIVENESS FOR TODAY? SUBMIT IT TO THE LORD CONFIDENTLY, KNOWING THAT HE WILL NOT HOLD BACK HIS GRACE AND GOODNESS.

TENDING THE GARDEN

*Oh, the joys of those who do not follow the advice
of the wicked, or stand around with sinners, or join in
with mockers. But they delight in the law of the LORD,
meditating on it day and night. They are like trees
planted along the riverbank, bearing fruit each season.
Their leaves never wither, and they prosper in all they do.*

PSALM 1:1-3 NLT

Do you delight in God's Word? Not just the Psalms, Proverbs, and host of favorite verses that come to mind because they warm your heart. How about God's commands? Do you delight in his call to obedience, holiness and sacrifice?

There's much of God's Word that isn't easy for us to wholeheartedly embrace. It can challenge us to do hard things: like confess our transgressions and love our enemies. But God's commands ultimately bring out the best in us. That's certainly cause for thanks and delight!

Dear Lord, thank you for showing us the way to righteousness. I pray that you will lead us away from those who revel in evil and keep us in your holy grip.

HAVE YOU EVER EXPERIENCED MOCKERY FROM OTHERS OVER YOUR FAITH? STAND FIRM IN THE LORD. HE WILL REWARD YOUR OBEDIENCE WITH HIS GOODNESS.

IN HIS NAME

Some trust in chariots and some in horses,
but we trust in the name of the LORD our God.
PSALM 20:7 NIV

Certainly in parts of today's world there exist Christians who suffer greatly for their faith, even suffering to the point of death. Such martyrs have a closer kinship than most of us to God's people of Biblical times, who faced battle involving powerful horses and chariots. Our battles might involve ostracism for being too *religious* or conservative in our ways. Regardless of who our foes are today, the name of the Lord is a guarantee that we will see victory in the end.

Lord God, when I consider your early followers, I know my life is comparatively safe and comfortable, and my battles are minor disappointments in life. Still, I know you honor my struggles for how they affect my life, and I thank you for reminding me to trust in you alone. I praise your holy name!

CAN YOU TAKE COMFORT THAT GOD WILL PROTECT YOU IN YOUR BATTLES? TRUST IN HIM ALONE TO BE YOUR DELIVERER.

MAY

We've passed through fire and flood,

yet in the end you always bring us out

better than we were before,

saturated with your goodness.

PSALM 66:12 TPT

THE WHOLE THING

You will seek me and find me, when you seek me with all your heart.
JEREMIAH 29:13 ESV

We are to love him completely and totally, and the amazing thing is that he knows when we're "all in." Halfheartedly worshiping God isn't going to cut it. One eye on the Lord and the other eye on our own way isn't going to work. The beautiful thing is that once we wholeheartedly give ourselves to Jesus, we are made new. His goodness will reign over our lives, and nothing can stand in the way of our eternal salvation and our being conformed to become more like him.

When we seek God, he never hides. He shows himself for who he is—worthy of our worship and our love.

Thank you, Lord Jesus, for loving me and giving me the hope of living with you forever. May I live out the rest of my days trusting you and only you.

WHAT ARE YOUR PRIORITIES IN LIFE? THINK ABOUT THE ETERNAL BENEFITS OF LOVING GOD COMPLETELY, AND LET THAT BE YOUR MOTIVATOR!

MY IMPORTANT JOB

Do not throw away your confidence; it will be richly rewarded. You need to persevere so that when you have done the will of God, you will receive what he has promised.

HEBREWS 10:35-36 NIV

It's pretty amazing that God has a specific role for each of us in his kingdom. Sometimes we lose sight of that, looking at our job for him as if we're one of millions of worker bees in a mass effort. But this is God we're talking about. Only he is able to organize life such that our contribution makes a difference the way it does. We should embrace that responsibility and feel confident and eager to do his will. Our individual efforts will be richly rewarded.

Thank you, Lord God, that what I do with my life matters to your kingdom. When I feel like my efforts don't matter, please remind me of the importance of my role. Please help me recognize my role! Sometimes even that is puzzling to me. Help me serve you with confidence and hear you when you say, "Yes. That's what I need you to do for me today."

WHAT DOES GOD NEED YOU TO DO FOR HIS KINGDOM TODAY? WHEN HE GIVES YOU A JOB, HE ALSO GIVES YOU EVERYTHING YOU NEED TO COMPLETE IT. JUST ASK HIM!

PERSONAL STASH

Do not store up for yourselves treasures on earth, where moth and rust destroy, and where thieves break in and steal. But store up for yourselves treasures in heaven, where neither moth nor rust destroys, and where thieves do not break in or steal; for where your treasure is, there your heart will be also.

MATTHEW 6:19-21 NASB

Are you a hoarder? You might think you're not, but if you have more than you need or can use in this lifetime, you might want to take another look. Are you focused more on making money so you can buy a bigger house and drive a fancier car than you are on your relationship with Christ? Remember that all of those things—the job, the mansion, and the wheels—can be taken away in a flash. However, your relationship with the Lord is yours to keep.

Dear Jesus, thank you for providing more for me than I'll ever need. Your love is more valuable than anything I could possibly earn. I pray that I will be content by living in your Word.

DO YOU HAVE MORE THINGS THAN YOU USE? MAYBE IT WOULD BE A GOOD IDEA TO GO THROUGH SOME OF THOSE THINGS AND BLESS OTHERS WHO NEED THEM MORE THAN YOU DO.

THE CHOSEN ONES

*You didn't choose me. I chose you. I appointed you to
go and produce lasting fruit, so that the Father will give
you whatever you ask for, using my name.*

JOHN 15:16 NLT

Even though we each chose to accept the gift of salvation
that Christ offers to everyone, Jesus told his disciples (and us)
that he has always known we would choose him. He chose us
before we even knew about his gift. And he chose us because
he knew we would bear fruit for him and his kingdom. Because
he chose us for that work, he promises that he and the Father
will help us in the effort. All we need to do is ask.

*Yes, Lord Jesus, I do ask for your help, today and always.
Thank you for choosing me and for working in my heart so
that I would, in turn, choose you. I want to live up to the honor
of being one of your chosen ones. Please put me where you
need me to be to increase the number of your followers. Help
me help others see that you have chosen them too.*

DO YOU KNOW SOMEONE WHO NEEDS TO KNOW
THEY'VE BEEN CHOSEN BY JESUS? SHARE THAT
ENCOURAGING WORD WITH THEM TODAY AND WATCH
HOW IT BRIGHTENS THEIR DAY!

JUST WHAT THE DOCTOR ORDERED

A cheerful heart is good medicine,
But a crushed spirit dries up the bones.
PROVERBS 17:22 NIV

Joy and happiness are gifts from God, but most of us allow external factors to determine our moods. Rather than let negativity continue to drag us down, it's better to turn to the great physician for support. His uplifting words are more powerful and healing than anything delivered by the world. The Lord wants us to enjoy the life he has blessed us with.

Oh, heavenly Father, thank you so much for your healing words that do more than put a smile on my face. I have peace and joy in my heart, knowing that you love me no matter what. Give me the ability to remember to focus on the true medicine of eternal salvation.

DO YOU LET EXTERNAL FACTORS DRAG YOU DOWN? EXPERIENCE GOD'S GOODNESS WHEN YOU TURN TO HIM FOR UPLIFTING.

NOT LOST AT ALL

*The Lamb at the center of the throne will be their
shepherd; he will lead them to springs of living water.
And God will wipe away every tear from their eyes.*
REVELATION 7:17 NIV

All we have to do is browse Facebook for a little while, or
talk with people at church, to learn of the loss of a loved one.
Maybe you're experiencing that in your own family. As difficult
as that loss is, one comfort we can take is the promise that,
for those loved ones who loved Jesus, every tear of pain or
sadness is gone. They are with Jesus, in eternal bliss, and God
has wiped away their tears.

*Dear Lord, it's still easy to bring back the sadness of losing
loved ones during my life. My own tears come readily,
especially if I consider the struggle faced before my loved
one died. But I thank you for reminding me that of the two of
us, my loved one is in the far better place. I might still cry, but
the one I lost is not lost at all. Thank you for the comfort and
eternal life you reserve for every one of us in heaven.*

DO YOU TAKE COMFORT THAT GOD EMBRACES YOU
WHEN YOU'VE LOST DEEPLY? EVERY TEAR SHED WILL BE
WIPED FROM OUR EYES AND WE WILL REJOICE AGAIN IN
ETERNITY.

RETURNING HOME

"So he returned home to his father. And while he was still a long way off, his father saw him coming. Filled with love and compassion, he ran to his son, embraced him, and kissed him."
LUKE 15:20 NLT

Most people know the parable of the prodigal son. The father was willing to put past mistakes behind and embrace his son with open arms. This is what Jesus has done for us no matter what we have done. He has thrown his arms around us and kissed us with his life changing grace.

We're no longer prodigals in his eyes. We're beloved daughters, wholly accepted, fully forgiven, worthy of his love and of all the eternal riches that come along with being a member of his family.

Thank you, Jesus, for giving your life for me. As the prodigal son returned home, I run to you for forgiveness and eternal love.

HAVE YOU EXPERIENCED YOUR OWN "RETURNING HOME" MOMENT? THANK THE LORD FOR HIS CONSTANT FORGIVENESS AND GOODNESS DEMONSTRATED IN YOUR LIFE.

A GOOD THING

"You have already been pruned and purified by the message I have given you."
JOHN 15:3 NLT

Jesus spoke the above words to his disciples in the midst of talking about how the vineyard keeper will prune the branches of his vine in order to be sure they are able to bear fruit. How lovely that he choose to assure them that, even though they may experience pruning they may not understand or enjoy, it is done so that they can better serve him, not because they have become unclean in his eyes.

Lord Jesus, thank you for your encouraging words in this verse. When something doesn't go the way I hope, it can be difficult to see through my disappointment. I might not recognize circumstances as helpful pruning, and I might even think I'm being punished for something I've done wrong. Far from it! You are tending to me with love.

HAVE YOU HAD A DISAPPOINTMENT THAT MIGHT ACTUALLY BE A GOOD THING? THANK THE LORD FOR HIS PRUNING IN YOUR LIFE, KNOWING THAT IT IS FOR THE BENEFIT OF BEARING GOOD FRUIT.

THE HOUSE THAT GOD BUILT

The temple I am going to build will be great, because our God is greater than all other gods. But who is able to build a temple for him, since the heavens, even the highest heavens, cannot contain him? Who then am I to build a temple for him, except as a place to burn sacrifices before him?

2 CHRONICLES 2:5-6 NIV

Does God need us to build him a temple? He doesn't need any of our material things, even though he does provide us with the ability to create and own them. Part of his plan is to show us the way to give generously to whatever and whoever promotes his kingdom. God wants us to work hard for what we have, to enjoy the goodness of the fruits of our labor, and to share with others. Those are our sacrifices to him.

Lord, thank you for the abilities you have bestowed upon me. I pray that I can honor you by using my possessions to your glory, and this includes sharing with others to promote your kingdom.

HOW CAN YOU USE YOUR BLESSINGS TO HONOR GOD? OFFER THEM BACK TO GOD TODAY AND ASK HIM TO SHOW YOU HOW TO USE THEM FOR HIS KINGDOM.

AS A MOTHER

I will extend peace to her like a river, and the wealth
of nations like a flooding stream; you will nurse and
be carried on her arm and dandled on her knees. As a
mother comforts her child, so will I comfort you; and you
will be comforted over Jerusalem.

ISAIAH 66:12-13 NIV

How lovely that the words God chose to express his absolute
love for Israel were words that symbolized a mother's love
for her child. Any of us who have been blessed as mothers,
or blessed by mothers, can identify with that unconditional,
unique love. When we think of how mothers love their children,
we can better understand that God's love is greater still.

Thank you, God, for loving me the way you love your chosen
nation, Israel. I thank you for my mother, Lord, and I thank you
for the opportunity to mother others. I pray for all women to
experience that kind of love in some fashion in their lives.

WILL YOU TAKE A MOMENT TO PRAY FOR OR ABOUT YOUR
MOTHER? GOD'S LOVE IS DEEPER THAN THE MATERNAL
BONDS OF MOTHERHOOD. TAKE COMFORT IN THAT
THOUGHT TODAY.

TRUE CHAMPION

Be strong and very courageous. Be careful to obey all the instructions Moses gave you. Do not deviate from them, turning either to the right or to the left. Then you will be successful in everything you do. Study this Book of Instruction continually. Meditate on it day and night so you will be sure to obey everything written in it. Only then will you prosper and succeed in all you do.

JOSHUA 1:7-8 NLT

Our definition of prosperity and success may be quite different from God's. Remember, the riches he's promised are those that don't wear out, can't be stolen, and will be stockpiled in heaven, as opposed to our garage. In other words, fame and fortune may not be waiting for us in this life, regardless of how hard we work or how carefully we study God's Word. If we find that discouraging, perhaps we've set our heart on the wrong view of what it means to succeed.

Success in God's kingdom means having a servant's heart, not having servants in our home. With God's help, may we prosper and succeed in all we do—for him.

Lord, I am grateful to be blessed with your holy Word. May I remember daily to use the tools you have provided to live my days according to your will.

HAVE YOU EVER TRIED TO LIVE YOUR LIFE WITHOUT THINKING ABOUT THE LORD'S WILL? IT'S NOT A GOOD PLAN. SUCCESS COMES WHEN WE FIND OUT WHAT GOD WANTS FOR US AND GO AFTER IT.

GOD'S VESSELS

He had no beauty or majesty to attract us to him,
nothing in his appearance that we should desire him.
ISAIAH 53:2 NIV

Just as Jesus didn't fit the majestic mold imagined by the people of his day, many people chosen by God to further his kingdom are written off today. We might not give attention to God's wisdom spoken through a particular person because we don't consider that person educated enough. Or maybe she doesn't fit the mold of the standard Christian wife and mother. Or maybe, God help us, we don't consider her successful enough by earthly standards to be used by God.

Lord Jesus, please touch my heart if I ever turn a deaf ear to someone you have chosen to share your wisdom or comfort with me. I want a discerning heart and mind. May I never make the mistake the people of your day did, to base value on outward appearance, rather than the God-blessed beauty of the heart.

HAS THE LORD SPOKEN TO YOU THROUGH SOMEONE UNEXPECTED LATELY? THANK HIM FOR THE INNER BEAUTY OF THAT PERSON TODAY.

DON'T WORRY; BE PRAYERFUL

"Do not be anxious, saying, 'What shall we eat?' or 'What shall we drink?' or 'What shall we wear?'"

We live in a fast-paced, pressure-filled, stressed-out culture. It's easy to fit right in. Our days become a To-Do list that never seems to get totally crossed off. No wonder anxiety is such a close companion. Often, we allow little things to become big things: making it to church on time, having the dessert we're baking turn out just right, losing five pounds before summer hits. We carry them all like oversized boulders, weighing down our hearts and minds.

God cares about the little things in our lives, as well as the big things, and he wants to free us from the anxiety of both. Let's ask him for perspective, as well as peace—and let the little things remain little in our lives.

Dear heavenly Father, thank you for providing so graciously. I turn my worries and concerns over to you so I can center my attention on your goodness and mercy.

ARE YOU A WORRIER? TURN THOSE ANXIOUS THOUGHTS OVER TO THE LORD, AND ASK HIM TO REPLACE THEM WITH HIS SUPERNATURAL PEACE.

HANG IN THERE

So let's not get tired of doing what is good. At just the right time we will reap a harvest of blessing if we don't give up.
GALATIANS 6:9 NLT

Some people have amazing stamina. They persevere in tough marriages, or tough jobs, or horribly harsh circumstances. And we look at them and wonder if they'll ever give up. The Bible tells us that those people have a rich harvest coming to them. They carry on, confident that the Lord will bless their faithfulness at the proper time. They should inspire us.

Precious Lord Jesus, I know I've given up at times when you might have wanted me to hang in there. Please forgive me and help me to stick with any projects, any relationships, any jobs that you want me to see to fruition. Help me to never grow weary.

WHAT CHALLENGE DO YOU HAVE THAT NEEDS GOD'S BLESSING AND ENCOURAGEMENT? ASK HIM FOR STAMINA TO KEEP GOING, AND LOOK FORWARD TO REAPING THAT HARVEST!

WONDERFUL GRACE

God, being rich in mercy, because of His great love with which He loved us, even when we were dead in our transgressions, made us alive together with Christ (by grace you have been saved).
EPHESIANS 2:4-5 NASB

What does it feel like to receive a box of chocolates or a bouquet of flowers? Not for your birthday. Not for your anniversary. Not even because you've had a bad day. Just because. That's the kind of gift we receive from God. His grace isn't earned or deserved. It's ours simply because God's love is so great.

But grace costs much more than a dozen roses or a pound of Godiva. It cost Jesus his life on the cross. What a gift—what a giver! All we can give in return is our love and praise. Let's take a moment to give that to God right now.

Thank you, oh Lord, for your grace and mercy. I know that everything you do for me is out of love. I pray that I may extend this to others so they can see you through my actions and words.

HOW DO YOU SHOW GRACE TO OTHERS? DEPEND ON THE LORD'S GRACE FOR YOURSELF AND WATCH HOW MUCH EASIER IT IS TO PASS ON TO OTHERS.

SURE FEET IN HIGH PLACES

*The Sovereign L*ORD *is my strength;*
he makes my feet like the feet of a deer,
he enables me to go on the heights.
HABAKKUK 3:19 NIV

How exciting is it to consider that we can be strong, thanks to God? We may not always feel we need that help, not when life is breezy and comfortable. But life is not always so, and sometimes we need strength and surefootedness to navigate. That's when we must remember to turn to the Lord, so we don't have to go it alone.

Lord God, you are my true source of strength—my strong
tower in times of trouble. Sometimes I can't imagine getting
through what others survive. But you will walk me through
anything. I'll carry on because you'll carry me.

IS THERE SOMETHING YOU NEED GOD'S HELP WITH TODAY? REMEMBER THAT GOD TRULY IS YOUR SOURCE OF STRENGTH. HE NEVER RUNS OUT, SO ASK HIM FOR AS MUCH AS YOU NEED.

CONFIDENCE BUILDER

The Spirit God gave us does not make us timid, but gives us power, love and self-discipline.
   2 TIMOTHY 1:7 NIV

We are more than what we seem. God's own Spirit lives inside us. His strength, wisdom, love—it's all at work within us. When we feel timid and small, not quite up to whatever task or challenge is in front of us, let's remember that we are more than what we seem.

We're not only beloved children of an almighty God, but walking, talking temples for his Spirit. We can hold our head high and move forward with confidence. Whatever we face today, we will not face it alone.

Dear God, thank you for being my wonderful Father who provides me with the power, love, and self-discipline that give me confidence in my everyday life. With this confidence, I pray that I can speak and act on your behalf to show the world that I am yours.

ARE YOU EVER SELF-CONSCIOUS OR TIMID? OVERCOME IT BY GRASPING HOLD OF THE FACT THAT GOD IS YOUR LOVING FATHER AND HE SURROUNDS YOU WITH HIS LOVE AND POWER.

EVERY KNEE, EVERY TONGUE

That at the name of Jesus every knee should bow, in heaven and on earth and under the earth, and every tongue confess that Jesus Christ is Lord to the glory of God the Father.

PHILIPPIANS 2:10-11 NLT

As believers living in an imperfect world, we become disheartened by how freely the Lord's name is used to curse people, things, and the most minor, annoying events. But the Word tells us in several different places that a time will come when everyone will kneel and acknowledge the sovereignty of Jesus Christ. We will do it joyfully, and others will do it as they should have all along—with an awareness of who this King truly is.

Praise you, Lord Jesus, for who you are. Hearing your name demeaned is painful, and I pray you will soon bring humility and awareness to those who have so little regard for the love and respect you deserve. I love you with all my heart.

COULD YOU PRAY TODAY FOR THOSE WHO DON'T YET KNOW OR RESPECT GOD? ASK HIM TO GIVE YOU BOLDNESS TO SHARE WHO HE IS TO THE WORLD EVEN IN THE FACE OF DISRESPECT.

GOODNESS OF GRACE

The grace of our Lord was poured out on me abundantly, along with the faith and love that are in Christ Jesus.
    1 TIMOTHY 1:14 NIV

Picture yourself after a long day of working in the garden, hiking a rocky canyon or serving at a soup kitchen. It's time to head home and hop into a hot shower. You know how good that shower feels? The grace God has poured on us is like a spiritual hot shower after a tough, gritty life.

God's gifts refresh us, as well as cleanse us, empower us, and allow us to fulfill our potential as the amazing women he has created us to be. Declare today a "spiritual spa" day and bask in the gift of God's grace.

Dear Jesus, I am grateful for your love and open arms, welcoming me into your kingdom. Your abundant grace gives me peace as I go through life each day. May I continue to stay focused on your goodness.

HOW HAVE YOU SEEN GOD'S GOODNESS? FOCUS ON THAT TODAY AND BE ENCOURAGED.

REMEMBERING OUR PLACE

Behold, I am insignificant; what can I reply to You? I lay my hand on my mouth.
JOB 40:4 NASB

Sometimes we joke about our confusion over God's will in a given situation. We ask, "Why doesn't he just *tell* me what to do?" That uncertainty was far more serious for Job when he lost everything of value in his earthly life. He also lost his patience, eventually, with God. When God reminded him who he truly was, Job was mortified at his arrogance. God loves us unconditionally and understands when we feel anger or frustration, but it's important to remember exactly who he is.

Heavenly Father, please help me to always respect and honor you for your generosity, forgiveness, and especially your omnipotence. I thank you for taking on earthly flesh as Jesus Christ so we could feel that connection with you. I pray I never take your extreme worthiness for granted.

WOULD YOU SAY YOU HAVE A HEALTHY "FEAR" OF THE LORD? DWELL ON THE RESPONSE OF JOB FOR A WHILE, AND REMEMBER WHO GOD IS.

SET FREE

Christ has truly set us free. Now make sure that you stay free, and don't get tied up again in slavery to the law.
GALATIANS 5:1 NLT

No one wants to be enslaved by anyone or anything, but we have to remember what true freedom is. God wants us to know his truth and be obedient to him. We must lay aside anything that takes our eyes off him, or we will forever be slaves to something—even slaves to God's law by living a legalistic life.

Living our lives by the letter of God's law, instead of by his "new command" to love God and one another, encourages us to slide back into trusting our own good deeds to win favor with him, instead of accepting the free gift of God's grace through Christ's sacrifice. We are free in Christ—free to live, love, and leave legalism behind.

Heavenly Father, thank you for freeing me from worldly sin by loving me unconditionally. I pray that I will leave what has me in bondage because only through you will I know and understand total freedom.

HAVE YOU EVER FELT LIKE A SLAVE TO SOMETHING WORLDLY? CHRIST DIED TO SET YOU FREE! REJOICE IN THAT FREEDOM TODAY.

NUMBERS

Though a man might prevail against one who is alone, two will withstand him—a threefold cord is not quickly broken.

ECCLESIASTES 4:12 ESV

We can certainly follow God and learn about Jesus and salvation and what that means in our lives if we choose to do it on our own. But community is so effective in keeping our foundation strong and our understanding sharpened. If you hope to make friends with like-minded people, there is really no better place than a strong, Bible-teaching church. There is strength in numbers!

Lord Jesus, I thank you so much for blessing me with my believing friends. When I need accountability, real love, and Godly advice, I know a group of people to embrace and who will embrace me. Please help me to be that for others as well.

DO YOU TAKE STEPS TO BUILD GODLY FRIENDSHIPS? GOD DID NOT INTEND FOR US TO BE ALONE IN THIS LIFE. REAP THE BENEFITS OF FIGHTING ALONGSIDE SOMEONE WHO IS LIKE-MINDED.

GOOD BREEDS GOODNESS

Do not those who plot evil go astray?
But those who plan what is good find love and
faithfulness.
PROVERBS 14:22 NIV

Have you ever known someone who dwells on the bad things in life and plots ways to get even? That's an unhealthy state of mind that can only bring bad things in return. When we spend time thinking about loving others and devising ways to share God's goodness, we are mirroring God's actions and intentions. This, in turn, opens our hearts to the blessings he has planned for us.

Dear Lord, thank you so much for loving me and being faithful in your immense goodness. Help me to turn away from bad thoughts and plans to get even with others who hurt me in any way. Help me to continue having loving thoughts and actions.

HOW HAS GOD SHOWN HIS LOVE AND FAITHFULNESS TO YOU? EXTEND THAT LOVE TO OTHERS EVEN WHEN IT'S DIFFICULT.

UNDER THE SKIN

Charm is deceptive, and beauty does not last; but a woman who fears the Lord will be greatly praised.
  PROVERBS 31:30 NLT

There is absolutely nothing wrong with hanging onto some of the outer beauty God blessed us with in our youth. We needn't feel we are insulting God by looking our best. But we should take comfort, especially as we age, in knowing our inner beauty will never fade. In fact, if we follow Christ's lead, our inner beauty will become far greater as we age and receive his gift of perspective. We aren't all naturally blessed with a gentle and quiet spirit. That's a far better goal than perfect skin!

Thank you, Lord, for the outer beauty you chose for me, whether it fits society's standards or not. I know so many women, especially those who have lived long enough to truly develop the grace of strength and gentleness, who just become more and more beautiful with time. Please help me to be such a woman.

ARE YOU ABLE TO SEE YOUR INNER BEAUTY? FEAR AND PRAISE THE LORD, AND YOU ARE BOUND TO FIND IT GROWING INCREDIBLY OVER TIME.

DESSERT, ANYONE?

"God did not send his son into the world to condemn the world, but to save the world through him."
JOHN 3:17 NIV

Parents everywhere have said, "If you're good, you can have dessert." Aren't you thankful that God didn't say that to us? We can never be good enough to earn the "dessert" of spending eternity with God in heaven. Out of his goodness, God chose to save us through his own sacrifice instead of through our own imperfect attempts to lead a godly life. Without him, that's impossible. Even with him, it can still be a struggle at times. But even then, God's grace and forgiveness come through.

As for our "dessert"? We don't know exactly what heaven will be like. But considering our amazing Creator, it can't be anything other than good.

Dear heavenly Father, thank you so much for forgiving me and bringing Jesus to wash away my sin. I pray that I never forget how you have made me guiltless without having to do anything to earn it.

HAVE YOU EVER FELT UNDESERVING OF YOUR BLESSINGS? YOU ARE! SO JUST ENJOY THE BLESSINGS YOU HAVE, KNOWING THAT YOU DON'T DESERVE THEM BUT HAVE BEEN GIVEN THEM ANYWAY.

LOOK DELIGHTED!

A cheerful look brings joy to the heart;
good news makes for good health.
PROVERBS 15:30 NLT

Have you ever caught yourself in the mirror when you hadn't expected to? Did you catch yourself scowling? That may be something that happens more often with age, but it would be nice if one's go-to expression was joyful. A smile makes such a difference to one's appearance—almost like a natural facelift. We're always quick to smile when we get good news, and if we believe in Christ's promises we have good news to last beyond a lifetime.

Thank you so much, Lord Jesus, for the good news of salvation you brought to my life. Please help that awareness pervade my being, bringing a constant, pleasant natural expression to my face. Certainly that kind of expression represents the inner joy of a life with you and is exceedingly inviting.

WHAT'S YOUR UNCONSCIOUS EXPRESSION? CHECK IT OUT! TRY TO MAKE IT ONE OF DELIGHT SO OTHERS WONDER WHAT YOU HAVE AND WANT IT FOR THEMSELVES.

TIME TO RELAX

Return to your rest, my soul,
for the LORD has been good to you.
    PSALM 116:7 NIV

Life for most of us is filled with busyness that keeps us hopping from the moment we wake up until it's time to go to bed. We have schedules and to-do lists that even Superman would find challenging. On top of all that, we have health issues, family concerns, and other things that keep us from going to sleep.

God wants us to turn our concerns over to him and rest, so he can refresh us, body and soul. When you get into bed tonight, take a deep breath, relax, and ask God to refresh you inside and out.

Thank you, Jesus, for offering me the rest and relaxation that my body and mind need. Lord, I know that I have gotten caught up in the chaos of life. I pray that I remember to let go of it and turn it over to you.

IS THERE A PROBLEM IN YOUR LIFE THAT KEEPS YOU AWAKE AT NIGHT? LEAVE IT AT GOD'S FEET AND LET YOURSELF REST IN THE PEACE THAT HE HAS FOR YOU WHEN YOU DO.

TRAINING WITH LOVE

Fathers, do not provoke your children to anger,
but bring them up in the discipline and instruction
of the Lord.
EPHESIANS 6:4 ESV

Most parents absolutely dote on their children. The love for them is unlike any other love experienced. Yet some parents get enjoyment out of making fun of their children, using downright sarcastic names for them, or pulling pranks on them that end in some kind of disappointment or humiliation. None of that behavior reflects love or nurturing. Parents are the most effective encouragers their children will ever have—at least they should be.

Thank you, Jesus, for children. I pray you will guide me in how I treat them, always training them in the way they should go, but also giving them love and a sense of value. May I never deliberately exasperate them. Please help me to mirror your unconditional love while guiding them in your ways.

DO THE CHILDREN AROUND YOU KNOW HOW IMPORTANT THEY ARE? TELL THEM TODAY AND WATCH A SMILE SPREAD ACROSS THEIR FACES.

SHOW A LITTLE LOVE

*In everything set them an example
by doing what is good.*
TITUS 2:7 NIV

We know we can't earn our way to heaven, nor are we expected to. However, we are still called to do the right thing out of love and respect for God. Doing the right thing is also a great way to show God's love to others. Even the smallest act can make another person's day. Being kind to a store clerk, holding the door for a young mom trying to enter a building with her small children, or getting something off a top shelf for someone in a wheelchair can make a big difference.

Jesus took time out of his busy schedule to play with children. Let's follow his example and allow a little extra time each day just to share our love—and his—in practical ways.

Lord, thank you for your mercy and understanding about my flaws and imperfections. I pray that I live my life for your glory and that I am able to show your love through my actions.

WHAT ARE SOME WAYS YOU CAN SHOW THE LOVE OF CHRIST TO PEOPLE YOU DON'T KNOW? MAKE A POINT TO DO THAT TODAY.

BANQUET

He has brought me to his banquet hall,
And his banner over me is love.
SONG OF SOLOMON 2:4 NASB

When we're hungry and someone sets out a spread of beautiful food, we're eager to taste all of the delicious flavors, aren't we? How much sweeter is that taste when we're led to the banquet hall by a God who loves us unconditionally? Sometimes we forget what comfort and peace we have right at our fingertips. We mustn't let any other "flavors" distract us from the delicious blessings he has for us.

Thank you, God, for the peace and joy you set out before me, just waiting for me to taste and enjoy. When I get too busy and distracted by everyday life and earthly gratifications, please gently guide me back to the truly good taste of your love and protection.

WHAT TASTE HAS HE BLESSED YOU WITH LATELY? SAVOR THE FLAVOR FOR A WHILE AND ENJOY ITS GOODNESS. ALL OF GOD'S BLESSINGS ARE DELICIOUS!

GIFT OF HEALING

"He himself bore our sins" in his body on the cross, so that we might die to sins and live for righteousness; "by his wounds you have been healed."
1 PETER 2:24 NIV

One of the worst sicknesses of all is sin, and we're all afflicted with it. However, God has given us the gift of healing through his Son. Unlike expensive doctor visits and health insurance, this is free because our Father loved us enough to take the pain and suffering upon himself so that we could be with him forever.

Being healed in this way is more than just being forgiven. God's touch can heal us from guilt, shame, and regret, so we can be strong enough and confident enough, to move forward toward a healthier, godlier, way of life.

Thank you, Lord Jesus, for giving me the greatest gift of all. Your goodness continues to astound me. I pray that no matter what happens in life that I will remember you are the ultimate healer.

HOW HAVE YOU BEEN HEALED? THANK THE LORD FOR HIS HEALING POWER AND GRACE OVER YOUR LIFE AND THE LIVES OF THOSE AROUND YOU.

JUNE

From your kindness you send the rain

to water the mountains

from the upper rooms of your palace.

Your goodness brings forth fruit for all to enjoy.

PSALM 104:13 TPT

HIS COMFORT

God blesses those who mourn, for they will be comforted.
MATTHEW 5:4 NLT

Many Bible scholars say that the mourning referred to in this verse is not mourning over earthly loss in life but over our own spiritual shortcomings. And certainly—especially after we truly accept Christ and understand how far we fall from his perfection, regardless of how hard we try—we do mourn. But we should always take comfort in Jesus's grace, which covers all of those shortcomings.

Lord Jesus, I am comforted, as you promised, every time I realize I've done it again—sinned against you and maybe a few other people in my life—but you stepped in long ago and cleared my name. I ask that you bless me with the humility I need to make amends with those I have wronged. That task is nothing compared to the sacrifice you made to comfort me.

DO YOU TAKE COMFORT IN KNOWING HE STILL WIPES YOUR SINS CLEAN? REST IN THE COMFORT THAT HE HAS READY FOR YOU WHEN YOU MOURN YOUR SPIRITUAL SHORTCOMINGS.

BODY FOR CHRIST

Do you not know that your body is a temple of the Holy Spirit within you, whom you have from God, and that you are not your own? For you have been purchased at a price. Therefore, glorify God in your body.
1 CORINTHIANS 6:19-20 ESV

As much as we need physical fitness for a healthy life, spiritual fitness is essential to stay connected with Jesus. Our bodies, minds, and souls aren't really ours. Our entire being belongs to Christ, who suffered the pain of persecution and laid down his life for us. It is now our job to glorify him with our gifts, and that starts with becoming spiritually fit. That includes spending time in prayer, getting better acquainted with God's Word and connecting with God's family through a local church.

We need to act on what we learn, putting God's love into action. Being spiritually fit is something that doesn't just happen on the inside. It should be visible from the outside, as well.

Dear Lord, thank you for the blessing of this earthly body. You allow me to delight in the sweet sights, sounds, smells, and feelings. I pray that I never take these blessings for granted.

HOW CAN YOU SHOW APPRECIATION FOR THE EARTHLY BODY THAT GOD HAS BLESSED YOU WITH? ASK HIM TO BLESS YOU WITH THE DESIRE FOR SPIRITUAL FITNESS TODAY.

NOTHING NEW

What has been will be again, what has been done will be done again;
there is nothing new under the sun.
ECCLESIASTES 1:9 NIV

If you read today's verse and those surrounding it out of context, it sounds quite defeating! There is nothing new, the world is full of weariness, neither the eye nor the ear is satisfied, and so on. But what Solomon is describing is the world—and life—without God. Without him in our lives, we and the earth are on a constant loop lacking significance. What a difference our Lord makes!

Thank you so much, Lord God, for creating us and this magnificent world. I am so grateful for my many blessings. But I recognize them as blessings from you, not just things that randomly happen. Without you in my life, it would have no meaning. I would have no meaning. But you tell me I am so loved that you sacrificed the one most precious to you. You amaze me.

CAN YOU REFLECT TODAY ON HIS IMPACT ON ABSOLUTELY EVERYTHING IN LIFE? ALLOW THIS AMAZING REVELATION TO GO DEEP INTO YOUR SOUL.

LIVING IN THE LIGHT

If we walk in the Light as He Himself is in the Light, we have fellowship with one another, and the blood of Jesus His Son cleanses us from all sin.

1 JOHN 1:7 NASB

What does light do? It helps us see things more clearly. It's also vital for helping things grow. That's what God's light does for us, as well. When we begin to see life from God's perspective, we can better sort out what's important from what's trivial, what's loving from what's selfish, and what's temporary from what's eternal.

As we allow this knowledge to influence the choices we make in life, we grow! We not only grow closer to God, but we become more mature in our faith. The more we mature, the more the world around us can see God's image more clearly through us.

Thank you, Lord Jesus, for washing our sins clean, for helping us see life through your eyes, and for helping us grow. Your ultimate sacrifice provides the light of truth that we need in order to appreciate the feast of your goodness.

HOW HAS GOD SHOWN YOU HIS LIGHT IN YOUR LIFE? RADIATE HIS LOVE TO THOSE AROUND YOU AS YOU BASK IN HIS LIGHT.

WHAT WOULD YOU DO?

"In the same way, let your light shine before others, that they may see your good deeds and glorify your Father in heaven."
MATTHEW 5:16 NIV

There is a reality television show called *What Would You Do*, in which unsuspecting people are set up in certain negative scenarios to see if they will do the noble thing if they are unaware that they are being watched. In a way, what Jesus espouses in today's verse is similar—we never know who (besides the Lord, of course) is watching our behavior. Our good deeds are like commercials for the Christian life and our Father in heaven.

Dear Jesus, I pray I will always mirror your reaction to circumstances around me, stepping forth to do the right thing or lend a helping hand, as if someone is always watching. Not only might a seeker see, I know you see. I pray I will never disappoint you with my choices.

WOULD YOUR BEHAVIOR CHANGE IF YOU KNEW THE WORLD WAS WATCHING? ASK GOD TO BLESS YOU WITH INTEGRITY, SO YOU CHOOSE WHAT IS RIGHT ALL THE TIME.

APP QUEST

Every prudent man acts with knowledge,
But a fool lays open his folly.
PROVERBS 13:16 NKJV

When we want to reach an unfamiliar destination, a map app on our phone can lead us there. It can also warn us when there's a detour ahead or traffic we should avoid. A wise driver learns to use this tool well. God's way, and his wisdom, are our "app" for traveling the road of life.

When we insist on heading our own way, chances are we're going to encounter potholes and dead ends along the road. Why not turn to God and his Word and ask for directions? It will make our journey smoother and lead us where our hearts truly long to go.

Lord, thank you for the ability to discern. I pray that you will guide me in all I say and help me use only words that will glorify you.

WHERE ARE YOU TRYING TO GO TODAY? WHAT DOES GOD'S WORD HAVE TO SAY ABOUT YOUR DESTINATION? TRY MAKING IT A JOURNEY GOD WOULD BE PLEASED TO ACCOMPANY YOU ON.

DISCIPLINE AND DELIGHT

Discipline your children, and they will give you peace of mind and will make your heart glad.
PROVERBS 29:17 NLT

Many of us have children or have had children under our care, whether ours or someone else's. Most know that feeling of not wanting to enforce discipline, either because it doesn't seem to be working or because giving in feels like the loving choice. But when children are grown and you loved them enough to discipline them, you will no doubt agree they are a delight.

Dear Father, I know I am your child, and there are times I need discipline, although I might feel like that discipline wouldn't be enforced if you truly loved me. I am sorry for being so childish in those moments, and I thank you for molding me day-by-day into a better Christian.

IS GOD DISCIPLINING YOU ABOUT ANYTHING TODAY? RECEIVE THAT DISCIPLINE AS HIS LOVE AND CARE FOR YOU. IT IS FOR YOUR GOOD.

RIPEST FRUIT

The fruit of the Spirit is love, joy, peace, patience, kindness, goodness, faithfulness, gentleness and self-control; against such things there is no law.
GALATIANS 5:22-23 NASB

Every fruit of the Spirit is a "good" fruit. However, notice that the first fruit on the list is *love*. This is significant because that's what all of our fruitful actions and thoughts should be rooted in.

When we wonder what the patient thing, the kind thing, or the gentle thing to do in any situation would be, we can start by asking ourselves what the loving thing to do would be. When we love well, all of these other fruits tag along, like a bunch of grapes all bound together by the vine.

Dear God, I pray that I am able to honor your desire to show the fruit of your Spirit in my life. Thank you for bringing your Son to show me the perfect example of love and how to live my life.

DO YOU THINK ABOUT THE FRUIT OF THE SPIRIT IN YOUR EVERYDAY LIFE? NOTICE IT AS YOU GO ABOUT YOUR DAY, AND THANK GOD FOR THE BLESSING THAT IS IN THAT FRUIT.

MOTIVATORS

Let us consider how we may spur one another on toward love and good deeds.
    HEBREWS 10:24 NIV

We may all know what our spiritual gifts are, or maybe we don't. Many churches try to help their congregants discover which gift they might be able to use to serve God. Sometimes the encouragers among us are the very ones who motivate us to serve him. Encouragement itself is a spiritual gift, and when it comes naturally to someone, we all reap the benefits. A kind word and an astute observation are often all we need to desire service for the Lord.

Lord, I know you bless each member of your church with a spiritual gift of some kind. I thank you for that, and I ask that you surround me with believers who choose to spur each other on toward deeds that build your kingdom.

WHAT GIFT WILL YOU USE TO SERVE GOD TODAY? IF YOU DON'T KNOW WHAT YOU HAVE TO OFFER, ASK THOSE WHO ARE CLOSEST TO YOU. BETTER YET, ASK THE LORD— AND DON'T STOP ASKING UNTIL YOU GET AN ANSWER.

TOUGH TO LOVE

"I say to you, Love your enemies and pray for those who persecute you."
  MATTHEW 5:44 ESV

The first impulse we have when someone hurts or betrays us is certainly not to love them. It's to get even. To distance ourselves from them. To grumble to others about them. To pray—but only to remind God what a horrible thing this person did and then give him a few choice ideas about what he could to do help settle the score.

Yes, this is one of many Bible verses that turns what we'd instinctively do in a given situation on its head. To love our enemies is to give them the opposite of what they deserve. Which is exactly what God did for us. He loved us when we'd turned our backs on him. With God's help, we can treat others the way he treated us—with exactly what they don't deserve, but truly need.

Lord, as difficult as it may be, I pray that I can find it in my heart to forgive those who hurt me. Rather than call them my enemies, I know I should see them as my opportunity to be more Christ-like in my actions, thoughts, and prayers.

HAVE YOU EVER BEEN HURT BY SOMEONE? PRAY FOR THEM TODAY, AND GIVE THEM THE GIFT OF FORGIVENESS.

CRAVINGS

Like newborn babies, crave pure spiritual milk, so that by it you may grow up in your salvation, now that you have tasted that the Lord is good.
    1 PETER 2:2-3 NIV

In other verses we're encouraged to put away childish things, but today's verse is a bit different. One way we *are* to be like children, even like newborns, is that we should experience a desire for spiritual learning as strong as a newborn's need for mother's milk. Once we've grasped that initial rush of the taste of the Lord, we should crave more of him.

Yes, Lord Jesus, I want to be totally overtaken with your goodness. Please nurture in me that desire to absorb everything I can about you. Instill a hunger in me that won't be satisfied other than by you and your Word.

IS YOUR HUNGER FOR HIM AS STRONG TODAY AS THE DAY YOU ACCEPTED HIM? DWELL ON HIS GOODNESS IN YOUR LIFE AND GET HUNGRY AGAIN!

I'M RICH

The blessing of the Lord brings wealth,
without painful toil for it.
    PROVERBS 10:22 NIV

People seem to have a warped idea of wealth and richness. Most of us assume it means having more money than we can spend, more possessions than we can use, more toys than we can play with, and a bigger house than we need. However, true wealth is what God has already blessed us with—his eternal love. The beauty of it all is that we don't even have to work for it. We own it simply by having faith in him. That is the most valuable gift he could have ever given.

I am thankful, Lord Jesus, that you have claimed me as your heir. Thank you so much for your richest blessings that I don't deserve. I pray that I am able to honor you by being your faithful servant.

HOW DOES GOD'S BLESSING COMPARE TO WORLDLY WEALTH? WEIGH THE TWO UP IN YOUR MIND AND HEART TODAY AND SEE HOW TRULY FULFILLING GOD'S WEALTH IS COMPARED TO THE WORLD'S.

CREATING

The LORD God formed the man from the dust of the ground and breathed into his nostrils the breath of life, and the man became a living being.
    GENESIS 2:7 NIV

It really is no great stretch for a Christian to accept that God created the universe out of nothing. He created a man from the dust of the ground. He created a woman from the rib of that man. And he created a spotless member of eternity from a hopeless sinner.

Thank you, God, for creating humanity and then doing what needed to be done to save humanity. Thank you, Jesus, for taking my place on the cross. And thank you, Holy Spirit, for breathing your life into my heart every day. I will never be able to repay my blessings, but I am so thrilled that I'll have eternity to try.

ISN'T IT AMAZING WHAT THE TRINITY HAS DONE FOR US? BE INSPIRED AGAIN BY THE INCREDIBLE GOD THAT CREATED THE WORLD AND EVERYTHING IN IT.

THIRST QUENCHER

As the deer longs for streams of water,
so I long for you, O God.
PSALM 42:1 NLT

Do we really thirst for God? Or do we simply enjoy having him in our lives because of all the blessings he brings our way? If that's where we are right now, that's not uncommon. Little kids act the same way. As babies, they long for the face of their mother because it means food and comfort. But as they grow, so does their love. They long to spend time with Mom just because they love her. When too much time goes by between visits, they can truly hunger for her presence.

Our hunger and thirst for God will grow along with our maturity. But maturity doesn't just happen. We have to make choices that foster our own spiritual growth. The more choices we make that honor God, the more mature we'll grow and the thirstier for his presence we'll be.

Dear Jesus, thank you for giving me the knowledge that you are all I really need. Pull me closer to you and help me see what I don't need or what may create a wedge between me and my love for you.

HAS THERE EVER BEEN SOMETHING YOU'VE WANTED MORE THAN ANYTHING ELSE? WAS IT AS FULFILLING AS YOU THOUGHT IT WOULD BE? MAKE IT YOUR DESIRE TO BE WITH GOD, AND THEN YOU WILL BE TRULY FILLED.

THE SON OF RIGHTEOUSNESS

For you who revere my name,
the sun of righteousness will rise
with healing in its wings.
And you will go out and leap
like calves released from the stall.
MALACHI 4:2 NIV

In this, one of the last verses of the Old Testament, God is making a promise to his people, and Jesus is that promise. The description of leaping like calves released from the stall is so appropriate to the joy one feels when understanding what a relationship with Christ is like. We are blessed to have Jesus available to us immediately upon accepting his gift of eternal life. We don't have to wait 400 years, as the Old Testament believers did, for the healing wings of our loving Savior.

Precious Jesus, I do feel uplifted and joyful when I reflect on how you love me. Please help me to always come back to that joy no matter where my day takes me. Thank you for being with me now. I love you.

DO YOU FEEL THE JOY OF KNOWING JESUS IS THERE FOR YOU? LET YOUR STEP BE LIGHTER TODAY AS YOU THINK ABOUT THAT.

ADOPTED DAUGHTER

"I will be a Father to you,
And you shall be My sons and daughters,"
Says the LORD Almighty.
    2 CORINTHIANS 6:18 NKJV

Often, adoptive parents tell their children that they're blessed because they were chosen. As God's adopted children, the same is true of us. God chose us. And when he did, we weren't on our best behavior. He saw us for who we truly were—the good, the bad, and everything in between.

God's love isn't based on what we do, but who we are. Just like adoptive parents and their children. Today, remind yourself that you are chosen. God loves you so much that his family wouldn't be complete without you in it.

Thank you, God, for choosing to adopt me. I know that you will always be there for me, even when I slip and fall. Your goodness knows no bounds.

HOW DID YOUR LIFE CHANGE WHEN GOD ADOPTED YOU? THINK OF THE BENEFIT YOU REAP IN BEING ADOPTED INTO GOD'S FAMILY, AND THANK GOD FOR THE GOODNESS IN HIS PLAN.

PARENTING SKILLS

Hear, my son, your father's instruction,
and forsake not your mother's teaching.
   PROVERBS 1:8 ESV

Not all of us had parents who taught us what we needed to know with regard to Christ's saving grace or even a wholesome life in general. Those of us who were raised by loving parents know we were blessed in that regard. God knows how we were raised, and while a father's instruction or a mother's teaching might fall short of what we needed, we can turn that around by parenting the way God would have wished for us.

Dear God, I want to honor you in my parenting skills and in how I behave with children. I ask that you help me to be a loving, wise teacher, always representing you as the greatest, most accepting parent I know.

DO YOU REPRESENT OUR HEAVENLY FATHER WITH THE CHILDREN IN YOUR CARE? YOU HAVE THE OPPORTUNITY TO SPEAK INTO THEIR LIVES IN A POWERFUL WAY, SO MAKE YOUR WORDS COUNT!

HOW DO YOU SPELL RELIEF?

He said to her, "Daughter, your faith has made you well. Go in peace. Your suffering is over."
MARK 5:34 NLT

We have all suffered something. It may be physical, mental, or emotional pain, but we've experienced difficult times that have made us wonder if we'll ever pull through. Jesus promises that when we put our faith in him, he will relieve our suffering. But that doesn't mean we'll be immediately healed like the people Jesus touched in the Gospels. It could happen. After all, with God nothing is impossible. But our suffering may also be relieved in other ways.

While we struggle with physical pain, God may provide the strength and peace we need to continue finding joy in life. While we're still mourning a loss, God may bring someone into our lives who understands our pain and can be a loving companion through it. Yes, God works in mysterious ways. But he is working, even when relief doesn't come the way we expect.

Lord, thank you for healing me from all of my ailments. All I need to do is believe and know that when I turn to you for hope, you will make good on your promise to deliver joy and peace. I have faith in you, dear Jesus.

HAVE YOU WONDERED IF YOUR SUFFERING WILL EVER END? BE ENCOURAGED TODAY THAT GOD IS WITH YOU IN YOUR SUFFERING. HE DOES NOT LEAVE YOU IN YOUR TIME OF NEED.

A NO-BRAINER

"What father among you, if his son asks for a fish, will instead of a fish give him a serpent?"
LUKE 11:11 ESV

One of the most terrific things about this verse is the wording directed so clearly at fathers. It almost sounds as if Jesus is saying, "Hey, this is a no-brainer. If you ask me to bless you, of course I'm going to bless you. I love you like you love your sons and daughters." He encourages us all to come boldly before him and ask for his blessings.

Thank you, Jesus, for the way you love us. Thank you for our fathers. Please help us to honor them and show them our love. Please bless those who didn't know their fathers or whose relationships with their fathers were strained. We look forward to the day we meet our perfect heavenly Father.

WILL YOU PRAY FOR YOUR EARTHLY FATHER TODAY? THANK THE LORD FOR ALL THAT YOUR EARTHLY FATHER HAS TAUGHT YOU ABOUT THE GOODNESS OF YOUR HEAVENLY FATHER.

TESTING WHAT'S GOOD

Do not treat prophecies with contempt but test them all;
hold on to what is good, reject every kind of evil.
1 THESSALONIANS 5:20-22 NIV

The world is filled with so many things that appear good and wonderful, but when held up to the Word of God, their brilliance fades. We're emotional creatures that are easily swayed by shiny, pretty things that make us feel good. That is why it's so important to stay immersed in the truth. We must hold everything up against God's pure light and compare it to what he says.

Just because someone tells us "this is what the Lord says" or "this is what this passage of Scripture means" doesn't make it true. We need to be discerning, prayerful, and steeped in our own study of Scripture to determine what is good—and what falls short.

Dear Lord, thank you for presenting the truth through your
Word. I pray that I continue to test worldly ideas by holding
them up to what is written in the Bible.

HAVE YOU EVER EXPERIENCED SOMETHING THAT SEEMED GOOD BUT WASN'T WHEN YOU TESTED IT BIBLICALLY? THANK GOD FOR HIS PERFECT TRUTH THAT SHINES LIGHT ON DARKNESS AND CONFUSION.

HANDS OFF

David also said to Solomon his son, "Be strong and courageous, and do the work. Do not be afraid or discouraged, for the LORD God, my God, is with you. He will not fail you or forsake you until all the work for the service of the temple of the LORD is finished."

1 CHRONICLES 28:20 NIV

These words from a father to a son are so lovely. David knew Solomon had a huge undertaking before him: the building of the Lord's temple. David couldn't do the job for his son. It can be difficult for parents to remain hands-off with their children's responsibilities. But we can help by encouraging them in their efforts and in God's love and support for them. Our experience with God's blessings carry a lot of weight.

Thank you, Lord, for children. May I always be an encourager to them when they face challenges. I pray my own attitude when facing challenges shows them that you will not forsake us when we have important tasks before us.

ARE YOU AN ENCOURAGER TO THE CHILDREN AROUND YOU? THINK OF HOW IMPORTANT THE WORDS ADULTS SPOKE TO YOU WERE WHEN YOU WERE YOUNGER. SHARE THE TRUTH OF GOD'S LOVE WITH THE CHILDREN AROUND YOU, AND WATCH THE POWERFUL IMPACT IT HAS ON THEIR LIVES.

JUST RIGHT

Let us not become conceited, or provoke one another,
or be jealous of one another.
GALATIANS 5:26 NLT

These days it's totally acceptable to act like we're "all that and a bag of chips"—even if inside we feel as though we'll never measure up to those around us. We're all vying to prove our worth. Yet we've somehow come to believe that we're worth more if we can make sure there are others who are worth less. Jealousy, conceit, putting others down—they're all tied to our pride.

Contrary to what modern culture, popular sitcoms, and even what our own gut often tells us, we're to humble ourselves instead of make ourselves appear bigger and better. Humility doesn't mean we need to make ourselves seem smaller or less important. It means we see ourselves as God does, for who we really are—no better or worse, no more, no less.

Dear God, teach what what it means to be humble. Help
me to see myself as you do—and thank you for who you've
created me to be.

HOW DOES IT FEEL WHEN SOMEONE ELSE CAN DO SOMETHING YOU ONLY WISH YOU COULD? THANK THE LORD FOR ALL THE UNIQUE GIFTS AND TALENTS HE'S WOVEN INTO YOU. BEING CONTENT BRINGS YOU MORE HAPPINESS THAN ANY TALENT EVER BRING.

WISE FORGETTING

*Then Peter came and said to Him, "Lord, how often
shall my brother sin against me and I forgive him?"*
MATTHEW 18:21 NASB

There's a big difference between forgiving and forgetting.
We are to forgive as Jesus forgives us. And we are to avoid
rehashing wrongs done to us or to our loved ones. If we
can't let those thoughts go—if we're keeping account of
wrongs against us—we probably haven't truly forgiven. But
the Lord blesses us with discernment as well. It's important to
listen for his guidance, and sometimes he guides us through
experience. Forgetting doesn't mean we should continue to
place ourselves where those wrongs will occur again.

*Lord, I find myself able to forgive wrongs, and I take hold
of any thoughts that bring those wrongs back to life for me.
I thank you, though, whenever you use the past to help
me avoid choices that might lead me back to those wrong
circumstances. Thank you for love and thank you for wisdom.*

ARE YOU STILL HOLDING ONTO PAST HURTS AND
BITTERNESS? ASK THE LORD TO HELP YOU FORGIVE AND
FORGET, BUT ALSO TO LEARN WHAT YOU NEED TO LEARN
IN EACH SITUATION.

CHOICES

Don't you realize that all of you together are the temple of God and that the Spirit of God lives in you?
    1 CORINTHIANS 3:16 NLT

If you were a caretaker responsible for the maintenance and protection of God's temple, what would you do? You'd make certain it was in good repair, that no one abused it or defaced it, that the temple itself was something pleasing in God's eyes. The only true "temple" left in the modern world designed to honor God is his Church. The way we care for our own bodies and for our relationships with our brothers and sisters is how we maintain the integrity, and beauty, of God's temple in this day and age.

One practical way to take your responsibility as caretaker seriously is to treat your own body kindly. That means getting enough rest, exercise, and proper nourishment to keep it at its best. How diligent of a caregiver will you be today?

Dear Lord, thank you for this body you have so generously provided me with. I pray that I am able to resist temporary unhealthy pleasures so I can stay healthy to share your Word with others.

DO YOU HAVE ANY UNHEALTHY HABITS THAT YOU NEED TO BREAK? ASK THE HOLY SPIRIT TO HELP GUIDE YOU INTO HEALTHY LIVING!

NO ONE CAN BOAST

Live in harmony with each other. Don't be too proud to enjoy the company of ordinary people. And don't think you know it all!

ROMANS 12:16 NLT

Nearly 300 years ago, Welsh minister Matthew Henry said of this verse, "Nothing is below us but sin." It's wonderful to consider that we are loved and given eternal life and amazing blessings by our heavenly Father when we embrace his Son. It's equally important to remember that all of that good stuff is from God, not from anything we do. We should avoid self-pride about our salvation. Nothing is more attractive than a humble Christian demonstrating God's love toward someone who doesn't yet know him.

Lord Jesus, I thank you for my salvation and for the role you play in every facet of my life. Please help me to reflect gratitude, not conceit, when I talk about you to unbelievers. Help me to demonstrate the peace you give freely to anyone willing to ask.

IS THERE SOMEONE WHO NEEDS TO SEE HUMILITY IN YOUR BEHAVIOR? MAKE IT YOUR GOAL TO LIVE IN HARMONY WITH THOSE AROUND YOU. THAT IS WHAT DRAWS PEOPLE TO CHRIST.

FILLED WITH JOY

You make known to me the path of life;
you will fill me with joy in your presence,
with eternal pleasures at your right hand.
PSALM 16:11 NIV

So many of the Psalms are beautiful promises of God's goodness, and this one pretty much sums it all up. The only way we can experience true joy is through him, and the extra wonderful thing about it is that this joy is eternal. It's something that can stay with us, bubbling just beneath the surface, even when times are tough.

Joy isn't dependent on our changeable circumstances. It's a byproduct of love, contentment, gratitude, and hope. In other words, it's a gift from God—a blessing that is ours when we're in the presence of our almighty, amazing, and eternally loving God.

Praise you, oh Lord, for bringing pure and righteous joy into my life. As I live with you in eternity, I will be forever grateful for what you have done for me, even though I don't deserve it.

WHAT BRINGS YOU JOY? DWELL ON THE ETERNAL PLEASURES THAT AWAIT YOU AND ALLOW JOY TO BUBBLE UP WITHIN YOU.

A WIDE TENT

Enlarge the place of your tent, and let the curtains of your habitations be stretched out; do not hold back; lengthen your cords and strengthen your stakes.
ISAIAH 54:2 ESV

God has always had big plans for each of us, and he asks us to prepare for, and recognize, them. Yes, those plans could very well include abundant blessings of family, friends, professional success, and rich experiences. But he may be asking us to enlarge our tents and stretch our curtains open because he wants us to be aware of opportunities to draw more people to him there. Either way, we are not to hold back—be open to the possibilities!

Dear Lord, I know all things are possible through you. Whatever role I am to play in your plans, I ask that you help me to be open and optimistic about that role. I don't want to hold back on anything you want me to do for your kingdom.

DO YOU KEEP YOUR "TENT" OPEN TO THE SEEKERS GOD SENDS YOUR WAY? BE HOSPITABLE TO THE STRANGERS AMONG YOU AND WATCH GOD MOVE IN WONDERFUL WAYS.

TRUE CONFESSION

*If we confess our sins, He is faithful and righteous
to forgive us our sins and to cleanse us from all
unrighteousness.*
    1 JOHN 1:9 NASB

We've all heard that confession is good for the soul. That's
not all it's good for. When we confess our sins before God in a
truly repentant manner, we're assured of his forgiveness. We're
washed squeaky clean, like a child being bathed by a loving
parent. Also like that child, chances are pretty good we'll get
dirty again soon.

Each and every day we need to have a heart-to-heart talk with
the Lord. How have we hurt him? Where have we fallen short?
Where do we need his help to change unhealthy habits once
and for all? God never tires of us coming to him or refuses
to bathe us in his grace. He's always there, waiting for his
children, with the fluffy towel of forgiveness in his hand.

*Thank you, Lord Jesus, for forgiving me for the sins I have
created—both in my mind and my actions. I am truly grateful
for the joy of knowing that I am always and forever in your
good graces.*

WHEN WAS THE LAST TIME YOU CONFESSED YOUR SIN TO
THE LORD? CONFESS NOW, AND FIND THE INCREDIBLE
FREEDOM AWAITING YOU.

THE ALABASTER JAR

Aware of this, Jesus said to them,
"Why are you bothering this woman?
She has done a beautiful thing to me."
  MATTHEW 26:10 NIV

How amazing those words must have felt to the woman who poured perfume on Christ's head, especially after suffering the verbal onslaught from his followers. Sometimes Christ moves us to do things for him that even his followers criticize as a waste. While we want to consider wise counsel from our church friends and even authority figures, sometimes Christ touches our hearts otherwise. We need to listen intently to what the Lord has to say specifically to us.

Lord, I know your followers want to do right in your eyes just as I do. Still, if ever your will is that I use my gifts in a way that lacks support from my fellow Christians, please give me discernment and assurance of your blessing. Don't ever let my actions be dictated solely by popular consensus instead of by your guidance and Word.

HAVE YOU EVER FELT THE LORD LEADING YOU AS HE DID THE GENEROUS WOMAN WITH THE ALABASTER JAR? BE EXTRAVAGANT IN YOUR SERVICE TO THE LORD. HE WILL BE BLESSED BY IT, NOT CRITICAL TOWARD YOU.

LOST SHEEP

"If a man has a hundred sheep and one of them gets lost, what will he do? Won't he leave the ninety-nine others in the wilderness and go to search for the one that is lost until he finds it?"
LUKE 15:4 NLT

We're all important to God, but there are times when he lets us graze on his Word while he turns to the open field of those who are lost. Human nature is such that we're more likely to go for the larger numbers to get the most bang for our buck.

God, on the other hand, sees us as individuals rather than groups, and he takes the time that's needed to pull each of us closer to him. He won't settle for saving a "majority." He loves the whole world, each and every individual. Jesus gave his life for us all, but he would have been just as willing to give his life for just one.

Thank you, Lord, for keeping such a close eye on me. I pray that I don't stray from your Word as I go about my everyday life.

HAVE YOU EVER BEEN THE SHEEP THAT STRAYS AND FELT GOD PULLING YOU BACK? REST ASSURED HE WILL COME AFTER YOU TO BRING YOU HOME. HE DOESN'T WANT ANY OF HIS SHEEP TO BE LOST.

JULY

Everything you do is beautiful,

flowing from your goodness;

teach me the power of your wonderful words!

PSALM 119:68 TPT

ENOUGH STRENGTH

He said to me, "My grace is sufficient for you, for My strength is made perfect in weakness." Therefore most gladly I will rather boast in my infirmities, that the power of Christ may rest upon me.

   2 CORINTHIANS 12:9 NKJV

I would imagine each of us could name the potential occurrence in life we would consider impossible to endure: a fatal diagnosis, an unfaithful spouse, the loss of a child. None of us needs to experience these things to know they would devastate us. But God promises that no matter how weak life might make us, he will always have enough strength to carry us through.

Father, I pray you will continue to bless me as you have, always upholding me in both good and difficult times. I know life can sometimes take shattering turns, and I thank you for the strength you provide in my weakest moments. I will never turn away from your strength, but will always reach for you and your grace.

IS THERE A CURRENT STRUGGLE YOU NEED GOD TO CARRY YOU THROUGH? ADMIT YOUR WEAKNESS TO THE LORD AND WATCH AS HE SHOWS HIS POWER THROUGH YOUR WEAKNESS.

TRAVELING LIGHT

*"Take nothing for your journey, no staff, nor bag,
nor bread, nor money; and do not have two tunics."*
LUKE 9:3 ESV

Jesus ordered his disciples not to carry anything extra
because it would be a burden as they went to the different
villages to heal the sick and spread the good news. As difficult
as it sounds, we are instructed to do the same. Our baggage
can come in the form of material possessions or emotional
issues that bog us down. It's time to let go of some of the stuff
that turns our focus away from him.

What does your heart cling to that you feel you can't live
without? Talk to God about it. Ask him to help you gain his
perspective about what you own, what you want to buy and
what you consider a necessity.

*Lord, thank you for providing what I need to love you, to
worship you, and to share your message with others. Please
deliver me from all of my unnecessary baggage that turns my
eyes away from you.*

DO YOU HAVE BAGGAGE THAT PREVENTS YOU FROM
GIVING ALL OF YOUR ATTENTION TO JESUS? LEAVE IT
BEHIND AS YOU DEVOTE YOURSELF TO THE LORD. YOU
WON'T MISS IT.

FREEDOM

There is now no condemnation for those who are in Christ Jesus, because through Christ Jesus the law of the Spirit who gives life has set you free from the law of sin and death.

ROMANS 8:1-2 NIV

Many of us take our freedoms for granted, but we aren't totally free in society because we are still bound by the laws of the land. The freedom that Jesus has bought for us gives us freedom in the truest sense of the word—because his laws are only for our good. They not only open the door for us to spend eternity with him, they allow us the freedom to live our lives to the fullest, to reach our potential and mature into the women God had in mind the day he created each one of us.

Forgive me, Lord, for taking my freedom in you for granted. Thank you for delivering me from my sin and imminent death. Through your amazing grace and goodness, I will experience the total freedom that you have already bought for me.

HOW DO YOU COMPARE YOUR WORLDLY FREEDOM WITH THE FREEDOM THAT JESUS GIVES YOU? THE FREEDOM FROM GOD IS A TRUE REASON TO CELEBRATE—THINK ABOUT THAT TODAY!

CELEBRATIONS!

The Lord is the Spirit, and where the Spirit of the Lord is, there is freedom.
    2 CORINTHIANS 3:17 NIV

No matter what struggles our nation endures, this is a fantastic country. As we gather with friends and family to celebrate our nation's independence, we can also celebrate the freedom Jesus brought to our lives. When Paul wrote the above, he was talking about the fact that we are unable to perfectly live to the letter of the law, but thanks to Jesus, we are free from condemnation. That's freedom worth celebrating every day!

Thank you, Jesus, for setting me free from my failings and the resulting penalty of my sins. Far from restricting, a life filled with you is a life of unfathomable freedom. Thank you, too, for blessing this country so abundantly. Please draw this nation to you, Lord, Jesus. We need you.

WHAT DO YOUR CELEBRATION TRADITIONS LOOK LIKE? TAKE A MOMENT TO REFLECT ON YOUR MANY FREEDOMS AND THANK GOD FOR THEM TODAY.

REMEMBER BEING BLIND?

There is only one Lawgiver and Judge, the One who is able to save and to destroy; but who are you who judge your neighbor?
    JAMES 4:12 NASB

For those of us not raised in the church, that period of time before we found Christ might have been full of thoughts and behaviors that would now shock us if we witnessed them in someone else. We may have experienced judgmental reactions by Christians before we followed Christ. As believers today, we should remember that and avoid a judgmental spirit towards those who are "blind." We must seek to mirror the inviting demeanor of Christ and the Christians who wooed us to him.

Lord Jesus, thank you for placing kind believers in my path to you. Please help me to represent you as welcoming, accepting, and inviting. Help my demeanor draw people to you, rather than shaming them or chasing them away. Remind me that the molding takes time and is solely in your hands.

IS THERE SOMEONE WHO NEEDS TO EXPERIENCE CHRIST'S KINDNESS THROUGH YOU? PUT YOURSELF IN THEIR SHOES AND DEMONSTRATE LOVE THE WAY YOU WOULD WANT TO RECEIVE IT.

OUR RIGHTS

Yet to all who did receive him, to those who believed in his name, he gave the right to become children of God—children born not of natural descent, nor of human decision or a husband's will, but born of God.

JOHN 1:12-13 NIV

God has granted us a birthright to his kingdom merely by believing in him. We are his children, not by our works or any good we have done. It's only through faith, God's grace, and Jesus' sacrifice that we're welcomed into the family of God. While other world religions judge followers based on their performance, Christ accepts us as the fallible humans that we are. We are blessed by his goodness rather than the other way around.

Heavenly Father, I am grateful to be called your child. Allow me to open my heart to my brothers and sisters in Christ in a way that is pleasing to you.

DO YOU EVER THINK ABOUT BEING AN HEIR TO GOD'S KINGDOM? PONDER ALL OF THE PRIVILEGES YOU HAVE AS A DAUGHTER OF THE KING! DON'T TAKE THOSE PRIVILEGES FOR GRANTED. INSTEAD, THANK THE FATHER FOR THEM AND BE BLESSED.

A STURDY WALK

Anyone who loves another brother or sister is living in the light and does not cause others to stumble.
1 JOHN 2:10 NLT

Loving our brothers and sisters in Christ sounds perfect, but we are not perfect. It takes the indwelling of the Holy Spirit for us to truly and consistently love one another, regardless of what happens in life. If we always seek the grace of the Holy Spirit, not only will we maintain unconditional love for our brothers and sisters, but we will also benefit from the stability that grace brings to our lives. There will be nothing that can make us stumble in our faith.

Lord God, I want to be strong and stable in my faith. I thank you for the Holy Spirit and for the inner grace I receive by having Jesus in my heart. I pray you'll make it easy for me to feel and show love for my brothers and sisters in Christ. I relish living in your light.

DO YOU SENSE LOVE AND GRACE FROM THE HOLY SPIRIT TODAY? PASS THAT ALONG TO THOSE AROUND YOU AND HELP KEEP THEM FROM STUMBLING IN THE DARKNESS.

QUENCHED THIRST

"If you knew the gift of God, and who it is that is saying to you, 'Give me a drink,' you would have asked him, and he would have given you living water."
JOHN 4:10 ESV

Just as Jesus spoke to the woman at the well, he speaks to us about grace. He knows everything about us—even our deepest, darkest, sinful secrets—yet he still forgives us and quenches our spiritual thirst. He provides exactly what we need, what our hearts truly thirst for, regardless of who we are and what we've done in the past.

Are you holding onto regrets? Are there things in your past you hope never come fully into the light? Jesus doesn't want to hold them against you. He wants to set you free from their hold on you. Bring your deepest regrets to him in prayer. Ask if there's anything you need to do today to make amends. Do what you can to make things right and allow Jesus to take care of the rest.

Thank you, Jesus, for quenching my thirst. As you spoke to that woman at the well, you speak to us through your Word. I know that you are my salvation, and for that I am grateful.

CAN YOU THINK OF TIMES WHEN YOU NEED GRACE? GOD HAS A WELL OF IT AVAILABLE, AND IT NEVER RUNS DRY! DRINK IN THE GRACE OF GOD TODAY AND BE QUENCHED.

FISHERS OF MEN

Then Jesus said to Simon. "Don't be afraid; from now on you will catch men." So they pulled their boats up on shore, left everything and followed him.

LUKE 5:10-11 NIV

Imagine the thrill felt by the disciples when Jesus called them into his service: to be addressed with such confidence and assuredness that they would successfully draw others to Christ and his offer of salvation. We should feel the same thrill today as the disciples did—and no less assurance. The Lord asks us to let him work through us to draw others to him. What an honor!

Dear Jesus, thank you so much for using someone I know to draw me to you. And I thank you for anything you may have done or said through me to draw anyone else to you. I pray I will always be open to opportunities to reflect the assurance that what you offer is real and absolutely essential.

IS THERE SOMEONE WHO NEEDS YOUR ASSURANCE THAT SALVATION IS REAL? SPEAK CONFIDENTLY TODAY AS YOU SHARE THE LOVE OF CHRIST WITH THOSE AROUND YOU.

WELL-TRAVELED PATH

Your word is a lamp to my feet,
And a light to my path.
PSALM 119:105 NKJV

Although the Bible helps guide us along the path God's provided for us in this life, it isn't a guidebook or instruction manual. It's much more. It's a love letter from someone who's loved us since before we breathed our first breath. God's love letter gives us some basic instructions on how to live in a way that's pleasing to him, and beneficial to us, but it doesn't address every situation and circumstance.

We need more light. We need to interact with the author himself. Only through God's Spirit can we truly understand, and apply, what we read. God also provides us with counselors and teachers who've walked his path longer than we have, know his Word more intimately, and can help us discern which way to turn when we're unsure. Let's begin with God's Word, but not stop there, when searching for God's light in our lives.

Thank you, heavenly Father, for lighting the path that you want me to travel. Without knowing you, I would be lost in darkness. In your goodness, you have given me clarity in my walk with you.

DO YOU FEEL LIKE YOU ARE "IN THE DARK" ABOUT AN IMPORTANT DECISION? ASK GOD TO SHED HIS LIGHT ON YOUR SITUATION AND LEAD YOU IN THE RIGHT WAY.

GLORY

We are citizens of heaven, where the Lord Jesus Christ lives. And we are eagerly waiting for him to return as our Savior. He will take our weak mortal bodies and change them into glorious bodies like his own, using the same power with which he will bring everything under his control.
PHILIPPIANS 3:20-21 NLT

Most of us have a friend or loved one who suffers (or suffered) from a physical disability or debilitating illness in life. God willing, those dear people, if old enough and able to decide, leaned on the Lord for strength and, more importantly, salvation. As heartbreaking as such circumstances are, today's verse is joyous. Knowing that Jesus transforms all of our bodies to the kind of glory he experiences? How can that not give us joy?

Dearest Jesus, thank you for the promise of glorified bodies. The sadness in my heart over my loved ones who suffered physically is lifted when I picture them with you, free of the restraints of earthly form. I know, too, they are in your caring arms. Such joy!

WHO COMES TO MIND WITH THESE WORDS? THANK THE LORD FOR HIS PROMISE OF GLORIFIED, PAIN-FREE BODIES FOR ALL WHO BELIEVE!

ALL THAT GLITTERS

He knows where I am going. And when he tests me,
I will come out as pure as gold.
    JOB 23:10 NLT

Even after Job lost everything he held dear to his heart—his children, his wealth, and even his health—he continued to trust God. Job's story has to be one of the most powerful lessons in the Bible. After all, he remained true to his Father in heaven rather than wallow in pity as so many of us would typically do. Much smaller things have turned people to bitterness, yet Job trusted God's goodness. Do we?

If you're struggling with difficult circumstances in your life, re-read the book of Job. Put yourself in his shoes. How well does your faith fill them? Talk to God about how your faith can shine as pure as gold.

Lord, heavenly Father, I pray that I am able to be more like Job and trust you. May my faith in you grow ever stronger so I may suffer more graciously rather than become embittered.

HAVE YOU EVER FELT THAT YOU WERE BEING TESTED? ASK GOD FOR THE STRENGTH TO SUFFER GRACEFULLY.

CAN'T COME SOON ENOUGH!

The Spirit and the bride say, "Come!" And let him who hears say, "Come!" Whoever is thirsty, let him come; and whoever wishes, let him take the free gift of the water of life.

REVELATION 22:17 NIV

There is something so exciting and anticipatory about today's verse. It is one of the last verses of the Bible, and it just feels like it's saying, "So that's the story. Let's go!" By the time we read this verse, we know all we need to know to fully lean on what God has in mind for our future. We know that future involves Christ's return, and he wants to take as many as possible to eternal life. We should feel excitement and an eagerness to let others know about that plan.

Come soon, Lord Jesus! When I look at the path the world is taking, I grow so eager for you to take your children to a safer, happier place full of light and love and free of evil. Please put the words in my mouth and bless me with behavior that will draw as many people to you as possible before your glorious return. That said: come!

DO YOU FEEL A THRILL WHEN YOU CONSIDER THE FUTURE WITH JESUS? THE JOY THAT AWAITS US THERE CANNOT BE FATHOMED, BUT WE CAN CERTAINLY LOOK FORWARD TO IT!

MORE THAN BREADCRUMBS

Then the LORD said to Moses, "I will rain down bread from heaven for you. The people are to go out each day and gather enough for that day. In this way I will test them and see whether they will follow my instructions."

EXODUS 16:4 NIV

How has God supplied manna in your life? What needs has he filled in unexpected ways? It's important to look back and remember when God has come through, because there will be times when we feel he's distant or silent—or perhaps not there at all. But just because we feel something is true doesn't make it so.

Regardless of what we feel, God is near, he cares, and he's at work in our lives. Our lives may not always look like what we pictured in our minds. Certainly the Israelites never pictured wandering around the desert for forty years and having their daily bread fall from the sky. But God continues to send manna to those he loves.

Lord, thank you for your faithfulness in providing for my needs. May I always remember your promises. Teach me to be grateful for all of the blessings you have brought. Your goodness is greater than anything I can ever imagine.

HAVE YOU EVER HAD SOMETHING YOU NEED ARRIVE IN THE NICK OF TIME, WHEN YOU DIDN'T EXPECT IT? CONSIDER IT MANNA—AND THANK GOD FOR HIS PROVISION.

EARTH RENEWED

You will go out in joy and be led forth in peace;
the mountains and hills will burst into song before you,
and all the trees of the field will clap their hands.
ISAIAH 55:12 NIV

As beautiful as our world is, it is a fallen world. We see so much beauty around us, but there are also dark, dangerous places. When the author of life returns and we experience his kingdom, our current world will look like it has been covered with a dark veil in comparison.

Come, Lord Jesus! Although I love my life and the many blessings you've brought upon me, and although I am amazed by the stunning nature of this world, I am so eager to meet you face-to-face and to experience this world free of sin and blemish. Please help me to be a good steward of this world and of the eternal gift of life that you've given while I await your return.

HOW DOES THE IDEA OF A PERFECT WORLD AFFECT YOU TODAY? LET IT ENCOURAGE YOU TO KEEP PRESSING INTO THE LORD AND ALL THAT HE HAS PLANNED FOR YOU.

CONTINUING THE WALK

Let it grow, for when your endurance is fully developed, you will be perfect and complete, needing nothing.
JAMES 1:4 NLT

Persevering for the long haul can be discouraging in a world where we've been conditioned to expect immediate results. From microwaves to text messaging to the drive-thru at our favorite fast food joint, we've come to expect that if we want something, it's available right now. Wanting to change our character, mend a relationship, or grow spiritually mature doesn't happen overnight—or without encountering a few bumps along the road. Trying to just hang on when we're tired and discouraged can make us feel like giving up is a viable option. Endurance can only grow as it's tested overtime.

When you're impatient for change, move your finish line. Make it your goal to keep pushing forward for one day, one hour, the next five minutes. Then start again. God's at your side, your cheerleader and coach. Every step draws you closer to developing endurance and to your goal.

Dear Lord, please help me stay on the path you've designed for me. I want to mature in my faith according to your plan, without the constant urge to hurry it along. I pray for the patience to get through the difficult times by drawing closer to you.

HOW DO YOU FEEL WHEN YOU HEAR THE WORDS, "BE PATIENT"? ALLOW THE LORD TO WORK THE FRUIT OF PATIENCE INTO YOUR LIFE, SO THAT YOU WON'T BE LACKING ANYTHING.

PHYSICAL AND SPIRITUAL ENERGY

*You prepare a table before me
in the presence of my enemies;
You anoint my head with oil;
My cup runs over.*
PSALM 23:5 NKJV

Those of us who have dieted through the years know how important it is to have enough energy from day to day. Low energy can signal a vulnerability to fatigue and illness. Today's verse follows David's verses about walking through the valley of the shadow of death. The Lord provides both physical and spiritual strength for us, among other blessings, to help us endure the hardships of our earthly life.

Thank you, Lord God, that you provide for me as you do. Please help me vigilantly feed both my body and soul in order to stay strong for the physical and spiritual challenges of life. Please keep my focus on the morsels of your goodness and grace, so that I will never be short of spiritual strength.

ARE YOU FEEDING BOTH YOUR SPIRITUAL AND PHYSICAL NEEDS? ASK THE LORD TO GIVE YOU WISDOM IN HOW YOU FEED YOURSELF SPIRITUALLY AND PHYSICALLY. HE CREATED YOU, AND HE KNOWS JUST WHAT IS BEST FOR YOU!

EMERGENCY RESCUE

God is our refuge and strength,
always ready to help in times of trouble.
PSALM 46:1 NLT

We immediately call emergency rescue when we witness an accident or a house on fire. But when we experience the deepest trouble that isn't visible to the eye, we often try to go it alone. We grit our teeth, square our shoulders and try not to let anyone see us cry. If we do seek help, we often turn first to our family and friends.

God is the perfect First Responder. Even our one-word prayer of "Help!" will never go unnoticed or ignored. God not only provides comfort, but strength, guidance, and a safe place to dry our tears. Call on him before all others. His response time can't be beat.

Lord, thank you for always providing the strength and comfort I need during difficult times. May I always remember to turn to you in both good times and bad. I know you will be there for me, no matter what.

WHAT DO YOU DO WHEN YOU NEED AN EMOTIONAL RESCUE? REMEMBER THAT GOD IS YOUR EVER-PRESENT HELP. HE WANTS YOU TO CALL OUT TO HIM IN YOUR TIME OF NEED.

SOLDIERS

"Greater love has no one than this, that one lay down his life for his friends."
    JOHN 15:13 NASB

Today's verse brings to mind the heroic efforts of our men and women in the military. Those who survive the war—but face the rest of their lives with a war-related physical or psychological disability—also need our prayers and appreciation. We should always strive to ensure our heroes have our prayers.

Dear God, thank you for bringing forth men and women brave enough to risk their lives to defend us and fight our battles for us. Please bless their efforts, keep them safe, and help us remember to pray for them and their families.

WILL YOU TAKE A MOMENT TO PRAY FOR OUR SOLDIERS TODAY? IF YOU KNOW A MILITARY FAMILY, FIND OUT WHAT YOU CAN DO FOR THEM TO SHOW THEM GOD'S LOVE TODAY.

ALWAYS LISTENING

This is the confidence we have in approaching God: that if we ask anything according to his will, he hears us.
  1 JOHN 5:14 NIV

God wants us to speak to him, to turn to him for our needs and wants. That doesn't mean we should request a list of things we expect him to do for us simply because it will make us happy. He makes it very clear that he hears us when we ask according to his will. If we're unsure of what that is, reading the Bible is a great place to start.

We know that anything that's in opposition to what God says cannot be God's will—or worthy of our prayers. But at times, that isn't obvious. Even Jesus added, "Not as I will, but as you will" (Matthew 26:39, NIV) after asking God to take the cup of crucifixion away from him. When in doubt, pray like Jesus.

Thank you, God, for listening to me when I pray. I know that my desires are not all pleasing to you, but you have provided me with everything that is truly good for me. May I always turn to you in prayer and never forget to consider your will.

WHAT DO YOU ASK GOD FOR? AND WHY? ASK GOD TO HELP YOU UNDERSTAND WHAT'S AT THE HEART OF YOUR PRAYERS, SO YOU CAN BETTER UNDERSTAND HOW TO PRAY ACCORDING TO HIS WILL.

TEN COMMANDMENTS

These are the laws you are to set before them.
EXODUS 21:1 NIV

Most of us have been taught that Jesus didn't come to do away with the Law but to fulfill it. Despite our obvious fallibility, God still expects us to try to obey the Ten Commandments. For some of us that requires strength and courage, and for others it simply requires watchfulness against slipping into sinful habits and behaviors. God promises us success if we strive for that obedience, and he will certainly support our efforts through the Holy Spirit if we just ask him.

Dear God, every day I try, and every day I fall short. So I do ask for your support and the constant indwelling of the Holy Spirit to help me keep from straying to the right or to the left on the path you've set before me. Thank you for the guidance of your commandments, and thank you even more for the saving sacrifice of your beloved Son.

WILL YOU SEEK HIS HELP TODAY AS YOU STRIVE TO STAY ON THE CORRECT PATH? HE IS MORE THAN WILLING TO OFFER YOU HIS HAND.

SOLID AS A ROCK

He is the Rock; his deeds are perfect. Everything he does is just and fair. He is a faithful God who does no wrong; how just and upright he is!
DEUTERONOMY 32:4 NLT

How many times have we heard the phrase, "That's not fair"? Kids say it when someone else has something they want. Coworkers say it when someone else gets a raise or promotion that they felt they deserved. Many things in our earthly life simply aren't fair. But the Bible tells us God always is.

God's love is perfect and his actions are just—even if it doesn't appear that way from our earthly perspective. When we're weighed down by what we see as unfair, we need to trust God's picture is much more accurate than our own. He will treat us justly, regardless of how we're treated by the world.

Lord, I know I'm guilty of wishing I had something someone else has and internalizing the lack of fairness about the situation. I pray that I will keep my eyes focused on you and on your perfection. I know that you are always fair in the most important way of all. You have never failed.

HAVE YOU EVER THOUGHT SOMETHING WASN'T FAIR? LEAVE IT IN THE HANDS OF GOD AND BE ENCOURAGED THAT HIS JUSTICE WILL ONE DAY TAKE CARE OF ALL OF LIFE'S UNFAIRNESS.

GOD'S COMPETENCE

Not that we are competent in ourselves to claim anything for ourselves, but our competence comes from God.
2 CORINTHIANS 3:5 NIV

Some people know at an early age what career they want to pursue. Some of us jump from job to job while we try to find what best suits our gifts. When we settle into the role God planned for us, we might not become wealthy, but he will use us in wonderful ways. If we find we are very good at what we do, it's important to remember where our competence comes from. Just like all other good and perfect gifts, competence is all about God, not us.

Dear Lord, I certainly am not perfect in what I do for a living, but I do appreciate when it all "works." I know that's you, not me. I can work as hard as I like, but competence is a gift that I appreciate and pray for daily.

HAVE YOU DEDICATED TODAY'S EFFORTS TO HIM? WATCH HOW MUCH BETTER YOU CAN BE AT YOUR JOB WHEN YOU LET GOD TAKE THE LEAD.

TRUE RICHES

Now that you belong to Christ, you are the true children of Abraham. You are his heirs, and God's promise to Abraham belongs to you.
GALATIANS 3:29 NLT

We are heirs of Abraham. That's good news! So, what did Abraham leave his "kids"? Just read the Old and New Testament. After all, "testament" means "will," as well as "witness."

We read that Abraham was promised a generationally long line of children—which includes us. All of those children are in line to receive God's gifts of everlasting love and eternal life. While some inheritances may include homes, cars, and life insurance policies, the riches we receive from God will outshine, and outlast, them all.

Thank you, Jesus, for making me wealthy as your heir in the truest sense of the word. I know that nothing earthly can compare to what you have in store for me. You have provided me with everlasting love that no amount of money can buy.

HAVE YOU EVER WORKED HARD FOR SOMETHING AND BEEN DISAPPOINTED? TAKE COMFORT AND JOY IN THE FACT THAT YOU WON'T BE DISAPPOINTED WITH GOD'S REWARD FOR YOUR HARD WORK.

STRENGTH THROUGH HIM

For the sake of Christ, then, I am content with weaknesses, insults, hardships, persecutions, and calamities. For when I am weak, then I am strong.
2 CORINTHIANS 12:10 ESV

Before we start our day, even if we specifically begin with God's work in mind, we not only glorify him but we strengthen ourselves if we take time to simply worship him for his almighty power. When we humble ourselves and thank him for who he is, his power is so much more evident to us all day long. That evidence is comforting, don't you think?

Almighty God, you are worthy of constant praise. I am so small and needy compared to you. Yet you still see such value in me that you are there for me always. You saved my life through the sacrifice of your Son. How can that be, Lord? Such power and love is hard to grasp and impossible to repay. But I will spend my life trying to live a life worthy of your grace.

DO YOU TAKE COMFORT IN KNOWING THAT HIS POWER COVERS ALL YOUR WEAKNESSES? LET HIM BE YOUR STRENGTH AS YOU GO ABOUT YOUR DAY.

JUSTICE FOR ALL

The LORD longs to be gracious to you;
therefore he will rise up to show you compassion.
For the LORD is a God of justice.
Blessed are all who wait for him!
ISAIAH 30:18

"Compassion" is more than kindness. It's a deep concern and empathy for the sufferings and hard times of others. This is what God has for us. When Jesus walked this earth, he walked in human shoes for over thirty years. He not only sees the difficulties we encounter, he knows how it feels to have to endure them.

Being able to share what you're going through with someone who's walked the same road is an immeasurable comfort, whether it's facing a life-threatening illness, the fall-out of divorce, or the grief of losing someone you love. Jesus is that kind of friend. He will never make light of what's weighing us down or make us feel as though we should be over this hurdle by now. He'll remain by our side, to listen and love, until every last tear is dry.

Lord, I am grateful that you love me enough to be gracious, compassionate, and just at all times. I wait for you with open arms, knowing that I have been blessed.

HAVE YOU SEEN GOD'S COMPASSION? LET THIS BE YOUR MOTIVATOR FOR SHOWING COMPASSION TO OTHERS.

HOLY GROUND

"Do not come any closer," God said. "Take off your sandals, for the place where you are standing is holy ground."

EXODUS 3:5 NIV

God wanted Moses to be sensitive—physically, emotionally, and spiritually—when he met him at the burning bush. Moses would soon deliver God's commands to his people, and his sensitivity needed to be fully alert. When we attempt to do God's work, to draw others to him, we need to pray for sensitivity as well. Only God knows where each person is, spiritually and emotionally, and we want to enable him to speak through us.

Heavenly Father, I thank you for any opportunity to draw others to you. Please help me to always be sensitive to the proper moment and the proper words. Thank you for allowing someone to do that for me on the most important day of my life.

IS THERE SOMEONE AWAITING THE RIGHT WORDS FROM YOU TODAY? LISTEN TO THE HOLY SPIRIT AND DON'T BE AFRAID TO SHARE WHEN HE PROMPTS YOU TO.

BEST LAID PLANS

"For I know the plans I have for you," says the LORD. "They are plans for good and not for disaster, to give you a future and a hope."
JEREMIAH 29:11 NLT

Most people like to make plans, but when things don't go according to how they think they should, they get frustrated or angry. We need to remember that God has already made plans for us, and they're greater than anything we'll ever come up with on our own.

We don't always see his plan as it unfolds, but it is there. And it's much bigger than planning lunch out on Friday or a dentist appointment next month. They are plans for our future. Plans that involve not just today, next month or next year. They're even bigger than plans for this life. They extend all the way into the next life as well.

Dear Lord, I pray that I can accept your plan for me without worrying that things aren't going my way. Thank you for the goodness of your design that is grander than anything I can create.

HAVE YOU EVER HAD YOUR PLANS GO COMPLETELY AWRY AND LATER DISCOVERED IT WAS BETTER THAN WHAT YOU INTENDED? SUBMIT YOUR PLANS TO THE LORD AND ALLOW HIM TO HAVE HIS WAY. IT WILL ALWAYS WORK OUT BETTER FOR YOU THAT WAY.

DELIVERANCE

My times are in your hands;
deliver me from the hands of my enemies,
from those who pursue me.
Let your face shine on your servant;
save me in your unfailing love.
PSALM 31:15-16 NIV

Despite the day-to-day uncertainty that David experienced in his life, he had eternal certainty that carried him through all circumstances. He knew God's hand was upon him, guiding him through both good times and bad. We all experience times when we feel alone, but if we can accept that God is with us, we can be content with the day, knowing the long term will be joyous.

Dear Lord, please help me to remember that you are there with me even during the rough days. I am fully aware of your presence when life goes well. But I want to appreciate that you are there for me through everything that I experience. I pray I will consider each day a blessing in your presence.

ARE YOU ABLE TO SENSE HIM EVEN WHEN TIMES ARE HARD? DON'T EVER DOUBT THAT HE IS WITH YOU. HE WILL NOT LEAVE YOU.

SAFE AND SECURE

Of Benjamin he said, "The beloved of the Lord dwells in safety. The High God surrounds him all day long, and dwells between his shoulders."
DEUTERONOMY 33:12 ESV

There's something so safe and comforting about being held in the arms of those we love. A simple hug has multiple physical and psychological benefits, such as lowering our blood pressure, increasing the production of "feel good" chemicals in our bodies (like oxytocin, serotonin, and dopamine), boosting our immune system, and calming our fears.

While it's true that a hug from God (when he surrounds us and we dwell between his shoulders) differs than those we usually receive, that doesn't mean they're simply metaphorical. Prayer, and meditating on God's Word can have a similar calming effect. So, head straight for God's arms. There's a hug with your name on it waiting for you.

I am thankful, oh Lord, for your tight grip on me as I go about my day. I find refuge in your loving arms and protection in knowing you are always with me. I pray that I can relax more and know that I don't have to keep my hectic pace that turns my attention away from you.

HAVE YOU EVER BEEN IN TOO BIG OF A HURRY TO RELAX AND TRUST GOD? TAKE SOME TIME TO SLOW DOWN AND REST IN GOD'S PRESENCE TODAY—EVEN IF ONLY FOR A FEW MINUTES.

WHO'S THERE?

Here I am! I stand at the door and knock. If anyone hears my voice and opens the door, I will come in and eat with him and he with me.
REVELATION 3:20 NIV

Many of us can remember the moment we heard Jesus knocking at the door and we actually opened it. He may have been knocking many times before, but until we were listening with the right attitude in our hearts, we didn't hear him or we chose to ignore him. He will not force himself through that door. He will always wait to be invited.

Lord Jesus, thank you so much for touching my heart and tweaking my ears so I finally heard you knocking. Thank you for bringing me to a place where I knew I needed desperately to open that door and invite you in. I'm so thrilled that you will never leave me.

CAN YOU TAKE TIME TO REFLECT ON THE DAY YOU INVITED HIM IN? REMEMBER IT WITH THANKFULNESS AND JOY IN YOUR HEART. GOD IS GOOD!

AUGUST

God, everyone sees your goodness,

for your tender love is blended

into everything you do.

PSALM 145:9 TPT

IT'S ALL GOOD

Since everything God created is good, we should not reject any of it but receive it with thanks.
    1 TIMOTHY 4:4 NLT

Everything that God created has a purpose, and he intended it all for good. However, what is good in one respect may not be in others. We have to keep everything in the context of his intentions. Some very good creations may become our poison if used in a way other than what God wanted. This includes digesting something that is merely meant for beauty or using the human body for something he's clearly instructed us not to do. When we follow God's design and commands, what he's intended for good, stays that way.

Dear God, thank you for providing so many things that are good. I pray that I will be able to follow your wishes and intentions on all of these delicious, sweet blessings.

CAN YOU THINK OF SOME CREATIONS THAT ARE GOOD FOR GOD'S INTENTION BUT BAD WHEN USED ANY OTHER WAY? LET YOUR MIND DWELL ON ALL THAT IS GOOD TODAY.

AS STRONG AS DEATH

Place me like a seal over your heart,
like a seal on your arm;
for love is as strong as death,
its jealousy unyielding as the grave.
It burns like blazing fire, like a mighty flame.
      SONG OF SONGS 8:6 NIV

No one needs to be convinced of what one person will do for another out of love. Although *Song of Songs* is about love between a husband and wife, representing God's love for his believers, this verse captures the passion of unconditional love that could be shared by any person for another. "As strong as death," the verse says. We all know people for whom we'd be willing to die. For Christ, that would be every single one of us, even those who don't yet understand or accept it.

Lord Jesus, your love is impossible to truly fathom. Thank you for loving all mankind to the point of death on the cross. It breaks my heart that you had to make that sacrifice for me, and it breaks my heart further that so many people ignore your sacrifice. I pray I will recognize ways to draw people to your truth.

FOR WHOM WOULD YOU SACRIFICE YOUR LIFE? GOD'S LOVE FOR US IS STRONGER THAN DEATH; IN FACT, IT DEFEATED DEATH! THINK ABOUT THAT TODAY, AND BE THANKFUL.

AT A CROSSROAD

My child, if sinners entice you, turn your back on them!
PROVERBS 1:10 NLT

Not all temptations look harmful. Consider the fruit in the Garden of Eden. Grabbing a piece of fruit seems like a pretty harmless choice. Okay, so God said not too. Maybe you misunderstood or he wasn't all that serious. After all, a ripe piece of fruit is pretty appealing, not to mention potentially tasty and nourishing.

But some things that appear to be harmless turn out to be quite the opposite. A little morsel of gossip. A little white lie. A little innocent flirting. Truth is, none of these are innocent or little. Each one leads us away from God, instead of closer to him. That's what temptation does, leads us off God's path onto a side road that winds up who knows where. But the closer we draw toward God, the more we can recognize a temptation for what it is—a dead end.

Dear Jesus, thank you for your many blessings. Give me the ability to discern what you want for me and the strength to turn away from what I shouldn't have.

HOW DO YOU OVERCOME YOUR TEMPTATION OR WEAKNESS? MAKE IT A POINT TO ASK GOD FOR STRENGTH AND COURAGE TO SAY "NO" EACH DAY.

NEVER

The LORD our God be with us, as he was with our fathers. May he not leave us or forsake us.
   1 KINGS 8:57 ESV

Sometimes we focus a little too closely on what we *don't* have. It's great to have goals, but there is definitely something to be said for appreciating the blessings of today. If we tell ourselves we would be happy *if only*, we're fooling ourselves and robbing ourselves of joy. When the "if only" is achieved, we'll just start looking for something more in order to find happiness. God's provisions and promises should bring contentment enough.

Thank you, God, for promising to be with me always. Thank you for the many ways you provide for me. I will always strive to become a better person and to live a productive life, but please help me focus on the blessings you've given me today and forever.

WHAT BLESSINGS DO YOU EMBRACE TODAY WITH CONTENTMENT? REST IN THE PROMISE THAT GOD WILL NEVER TURN HIS BACK ON YOU OR WALK AWAY.

THE BEST SERVICE EVER

"Even the Son of man did not come to be served, but to serve, and to give his life as a ransom for many."
MARK 10:45 NIV

So much of the worldly view of servanthood is negative. It connotes inferiority. How often have you eaten at a restaurant and wanted to get your waiter's attention—but have forgotten what he or she looks like? It's because we don't take a good look. We regard those who serve us more like a soda machine; we put our money in and what we want pops out.

Jesus showed us through his example that being a servant is the highest, most godly, position we can hold. Pay attention to what you can do to serve others today. And instead of seeking, or expecting, a "tip," such as thanks or praise for a job well done, go one step farther and serve others in secret, behind the scenes. It's a lesson in love and humility God loves for us to learn.

Lord, although I know that nothing I do is perfect, I pray that I will serve you in a way that is pleasing and honorable. Guide me in my service and allow this to be a testimony so that others will see you in me.

HOW HAS THE LORD ALLOWED YOU TO SERVE HIM? TAKE DELIGHT IN YOUR ABILITY TO SERVE GOD THROUGH SERVING OTHERS.

MIGHTY TO SAVE

Who is this who comes from Edom, With garments of glowing colors from Bozrah, This One who is majestic in His apparel, Marching in the greatness of His strength? "It is I who speak in righteousness, mighty to save."
ISAIAH 63:1 NASB

There have always been Christians who have been persecuted for their faith—seriously persecuted, not just ostracized, as some of us may have been. Today is no exception, and our hearts break to hear of those suffering for their love for Christ. But Isaiah's vision was of the returning Christ who will defend them all. How gripping it is to consider his righteous return, full of splendor, might, and eternal salvation!

Come, Lord Jesus! Thank you for your promises. I pray for those around the world who struggle, suffer, and even die because of their love for you. I eagerly await your return, and I want so much to see the joy on the faces of your martyrs.

CAN YOU SPEND SOME TIME TODAY PRAYING FOR THOSE WHO ARE FACING PERSECUTION FOR THEIR BELIEF IN GOD? THANK GOD FOR HIS AMAZING GRACE AND STRENGTH TO PERSEVERE.

WHAT DO YOU SEE?

"I don't know whether he is a sinner," the man replied.
"But I know this: I was blind, and now I can see!"
JOHN 9:25 NLT

How well do you know Jesus? Whether you've just recently placed your faith in him or followed him for years, there's always more to know. We can't fully understand the immensity of who God is and the complexity of how he works, until we get to heaven. Even then, who really knows if there will still be mystery in his majesty? But we don't have to know everything about him to love him—or to follow him.

Just by what we read in the Gospels, we can tell that Jesus is someone unique to history, someone worthy of our love, our trust, and our faith. Let's act on what we know, be it little or much. The more time we spend with him, the wider he'll open our eyes, and hearts, to his beauty and blessings.

Heavenly Father, I pray that my vision will be focused on you. Remind me of what is truly important. You are the healer of human frailties. You know what we need and where we are lacking.

WHAT IN THIS WORLD HAVE YOU BEEN BLINDED TO? FOCUS YOUR VISION ON THE LORD TODAY AND BE REMINDED OF WHAT IS TRULY IMPORTANT.

HASTY DECISIONS

So after waiting patiently,
Abraham received what was promised.
HEBREWS 6:15 NIV

It's wise counsel not to make impulsive decisions. It is much better to exercise caution and introspection. If we turn to, and wait on, the Holy Spirit, with whom we were blessed for such occasions, we might find our decisions and their consequences different—and better—than they would have been otherwise.

Holy Spirit, thank you for filling my heart daily. Thank you for the guidance and common sense you offer me to keep me safe, healthy, contented, and in your will. When I start to act under the wrong motivations, please nudge me and remind me to focus on your direction.

IS THERE A DECISION YOU NEED TO PRAY ABOUT TODAY? TAKE TIME TO SEEK THE LORD'S ADVICE, OR GET COUNSEL FROM SOMEONE YOU TRUST AND RESPECT.

FOOL'S GOLD

"The thief's purpose is to steal and kill and destroy. My purpose is to give them a rich and satisfying life."
JOHN 10:10 NLT

What makes life rich and satisfying? Depending on who you ask, answers could range from fame and fortune to having children to running your own business. But what would your answer be? Would it be anything like the answer Jesus would give?

The riches knowing God brings our way not only deliver eternal satisfaction, but they're a treasure that can't be stolen. If the things you're trusting in to make your life rich and satisfying can be lost, destroyed, or stolen, chances are they aren't God's best. They are fool's gold. They look enticing and valuable. But they promise more than they can deliver. God never does.

Father, help me place my hope and faith in you rather than anything else. I want your riches to be my heart's true desire. No matter how much the rest sparkles and shines, it is nowhere near what you have promised.

HAVE YOU EVER HAD ANYTHING STOLEN? DOESN'T IT FEEL GOOD TO KNOW THAT NO ONE CAN TAKE AWAY THE RICHES GOD'S GIVEN YOU, INCLUDING YOUR SALVATION?

PHILADELPHIA

Be devoted to one another in brotherly love. Honor one another above yourselves.
ROMANS 12:10 NIV

Paul shared the above counsel in discussing how believers should treat one another. It should be fairly easy to feel devotion to and honor for fellow believers. But often we need to step outside our comfort zone to do that, and this is not news to the Lord. If we find ourselves called but challenged, the Holy Spirit stands ready to guide us and provide the devotion and honor we need to demonstrate. We only have to ask.

Holy Spirit, thank you for being there for me whenever I ask you to fill me with the grace needed to follow your will. I pray I will always be able to show compassion and respect for my fellow believers. Please help me in that.

DO YOU GO TO THE HOLY SPIRIT WHEN YOU FEEL CHALLENGED TO LOVE YOUR FELLOW BELIEVERS? BE DEVOTED TO THOSE AROUND YOU, AND SHOW THEM THE TRUE LOVE OF GOD.

LOOK FOR THE NEXT EXIT

The temptations in your life are no different from what others experience. And God is faithful. He will not allow the temptation to be more than you can stand. When you are tempted, he will show you a way out so that you can endure.

1 CORINTHIANS 10:13 NLT

We've all wanted to do the "wrong" thing. Eat the extra cookie. Buy the shoes we can't afford. Respond in anger to our children. Exceed the speed limit—until we see a police car. Yes, there are things that can stop us in our tracks when we're tempted to go the wrong way.

God promises there will always be an "exit" available to us. But we have to choose to take it. That can mean refusing to "friend" an old beau on social media who still makes your heart beat a little faster. Or maybe joining a support group that can help you break a longstanding addiction. Are you headed the wrong direction in any area of your life right now? Take the next exit. God's placed it there, within reach.

Lord, regardless of what tempts me away from your will, I pray that I have the courage to say no. I am blessed to be called yours, and I don't want anything to turn my attention away from you because nothing Satan can tempt me with is anywhere near as good as what you have promised.

WHAT TEMPTATION IS TUGGING AT YOUR HEART RIGHT NOW? WHAT EXIT DO YOU HAVE? ASK GOD FOR THE STRENGTH AND RESOLVE NEEDED TO FOLLOW THROUGH.

THE BAD COLUMN

Who can discern his errors? Forgive my hidden faults.
PSALM 19:12 NIV

One of the most common misconceptions unbelievers have is that they live comparatively "good" lives, so their need for a Savior is nonexistent. But David was well aware he was a sinner. He was aware that he didn't even know what all of his sins *were*, there were so many. He's wise to request forgiveness for the hidden sins, as well as those he recognizes. We should be so smart (and humble)!

Thank you, Jesus, that you came to save me from myself! Before recognizing my need for you, I thought I had enough checks in the good column to outweigh the bad. You were so patient in waiting for me to realize I'd never get the bad column clean because I didn't even know everything it entailed. Thank you.

ARE YOU JOYOUS ABOUT HIS FORGIVENESS TODAY? THANK THE LORD FOR FORGIVING ALL OF YOUR SINS—HIDDEN AND OPEN. REMEMBER THAT JESUS IS THE ONLY WAY TO SALVATION.

NEW YOU

You were taught, with regard to your former way of life, to put off your old self, which is being corrupted by its deceitful desires; to be made new in the attitude of your minds; and to put on the new self, created to be like God in true righteousness and holiness.

EPHESIANS 4:22-24 NIV

We are born into this world wanting to get our way. We want what we want, when we want it, and that means now! We have strong desires that may not be pleasing to God… that is, until after we turn our lives over to him and accept that his way is the only one that is righteous and holy.

This new way may not feel comfortable at first. After all, people around us may be accustomed to the "old" us: the one who gossips, drinks a bit too much, or is the first to laugh at an off-color joke. But as God changes our attitudes, our lifestyle follows suit. Little-by-little or overnight, God's makeover will make us more beautiful inside and out.

Lord, I pray that I will do as you commanded in shedding my old self in favor of the new self that you want me to be. Thank you for giving me a new attitude and desires that are pleasing to you.

WHAT IS ONE THING YOU'VE CHANGED SINCE TURNING YOUR LIFE OVER TO GOD? CONSIDER HOW IT HAS CHANGED YOUR LIFE FOR THE BETTER.

THE LITTLE THINGS

If you give even a cup of cold water to one of the least of my followers, you will surely be rewarded.
MATTHEW 10:42 NLT

This verse is so full of promise. Many of us carry a burden of guilt about not doing enough for the kingdom. We don't go on mission trips, we don't work in the nursery on Sundays, or we don't try to become leaders in Bible study groups. Jesus assures us that while all of those efforts are worthy of great reward, he will not ignore any serving gesture we make for him. A word of encouragement, a meal for someone in need, a hug—anything we do to serve as his disciples. A reward is coming even for those things.

Jesus, I want to serve you well, and sometimes I feel frustrated or a little guilty that I don't do as much as others. But I thank you for recognizing every effort I do make to comfort or uplift people in your name.

WHAT HAVE YOU DONE LATELY IN HIS NAME? THINK OF SOME SMALL WAYS IN WHICH YOU CAN HELP THOSE IN NEED.

THE COMMON MAN...AND WOMAN

Jesus said to him, "Go your way; your faith has made you well." And immediately he recovered his sight and followed him on the way.

MARK 10:52 ESV

The blind man who was healed by Jesus wasn't anyone special—not a celebrity, political figure, or religious leader. He was simply a man in the crowd. Jesus loves all of us the same, whether we're one of many or someone considered *special* by the world's standards. His goodness transcends public opinion. So should ours.

Does our love cross social, racial, political, and religious boundaries? Are we willing to serve "the least of these"? If our circle of friends were a box of chocolates, would they all look and taste exactly the same? There is no hierarchy, or uniformity, in God's family. Jesus died for the rich, the poor, the cynical, and the sincere—regardless of IQ, income bracket, country of origin, or religious affiliation. No man, or woman, is "common" in God's eyes.

Heavenly Father, only you have the vision to see everyone and everything so clearly through the eyes of love. Help me see others the way you do.

HAVE YOU EVER FELT INSIGNIFICANT WHILE IN THE MIDST OF "IMPORTANT" PEOPLE? KNOW THAT GOD DOES NOT JUDGE BY THE WORLD'S STANDARDS. HE PLACES GREAT IMPORTANCE ON YOUR LIFE.

HIS PERFECT WILL

Be joyful in hope, patient in affliction, faithful in prayer.
  ROMANS 12:12 NIV

When we find ourselves at a crossroads and neither of the available outcomes is ideal or within our control, it can be difficult to know what to pray for. The key is to accept that neither outcome is beyond *God's* control. Our wisest action is to request that God will enable us to accept whatever his will is in the circumstances. An amazing amount of peace lies in that submission.

Heavenly Father, I often forget that I'm not in total control of my circumstances or those of my loved ones. I know you listen to our petitions, but please help me embrace the peace of knowing and accepting that your will always leads to the best outcome even if I can't understand it at the moment.

IS THERE A CIRCUMSTANCE YOU NEED TO GIVE UP TO HIS WILL? LET HIM HAVE IT AND RELAX IN THE PEACE THAT FOLLOWS.

WALK WITH ME

As they walked along they were talking about everything that had happened. As they talked and discussed these things, Jesus himself suddenly came and began walking with them.

LUKE 24:14-15 NLT

Ever since Jesus came to earth, he has walked with us, and he promises to continue to do so. He is always there beside us, and he listens to everything we tell him, yet he doesn't intrude. If we don't pay attention to his presence, we are missing out on the best opportunity to have the best friend for life.

Why not take a walk today and talk with Jesus? Leave your music at home and simply enjoy the world God's made in the company of its very own Creator. It's not only a spiritually refreshing way to start the day, but it's beneficial mentally and physically as well. So, put on your walking shoes and get started. When we walk and talk with Jesus, no subject is out of bounds.

Jesus, my dearest friend, I thank you for walking alongside me every second of every day. I know that I should always be aware of your presence, but sometimes my attention is diverted elsewhere. I pray that my relationship with you will continue to grow stronger.

WHO IS YOUR BEST EARTHLY FRIEND? INCLUDE JESUS IN YOUR RELATIONSHIP AND WATCH IT GROW EVEN DEEPER.

INSERT FOOT IN MOUTH?

Even a fool is counted wise when he holds his peace;
When he shuts his lips, he is considered perceptive.
PROVERBS 17:28 NKJV

Perhaps Mark Twain knew he was paraphrasing today's verse when he said, "It is better to keep your mouth closed and let people think you are a fool than to open it and remove all doubt." Of course, we're not expected to spend our lives muted, but not every thought needs to be shared with the world—especially if we've given it too little forethought. One reason Bible study is excellent is because it helps us know how God would like us to respond, if at all.

Thank you, God, for the wisdom you share with us through your Word. Please keep me drawn to studying and following its guidance. I want to be discreet and diplomatic, but more than anything, I want to be squared with your Word when I speak.

DO YOU THINK BEFORE YOU SPEAK? TRY WAITING A FEW SECONDS BEFORE THOUGHTS TUMBLE OUT OF YOUR MOUTH TODAY, AND SEE HOW MUCH WISER YOU FEEL.

GOD WHO?

Since we are receiving a Kingdom that is unshakable, let us be thankful and please God by worshiping him with holy fear and awe.

HEBREWS 12:28 NLT

How do we worship with "holy fear and awe"? We see God for who he really is. Or, at least, we see him as clearly as we possibly can in this world. We don't paint a picture of who we want God to be, a benevolent grandfather who gives us everything our hearts desire—or who the God we fear he may be, a harsh taskmaster waiting to slap our knuckles with a ruler every time we step out of line.

We don't pick and choose the Bible verses we're going to use to create the heavenly Father who most closely resembles us. We worship God for all we know and understand (and for what we don't), for his unequaled power, tempered by his never-ending love. We come to him acknowledging how big he is and how small we are. That's what holy fear and awe is all about.

Lord, may I count my blessings each day and never forget that it all starts with the kingdom you have provided. I am in awe of you and your greatness, and there is no doubt in my mind that you are all I need.

WHAT DO YOU MOST FEAR, AND ARE MOST IN AWE OF, ABOUT GOD? SEARCH GOD'S WORD TO SEE IF IT SUPPORTS WHAT YOU FEEL.

SPIRITUAL WEAPONS

The weapons we fight with are not the weapons of the world. On the contrary, they have divine power to demolish strongholds.
2 CORINTHIANS 10:4 NIV

There are certainly times and places where actual military weaponry serves as a protection and a blessing, especially in today's world. But today's verse addresses the weapons we have at our disposal daily to conquer the evil in our immediate midst. Jesus is all powerful, and he blesses us with love, faith, and his Word. We must always be in prayer, asking for these weapons to serve him well.

Lord Jesus, thank you for the spiritual weapons you place at my disposal to conquer the evil around me. Thank you for our brave military forces, as well. Please bless them and keep them safe. May we fight the good fight against evil in this world until the day you return to us.

WILL YOU EMBRACE THE WEAPONS HE HAS GIVEN YOU? TAKE THEM UP AND FIGHT THE GOOD FIGHT OF FAITH!

EXTRA! EXTRA! TELL ALL ABOUT IT!

We bring you the good news that what God promised to the fathers, this he has fulfilled to us their children by raising Jesus, as also it is written in the second Psalm, "You are my Son, today I have begotten you."
ACTS 13:32-33 ESV

What do we do when something wonderful happens? We want to share the good news! The birth of a child, a new job offer, a marriage proposal, a graduation, or highly anticipated move—whatever fills us with joy is something we don't want to keep to ourselves.

All of us like to hear good news, and God has provided the best news of all: he has adopted us. As soon as he became our Father, we instantly inherited a place by his side for eternity. That's not only good news, but the best news ever. How can we share it with those around us?

I am grateful, Lord, for your willingness to adopt me and love me enough to forgive my sin. Life with you for eternity is the biggest show of your love and goodness I can imagine. May I protect it with my faith and desire to do your will.

WHAT IS YOUR NORMAL REACTION TO GOOD NEWS? THINK OF THE GREAT NEWS THAT GOD IS YOUR FATHER, AND JUMP FOR JOY!

BETTER IS ONE DAY IN HIS HOUSE

*A thousand years in your sight
are like a day that has just gone by,
or like a watch in the night.*

PSALM 90:4 NIV

There is something comforting about the way this verse drives home the difference between our finite perception of time and God's infinite eternity. Like everything else about God, his reality is incomprehensible. We are simply too small to get it. Life here on earth is often inexplicably wonderful. But it is *nothing* compared to what he has awaiting us.

Dear God, we'll never be able to understand time as you designed it—not until you return. What work and joy do you have planned for us in eternity? I can't wait to find out!

HOW DO YOU IMAGINE ETERNITY WITH THE LORD? ONE THING YOU CAN COUNT ON: IT WILL BE MUCH BETTER THAN YOU CAN EVEN DARE TO IMAGINE.

INNER BEAUTY

The LORD said to Samuel, "Don't judge by his appearance or height, for I have rejected him. The LORD doesn't see things the way you see them. People judge by outward appearance, but the LORD looks at the heart."
  1 SAMUEL 16:7 NLT

Picture yourself at a beauty pageant. All those lovely women walking across the stage in their stunning gowns and skimpy swimsuits, displaying their amazing bodies and flawless features. Each one would display her God-given talents and hard-earned skills in the talent competition before the audience and judges. Who would you choose to receive the crown?

Now, imagine God was the judge. Chances are it would be hard for us to tell who the winner would be. That's because God's take on beauty is so different from our own. He sees us from the inside out. What can we do to make our heart more beautiful? Reflect God's own image more clearly in our lives. What area of our heart is most desperately in need of a makeover?

Jesus, your unfailing ability to see past the exterior gives me the confidence and hope that keeps me going day in and day out. I pray that others are able to overlook my outward appearance and see your goodness through me.

HAVE YOU EVER JUDGED PEOPLE BASED ON THEIR OUTWARD APPEARANCE OR BEEN JUDGED BY YOURS? TAKE COMFORT IN KNOWING THAT GOD SEES THE TRUE BEAUTY INSIDE OF YOU!

SHINING LIKE THE SUN

As the men watched, Jesus' appearance was transformed so that his face shone like the sun, and his clothes became as white as light.

MATTHEW 17:2 NLT

As if being one of his disciples wasn't honor enough, Peter, James, and John experienced the privilege of seeing Jesus in his transfigured state. I think we all have ideas of what heaven will be like, even though we can't truly know until we're there. But, assuming this is what we'll see in heaven, what a treasure of information this verse holds! Seeing him face-to-face is hard to fathom: imagine light emanating from him like it does from the sun!

I can't wait, Jesus, to meet you face-to-face. Thank you that my loved ones and I will be privileged the way your disciples were. I pray you will help me remember this image of you and carry it with me as a source of encouragement and strength through every day until I get to join you in heaven.

DO YOU IMAGINE THE DAY YOU'LL SEE HIM IN PERSON? THINK ABOUT THE LIGHT AND WARMTH OF HIS PRESENCE AS IF YOU WERE BASKING IN THE SUN. IT WILL BE GLORIOUS!

REFRESHMENT BREAK

He makes me lie down in green pastures,
he leads me beside quiet waters, he refreshes my soul.
He guides me along the right paths for his name's sake.
PSALM 23:2-3 NIV

Longing to become a woman who reflects God's image in what we say and do can lead us to believe that life is one big improvement plan. We strive to be more patient, speak kindly, serve others, and love well. And that's just a start. But life is more than a refining process. It's a gift. Like a literal gift, we're to open it and enjoy what's inside.

Some gifts are useful, tools we need to get a job done. Others are given simply for our enjoyment. We need both to live a balanced life. God gives us bubble bath, as well as blenders. Today, open the gift of silence, solitude, and reflection. Ask God to quiet your mind as well as your heart, and lead you to a place of peace and rest.

Lord, even when I'm feeling down or discouraged by life's circumstances, I know you are there to give me comfort. I pray that I will be still and bask in the warmth and comfort of your loving arms.

HAVE YOU EVER FELT AS THOUGH YOU WERE TOO WEARY TO TAKE ANOTHER STEP IN LIFE? ALLOW GOD TO LEAD YOU BESIDE THE STILL WATERS WHERE HE CAN REFRESH YOUR SOUL.

MERCY

You must show mercy to those whose faith is wavering.
    JUDE 1:22 NLT

We may know believers who doubt that God's love for them is unconditional. We may know seekers who think salvation can't possibly be as simple as it sounds. Or we may know people who allow their doubt to lead them toward false teaching. Jude cautions us to lovingly draw doubters toward God's Word, rather than ridiculing or talking down to them. We should try to emulate Christ's respectful approach.

Dear Jesus, please put the right words in my mouth when I come across believers who struggle with doubt, or people seeking in the wrong places. I want to say the words that people need to hear in order to understand their need for you, and only you.

IS THERE SOMEONE JESUS WANTS TO REACH THROUGH YOU? ASK HIM HOW YOU CAN ENCOURAGE THEM TOWARD HIS WORD TODAY.

VIVA LA DIFFERENCE

Then Peter began to speak:
"I now realize how true it is that God does not show
favoritism but accepts from every nation the one who
fears him and does what is right."
  ACTS 10:34-35 NIV

We often find that we surround ourselves with people who make us feel comfortable. Those who dress differently, speak with a different accent, eat different food, or do things we aren't used to are often on the outside looking in.

We need to remember that in God's goodness, he considers *all* who love him as his children. We are brothers and sisters and should treat each other as such. That starts with looking others in the eye and offering a sincere smile that says, "You are accepted here." If you're used to keeping your distance from those who are different from you, even this small step may feel risky at first. But love is always a risk. One that God asks us to take.

Lord, I pray that I will embrace the differences and allow
people I'm not familiar with into my heart. We are all brothers
and sisters in Christ, and I know that you want me to accept
them into the family of believers as you have.

DO YOU KNOW SOMEONE WHO IS DIFFERENT? CONSIDER HOW YOU CAN MAKE THEM FEEL MORE AT HOME WITH YOU THE NEXT TIME YOU SEE THEM!

FREEDOM FROM DEATH

Because God's children are human beings--made of flesh and blood--the Son also became flesh and blood. For only as a human being could he die, and only by dying could he break the power of the devil, who had the power of death. Only in this way could he set free all who have lived their lives as slaves to the fear of dying.

HEBREWS 2:14-15 NLT

How atheists manage to go through each day without living in mortal fear is a wonder. At any moment, according to their belief system, something may take their lives, and… that's it: the end. Even as believers, most of us have a natural fear of actually dying. But we have no fear of what happens next, thanks to Jesus. For us, death is a walk through the door to eternity. We are no longer slaves to fear.

Thank you, Lord Jesus, for sharing in my humanity in order to show yourself to me and to make the ultimate sacrifice, freeing me from the power of death. Please help me to share the good news of that gift with others, especially those who haven't embraced you and thus have good reason to fear death

DO YOU FEAR DEATH? LET TODAY'S VERSE BRING YOU COMFORT.

POWER OF PRAYER

The prayer of faith will save the sick, and the Lord will raise him up. And if he has committed sins, he will be forgiven.

JAMES 5:15 NKJV

Prayer is a great mystery. We don't understand how it really works and why God seems to move in miraculous ways through the power of prayer in one circumstance, yet seems to remain silent and uninvolved in another. The words we choose, the size of our prayer circle, the fervor behind our request or even how frequently we come to God with our prayer is not the key to a "successful" prayer life.

God's answers are in line with God's will. In other words, he acts as he sees fit. That doesn't mean prayer is unnecessary or ineffective. It's greatest gift is drawing us closer to our heavenly Father. The closer we are to him, the more we see life from his perspective. The answer to our prayer may ultimately be that we're at peace with whatever answer God brings our way.

Dear Lord, you are the great physician. I come to you with this prayer for forgiveness and healing. Only you know how deeply I need both.

WHAT ANSWERS HAVE YOU SEEN TO RECENT PRAYERS? SPEND SOME TIME TODAY THANKING GOD THAT HE HEARS YOU WHEN YOU PRAY.

UNTO THE LORD

Work with enthusiasm, as though you were working for the Lord rather than for people. Remember that the Lord will reward each one of us for the good we do, whether we are slaves or free.

EPHESIANS 6:7-8 NLT

Most of us have, at some point in life, worked jobs we didn't enjoy. Or we may have worked under less-than-pleasant supervisors. In those situations, it can be difficult to give the job our best efforts. But we represent Christ, especially if our co-workers know we're Christians! It truly does make it easier to work well when we consider ourselves to be working for Christ. God loves a hard worker, and we want to feel good about giving him our best.

Heavenly Father, sometimes it's just difficult to get up and go to work. Sometimes the work is tedious. It would feel so nice to just stay home and relax. But thank you, Lord, for being my motivation for doing a good job. I hope my efforts today are pleasing to you, and I hope I represent you well in front of my co-workers.

ARE YOU AWARE OF HIS APPRECIATION WHEN YOU WORK HARD? DO YOUR JOB FOR HIM TODAY AND FEEL HOW MUCH MORE SATISFYING IT IS.

HEART OF FORGIVENESS

Be kind and compassionate to one another, forgiving each other, just as in Christ God forgave you.
EPHESIANS 4:32 NIV

It's difficult to give up hard feelings for others in this world where people hurt each other, cut us off on the road during rush hour traffic, and throw us under the bus for their own personal or professional gain. But God calls us to be kind and to forgive. Even though it's not easy, forgiveness isn't just something we do for those who've wronged us. We also do it for ourselves.

Forgiving others frees us from the weight of carrying resentment or a grudge around with us every day. Can you feel the weight of those right now? Talk to God about whoever has hurt you. Ask him to give you the desire, strength, and wisdom you need to fully forgive, even if you have to do it over and over again until you can finally let go—and set yourself free.

Thank you, God, for forgiving me of my sin. I pray that I will extend this same heart of forgiveness toward those who hurt me or say terrible things about me. May I set an example for others in the name of Christ.

DO YOU FIND IT DIFFICULT TO FORGIVE OTHERS? SET YOURSELF UP TO ENJOY GOD'S GOODNESS BY LETTING GO OF PAST HURTS AND OFFENSES. YOU WILL FIND INCREDIBLE FREEDOM IN THE PLACE OF FORGIVENESS.

SEPTEMBER

The rarest treasures of life

are found in his truth.

That's why I prize God's Word

like others prize the finest gold.

Nothing brings the soul such sweetness

As seeking his living words.

PSALM 19:10 TPT

THE KEY

The Lᴏʀᴅ will guide you continually, giving you water when you are dry and restoring your strength. You will be like a well-watered garden, like an ever-flowing spring.
ISAIAH 58:11 NLT

Sometimes we need guidance and it doesn't always come from the Sunday sermon or comments by fellow Christians. The Lord encourages us to seek guidance from him right in his Word. A Bible concordance is an excellent means of pinpointing what God says about specific issues and concerns. We are wise to make use of it.

Dear God, I thank you for the times you answer my prayers and questions through my pastor's teaching or through advice from my Christian friends. But I know your Word is the key. It is the truth, always. Please guide me to read the passages that will give me the guidance you want me to have at given moments.

HOW DO YOU MOST OFTEN SEEK GOD'S GUIDANCE? SEARCH HIS WORD FOR ANSWERS AND YOU WON'T BE DISAPPOINTED!

FAMILY MONOGRAM

See, I have engraved you on the palms of my hands;
Your walls are ever before me.
ISAIAH 49:16 NIV

Monogramming is one way people establish possession of something—from towels to apparel. Many people monogram luggage, phone cases, kids' backpacks or other items to send a message that says, "This is mine, not yours" to others in case they misplace their belongings.

Jesus doesn't lose anything that he has claimed as his, including us. We are in his constant care. But like a parent who carries pictures of their children in their wallet, he has marked us as his own. We carry his name, "Christ" with us wherever we go. What a privilege and a blessing it is to be his.

Thank you, Lord Jesus, for claiming me as yours. Please direct me to look up toward the heavens during difficult times when I feel invisible or insignificant, and remind me that I will never be seized from your almighty grip.

WHAT EVIDENCE HAVE YOU SEEN OF THE LORD CLAIMING YOU FOR HIS OWN? PONDER THAT FOR A WHILE AND LET IT ENCOURAGE YOU TO PRESS INTO HIM TODAY.

IT'S NEVER TOO SOON

Seek the LORD while he you can find him. Call on him now while he is near.
ISAIAH 55:6 NLT

So many people assume that Jesus will always be available, so they can take their time deciding whether they need him in their lives or not. The word "while" in this verse sounds like very, very strong encouragement to accept Christ now. We never know what a day will entail.

Precious Lord Jesus, I thank you so much that you touched my heart when you did, and I will never take you for granted. I pray that all people will understand their urgent need for salvation through you. Please impress upon my unsaved friends and loved ones that nothing is more important in life than you.

IS THERE SOMEONE YOU KNOW WHO HAS BEEN ON THE FENCE FOR TOO LONG? ENCOURAGE THEM TO TAKE A STEP TOWARD THE LORD TODAY.

SOURCE OF WISDOM

The LORD gives wisdom;
from his mouth come knowledge and understanding.
    PROVERBS 2:6 NIV

Some people think that wisdom comes from education and books written by man, but believers know that it comes from allowing God's Word to take over. Reading the Bible, studying it, pondering it with an open heart, and prayerfully allowing it to guide our lives shows great wisdom—and provides it, as well.

We can be smart as a whip, but unless we are wise, we will lack understanding as to what's truly important and how we can best align our lives with it. Wisdom is taking knowledge and knowing what to do with it. We can know full well the error of someone's argument, but only with wisdom can we find the words, and the compassion, that will allow us to help that person see the error of his or her ways, and motivate them toward positive change.

Thank you, Jesus, for giving us all the answers we need to live a holy life. Please keep me focused on your wisdom and not the noise of the world.

DO YOU LISTEN MORE TO GOD'S WORD OR MAN'S LIMITED WISDOM WHEN MAKING DECISIONS? YOU WILL FIND THAT BETTER DECISIONS ARE MADE WHEN YOU LISTEN TO THE WISDOM FROM ABOVE.

VERIFYING THE TRUTH

Now the Bereans were of more noble character than the Thessalonians, for they received the message with great eagerness and examined the Scriptures every day to see if what Paul said was true.
ACTS 17:11 NIV

While some may feel that they would be exhibiting a rebellious nature by comparing what their pastors teach with what is said in the Scripture, this verse commends the Bereans as having noble character for doing just that. Paul was no slouch with regard to preaching, but the Bereans kept in mind that he was just a man. We should always have our focus on God's Word first.

Thank you God, for the pastors and teachers you bring into my life. Bless them in their efforts to represent you and spread your Word. Thank you also for making your Word available to all of us. I don't take that privilege for granted. Please help me to understand the intent and the meaning of everything you have told us.

DO YOU COMPARE WHAT YOU'RE TAUGHT WITH WHAT GOD TEACHES? IT'S A GOOD HABIT TO GET INTO TO MAKE SURE YOU AREN'T ACCEPTING FALSE TEACHING.

HIGHER EDUCATION

Show me your ways, LORD, teach me your paths.
Guide me in your truth and teach me,
for you are God my Savior,
and my hope is in you all day long.
PSALM 25:4-5

So many of us consider education important in our lives because it enables us to accomplish our professional goals. The same applies to learning about God. It's of utmost importance because God is our eternal teacher. What he has to teach is the pinnacle of higher education. Knowing about God, by reading the Bible, listening to a message on a Sunday morning, or attending a Bible study or women's retreat, helps us better recognize God's character and see his hand at work in the world around us. Even so, knowing *about* God isn't as important as knowing God—the same way that knowing all about our best friend isn't the same as knowing her.

To know someone, we need to spend time with them. So, before we read the Bible or head to church, let's invite Jesus to join us. It's our Savior, not theology, that ultimately changes our lives and our destiny.

Thank you, God, for showing me your ways and teaching me your truth. As long as I stay focused on you and learn more about you, I will continue to enjoy your goodness.

DO YOU SPEND TIME EACH DAY LEARNING MORE ABOUT THE LORD? THERE IS AN INFINITE MEASURE TO LEARN— AND IT'S ALL GOOD BECAUSE GOD IS GOOD.

HEARING STRAIGHT FROM JESUS

They said to the woman, "It is no longer because of what you said that we believe, for we have heard for ourselves, and we know that this is indeed the Savior of the world."

JOHN 4:42 ESV

It's a privilege anytime we're able to be a part of someone's path to salvation, so if we can share about what salvation is, that is to be honored. But true salvation comes as a result of a connection between a new believer and the Lord. So a part of any effort we make should be to encourage a seeker or new believer to pray and read the Gospel.

Lord Jesus, the woman at the well proved to be such an integral part of the salvation of those who heard her and then wanted to hear from you. Thank you for any time you've used my behavior or words to incite someone to want to hear from you. Please help me to play that part with every seeker I know.

DO YOUR WORDS AND ACTIONS PIQUE CURIOSITY ABOUT JESUS IN SEEKERS? THINK ABOUT HOW YOU CAN MAKE THAT HAPPEN AS YOU GO ABOUT YOUR EVERYDAY BUSINESS.

WALK THE TALK

He told them, "Go into all the world and preach the Good News to everyone."
   MARK 16:15 NLT

God has given us the amazing opportunity to share his message with everyone we come into contact with. We don't have to go someplace exotic or scary. All we have to do is show his love by speaking the truth and shining his light on those we encounter, even if it's while shopping in the grocery store.

When we walk in God's ways, we'll stand out like a fine Belgian chocolate in a world of cheap carob chips. God's love shining through us will attract people to us. They'll have questions as to why we chose to forgive, showed hospitality to a stranger, or generously donated a portion of our hard-earned money to help people around the world. That's an open door to share how God has changed our lives and our hearts. When what we preach lines up with how we live, that's truly good news.

Dear Lord, I am delighted that you have called me to share your Word with others. I pray that I see the opportunities to tell people about you and to treat them with the respect due my brothers and sisters in Christ.

HOW CAN YOU SHARE YOUR FAITH WITH OTHERS TODAY? THINK ABOUT THE SIMPLE WAYS YOU CAN SHOW JESUS TO THOSE AROUND YOU.

STUMBLING BLOCKS

Let us stop passing judgment on one another. Instead, make up our mind not to put any stumbling block or obstacle in your brother's way.
ROMANS 14:13 NIV

There are a couple of cautions for believers in this verse. We often jump right into judging those who live outside faith in Jesus. That is so uninviting. And Jesus says it's wrong. We have many freedoms as believers, but we need to be cautious around believers who feel they're sinning if they exercise those freedoms. We don't want to put them in a position of judging themselves harshly for behaviors they would not have exhibited were it not for our example.

Dear Lord, please help me to be sensitive to unbelievers and believers alike. Give me the discipline to be loving and sacrificial when the circumstances require it. Help me to be more like you.

ARE YOU ABLE TO DO WITHOUT WHEN IT HELPS YOUR BELIEVING FRIENDS? THE SACRIFICE IS WELL WORTH IT.

BLESSINGS OF A FRIEND

Perfume and incense bring joy to the heart,
And the pleasantness of a friend springs from their
heartfelt advice.

PROVERBS 27:9 NIV

We were made for friendship. Even though Jesus was God, he had a circle of friends with whom he walked and talked, celebrated and mourned, laughed with, cried with and shared his heart, as well a meal. We will connect with some of our friends more deeply than others. Jesus had Peter, James, and John.

Who is in your inner circle? What special gifts does each bring to your relationship? How do they help you see God, and the world, in a way that differs from your own point of view? Invite your friends to challenge you as well as make you laugh. Those who know us best see our weaknesses as well as our strengths. They can be just the mirror we need to take care of that proverbial spinach between our teeth in regard to our character.

Thank you, God, for the friends you've brought into my life.
Help me be as much of a blessing to them, as they are to me.

DO YOU HAVE A FRIEND WHO TOTALLY "GETS" YOU?
THANK GOD FOR THE BLESSING OF HIS FRIENDSHIP TODAY.

PROMISES

I will certainly bless you. I will multiply your descendants beyond number, like the stars in the sky and the sand on the seashore.

GENESIS 22:17 NLT

There are many promises in the Bible that have come to pass, and there are promises that have yet to be fulfilled. But they are God's promises, and they *will* come to pass. When we experience struggles during our earthly life, it helps if we focus long term and remember God's promises. They give us strength and hope.

Dear God, your promise of salvation is the most important one, and I look forward to the fulfillment of your promises with regard to eternity and your second coming. Please help me to keep a long-term view of this life so I can represent you as a person of hope and faith.

IS YOUR LONG-TERM FAITH AND HOPE EASY FOR OTHERS TO SEE? RELY ON THE PROMISES OF GOD TO GIVE YOU THE STRENGTH YOU NEED TODAY.

MOUNTAINS AND MOLEHILLS

He replied, "Because you have so little faith. Truly I tell you, if you have faith as small as a mustard seed, you can say to the mountain, 'Move from here to there,' and it will move. Nothing will be impossible for you."
MATTHEW 17:20 NIV

So many of us see our problems as being insurmountable. We wallow in the depths of despair and worry about every little thing that comes before us. Even our biggest concerns are small for God. But he doesn't treat them that way. What matters to us, matters to him.

What are the mountains in your life, today? Like a summit that seems insurmountable, God will help you over it, around it, through it, or he will remove it altogether. We'd all prefer the latter, but God gives us the strength to handle the other options, as well. It all begins with prayer. When we pray, God gives us perspective. He helps us tell the mountains from the molehills and respond to each in kind. So, take your tiny mustard seed of faith and plant it firmly in God. He'll make sure you get where you need to go.

Lord Jesus, thank you for the power of prayer. Teach me to lean on you with the faith that you have commanded and free me from worry.

DO YOU EVER WORRY ABOUT THE NEXT STEP IN YOUR LIFE? BELIEVE THAT GOD'S PLAN FOR YOU IS GOOD, AND TRUST HIM TO BRING ABOUT THAT PLAN IN HIS TIME.

PEACE AND CONFIDENCE

The fruit of righteousness will be peace;
the effect of righteousness
will be quietness and confidence forever.
    ISAIAH 32:17 NIV

The quietness and confidence Isaiah speaks about has to do with the peace that overrides all concern and uncertainty we experience in our day-to-day lives. We may experience frustration, fatigue, and far worse—illness, strife, or loss. But overriding these circumstances is the eternal peace granted us when we truly accept that we have been given an eternal future with the Lord and our fellow believers.

Dear God, I know sometimes I complain and plead and otherwise show my discontent. And sometimes it's far worse than discontent—despair or near abandonment of hope. But in my heart I always know the peace of eternal grace and life with you. Please help me to live a righteous life so that peace will be quiet and strong in my heart.

DO YOU TURN TO GOD WHEN YOU DESPAIR? MAKE IT A POINT TO SEEK HIM OUT FIRST WHEN YOU FEEL LIKE YOU ARE LOSING HOPE. HE IS THE SOURCE OF PEACE AND CONFIDENCE WE SO DESPERATELY NEED.

PICK ME

Then I heard the Lord asking, "Whom should I send as a messenger to this people? Who will go for us?" I said, "Here I am. Send me."
ISAIAH 6:8 NLT

Just as God called on Isaiah to go forth and speak for him, he is calling us to do the same. Even the newest believers who are willing to stand up for their faith can be great spokespeople for spreading the Good News. Remember that no one is perfect, but God can use even flawed talents when our desire is to share the gospel with a willing heart.

It's our willingness, not our Bible knowledge, talent, charisma, or speaking ability that makes us the perfect candidate to be God's messenger. Even if you're the kind of person who'd be the last one to raise your hand and volunteer in a group, this is your chance to shine. Raise your hand, open your heart, and tell God, "Here I am. Send me—wherever, whenever. I'm ready, because I'm yours."

Lord God, thank you for implanting your message in my heart. I pray that I will take opportunities as they arise to spread your message and share your mighty love with others.

HOW HAS GOD USED YOU TO SHARE HIS MESSAGE? ACCEPT YOUR IMPERFECTIONS AND RELY ON GOD'S GRACE TO SPEAK THE WORDS THAT NEED TO BE SPOKEN.

IMPERISHABLE

You know that it was not with perishable things such as silver or gold that you were redeemed from the empty way of life handed down to you from your forefathers, but with the precious blood of Christ, a lamb without blemish or defect.

1 PETER 1:18 NIV

One of the things a lot of us marvel at, after we've spent some time surrounding ourselves with the love of Jesus and the wisdom of God, is the fact that there was a certain emptiness to our lives before. And we didn't even recognize it for the most part. For many of us, it's only when we look back that we realize something truly precious was missing. If we ever start feeling that emptiness again, it's time to stop and immerse ourselves in his grace and teaching as if it's brand new again.

Thank you so much, Jesus, for filling the void I didn't even know was in my life. Every once in a while I start to feel like maybe I'm losing that fullness. When that happens, please remind me to turn my focus on you, your blessings, and your Word. Help me to always stay connected with your imperishable gift of life and love.

DO YOU FEEL A LITTLE EMPTY TODAY? ASK THE LORD TO FILL YOU WITH HIS SWEET PRESENCE AND THANK HIM FOR THE GIFT OF LIFE.

JESUS, OUR FRIEND

No longer do I call you servants, for the servant does not know what his master is doing; but I have called you friends, for all that I have heard from my Father I have made known to you.

JOHN 15:15 ESV

It's never fun to be an outsider looking in. That's how servants probably feel while taking care of their masters. We have been pulled from servanthood to a new relationship with Jesus, so we are now part of his inner circle of friends. What an honor, privilege, and (honestly) rather daunting role. The fact that Jesus is a friend to us is mind-boggling and exciting. The fact that he considers us a friend, well, that's just downright humbling.

To have the God of the universe, the one who made the lame walk and the blind see, the one who created the cosmos and rose from the dead, invite us into his circle of friends should remind us every day how blessed we are—and how much we are worth in Jesus' eyes. The word *friend* has never sounded so sweet.

I am eternally grateful, Lord Jesus, to know that you are my friend in the ultimate sense of the word. Show me how to be a faithful friend in return.

HAVE YOU EVER FELT LEFT OUT? ENJOY THE FRIENDSHIP OF GOD AND HIS PERFECT LOVE TODAY. YOU'RE NEVER AN OUTSIDER TO HIM.

A PLACE FOR ME

"My Father's house has many rooms; if that were not so, would I have told you that I am going there to prepare a place for you?"
JOHN 14:2 NIV

If we don't think specifically enough about heaven, we might picture it as a vast, open space of clouds, blue sky, and happy people all dressed in white choir robes. Consider how exciting Jesus's comment is, then, about heaven containing many rooms. We don't know what that means, other than the fact that there is room for all of us, and our place is guaranteed. But heaven is indescribable. There must be so much to it—much space, much variety, and much, much joy.

Precious Jesus, I would have no eternal home, had you not sacrificed your life for my sins. I know the promise you made your disciples is a promise to me as well. I can't wait to see what heaven entails and what my role will be there. Please help me focus on the place that you have prepared for me!

HOW DOES A HEAVENLY PERSPECTIVE MAKE YOUR DAY MORE BLESSED? THINK ABOUT THE MANY ROOMS AND HOW JESUS HAS SPECIALLY PREPARED EACH OF THEM. THERE IS EXCITEMENT WAITING FOR US IN ETERNITY!

MORE THAN ENOUGH

How great is the goodness
you have stored up for those who fear you.
You lavish it on those who come to you for protection,
blessing them before the watching world.

PSALM 31:19 NLT

Lavish is a lovely word. It brings to mind opulent palaces, designer gowns, and jewelry that's insured for more than your home. But *lavish* is not just an adjective, it's also a verb. It's an action which God chooses to do to us—lavish his goodness on our lives. He's more than generous. He's extravagantly abundant when it comes to blessing us with good things. His storehouse never runs out, because his love never does. That means our thanks and praise should flow just as freely.

Kind of like little kids, it's easy for us to grow accustomed to a parent who continually lavishes us with good things. Kids rarely consider the house they live in, the food in the fridge, or the bed they sleep in as cause for thanks. Are we doing the same with God? What is he lavishing on you today?

Thank you, Lord Jesus, for blessing me in more ways than can be counted. Help me not grow so accustomed to your goodness that I take it for granted.

HAVE YOU EVER HAD TO LIMIT THE NUMBER OF PEOPLE AT AN EVENT YOU WERE HOSTING BECAUSE YOU DIDN'T HAVE ENOUGH ROOM? THAT WILL NEVER HAPPEN IN GOD'S KINGDOM! HE HAS ROOM FOR EVERYONE WHO WANTS TO JOIN HIM.

THAT ONE STEP

The Christian wife brings holiness to her marriage, and the Christian husband brings holiness to his marriage. Otherwise, your children would not be holy, but now they are holy.

1 CORINTHIANS 7:14 NLT

Many of us have sisters in Christ whose husbands have not embraced his gift of eternal life. We must always keep those couples in prayer and pray for the believing spouse to represent Christ as gentle, forgiving, and accepting. That is so difficult if husbands are belligerent to the Christian faith. To be challenged by the person you love most here on earth must be very difficult.

Dear Lord, thank you for those wives who carry on with their devotion to you, especially when their husbands reject you. Please bless those women who need and want to draw their loved ones to you. And please touch the hearts of unbelieving husbands so that through their wives they will see that all are children of God if they just take that one step and believe.

DO YOU KNOW SOMEONE WHO NEEDS THIS PRAYER TODAY? ASK GOD TO GIVE THEM EXTRA GRACE IN THEIR CIRCUMSTANCE TO SHOW GOD'S LOVE AND GOODNESS.

THE POWER OF CHOCOLATE... AND FAITH

You are all sons of God through faith in Christ Jesus.
GALATIANS 3:26 NASB

There are many benefits to our faith in Christ. Some of them, believe it or not, are similar to chocolate. Chocolate contains phenethylamine (say that ten times fast!), which is a mood elevator and antidepressant. It gives us a sense of well-being, like being in love. When we place our faith in Christ, we not only receive forgiveness, eternal life, and the honor of being called children of God—but we receive peace, love, and joy as an extra bonus. Talk about a mood elevator!

But there's more. Chocolate also contains theobromine, which stimulates the heart muscle. Faith does the same with our figurative heart. It kindles empathy, compassion, and kindness as we interact with others, not to mention how it nudges us to act sacrificially, just like Jesus did for us. Granted, faith is obviously better than chocolate on so many levels. But now, when you eat a piece of chocolate, you can use it as a touchstone, a tasty reminder of faith's power in your life.

Lord, I am blown away by how much my faith in you has the power to change every area of my life. Please show me any areas I haven't yet allowed faith to transform.

ARE THERE ANY OTHER THINGS ABOUT CHOCOLATE THAT BRING GOD TO MIND? FINDING TOUCHSTONES THAT HELP TURN OUR MINDS TOWARD "HEAVENLY THINGS" ARE ALWAYS WELCOME.

A HEALTHY HABIT

How sweet are your words to my taste,
sweeter than honey to my mouth!
   PSALMS 119:103 NIV

Many of us fit the stereotype of having a sweet tooth, especially with regard to chocolate. Just thinking about it can make the craving grow. We can definitely fall into a habit of having sweets after every meal, or as we watch television at night, or when we go to the movies. How terrific if we have equally strong cravings for God's Word. If we try, we can develop the habit of needing to hear from him through his Word when we get up in the morning, when we take a lunch break, and when we settle in for the night.

Dear Father, I know your Word truly is better than any sweets I may crave during my day. Please help me to develop the habit of turning to you when I get up, when I take breaks, and when I get ready for bed at night. With you, my dreams will surely be sweet.

WHEN DO YOU INDULGE IN THE LORD'S SWEET WORD? THE MORE YOU DIVE IN, THE MORE ADDICTED TO HIS WORD YOU WILL BECOME. HIS WORD IS LIFE!

ALL DRESSED UP

I will greatly rejoice in the LORD; my soul shall exult in my God, for he has clothed me with the garments of salvation; he has covered me with the robe of righteousness, as a bridegroom decks himself like a priest with a beautiful headdress, and as a bride adorns herself with her jewels.

ISAIAH 61:10 ESV

Here the Bible compares our salvation to the garments worn at a wedding: costly, beautiful, and reserved for a special occasion. That occasion celebrates a unique relationship, a lifelong love between a husband and wife. Our salvation is born of a commitment to love as well. Only it's one that will last throughout eternity.

Like marriage, our relationship and experience with God differs from that of everyone else. Perhaps there was a specific moment when you chose to say the words, "I'm yours." Or perhaps your love of God is something that's grown slowly through the years, like childhood sweethearts who seemed destined to spend their lives together. Regardless of how you came to know and love God, your salvation is a wedding gift that can never be returned. Your eternity's secure in the hands of the one who loved you long before you even knew he was there.

Lord God, I am grateful that you love me enough to prepare me for life with you in heaven. I'm yours, today and forever.

ARE YOU DRESSED AND READY TO GO FOR WHEN HE TAKES YOU? THERE IS NOTHING BETTER THAN SPENDING ETERNITY WITH JESUS.

BREATH OF HEAVEN

He breathed on them and said,
"Receive the Holy Spirit."
JOHN 20:22 NIV

When God created Adam, he breathed life into him and mankind began. Similarly, after his resurrection, Jesus breathed on the disciples and they were filled with the Holy Spirit. The same happens to us as we are born and then reborn upon accepting Jesus into our hearts. We were dead in our spirits until Jesus gave us new life.

Lord Jesus, thank you for giving me life, both earthly and eternal. I know that all life is precious, and I thank you in particular for rebirth and the Holy Spirit. I pray you will help me to lead others to understand their need for the breath of heaven you offer.

DO YOU KNOW SOMEONE WHO NEEDS TO HEAR ABOUT JESUS' BREATH OF LIFE? ASK GOD TO GIVE YOU AN OPPORTUNITY TO SHARE IT WITH THEM SOON.

JUST LIKE SHEEP

When Jesus went ashore, He saw a large crowd, and He felt compassion for them because they were like sheep without a shepherd; and He began to teach them many things.

MARK 6:34 NASB

Sheep need help. They have a lousy sense of direction and can get lost even in familiar surroundings. They like to follow the crowd, even if the flock is heading straight for the middle of the highway. They need shelter from the wind, snow, rain and heat.

Pretty much their only defense mechanism when they're in danger is to run. Like sheep, we need a good shepherd, someone to guide us and guard us. Someone who will show us the way home.

Lord, thank you for never turning your back on a single soul who needs you. I am grateful that you have given me the comfort and love that I need. I pray that I will take advantage of opportunities to share the goodness of what you have taught me through your Word.

WHAT CAN WE LEARN FROM JESUS ABOUT SHEPHERDING OTHERS? WITH GOD'S HELP, BE A SHEPHERD TO SOMEONE WHO NEEDS A BIT OF GUIDANCE TODAY.

ZIPPING IT

It is foolish to belittle one's neighbor;
a sensible person keeps quiet.
PROVERBS 11:12 NLT

The saying goes, "Speech is silver, but silence is golden."
We women love a good chat. But sometimes the chat isn't so
good. It's amazing how quickly we can get sucked into gossip
without even seeing it coming. We're not going to get along
with everyone we meet in life, but there's much to be said
for holding our tongues. We should be comfortable saying
everything we say about others in their presence; otherwise,
we shouldn't be speaking about them at all.

Dear Jesus, please help me recognize when I'm stepping into
a gossip fest before I'm knee deep! I know my speech and
behavior represent you. I lean on you for the wisdom to know
when to hold my tongue. Remind me of my own imperfections
when I want to talk about those of others.

DO YOU TRY TO AVOID GOSSIP? THINK ABOUT HOW
MUCH GRACE THE LORD HAS GIVEN YOU FOR ALL OF
YOUR WEAKNESS AND IMPERFECTIONS, AND OFFER THAT
SAME GRACE TO OTHERS.

MOVING FORWARD

Forget the former things; do not dwell on the past.
ISAIAH 43:18 NIV

We all have a past—some of it wonderful and some we'd prefer to forget. One of the greatest gifts that God has given us is the ability to look to the future and leave the past behind. This gives us the freedom to focus our attention on where he wants us to go, instead of where we've been. Sometimes we drag past trash right along with us, like a car that gets an old fast food bag caught in its grill and carries it along for hundreds of miles. Once a driver notices, what does he do? Gets rid of it. So should we.

If there's any trash from your past that keeps tripping you up and getting underfoot, talk to God about it. Get counseling if need be. It has no place in the present. Leave what's behind you… behind.

I am forever grateful to you, oh Lord, for removing the shackles of my past and giving me the freedom for my future. I pray that I will walk away from the shadows that threaten to hold me back from what you have called me to do.

HOW HAVE YOU LET GO OF THE PAST AND LOOKED TO THE FUTURE? ASK GOD TO HELP YOU SEE YOUR PAST FROM HIS PERSPECTIVE AND THANK HIM FOR NOT HOLDING YOUR PAST AGAINST YOU.

KEEP IT AFLAME

Fire shall be kept burning continually on the altar;
it is not to go out.
LEVITICUS 6:13

God's people in Old Testament times were required to do many things to maintain their connection with God. The altar fire was to serve as a constant reminder of God's presence in the temple. While that isn't required of us today, hopefully we are always aware of God's presence within our hearts. We must seek him daily to keep that fire burning.

Holy Father, you are amazing and powerful—the most important aspect of life. I ask that you help me keep a fire for you burning in my heart. Everyone's enthusiasm weakens at times as they become distracted by other matters in life. Please enflame the embers for me when I struggle to feel connected to you. Don't ever let me neglect you. I don't want to feel I've let the fire go out.

DO YOU NEED GOD TO STOKE THE FIRE AGAIN FOR YOU?
ASK HIM TO HELP YOU KEEP BURNING STRONG FOR HIM.

LIGHT OF THE WORLD

He has rescued us from the kingdom of darkness and transferred us into the Kingdom of his dear Son.
COLOSSIANS 1:13

Don't you hate it when it's late at night, you're in unfamiliar surroundings and you can't locate the light switch? You fumble around. You can't get your bearings. You stumble over things. That's the kind of life we lived before Jesus came to our rescue. When we chose to follow him, it's like he turned on the light and we could finally see where we are.

We could see our sin more clearly too. But that was only so we could understand how great Jesus' gift of forgiveness really is. In God's kingdom, we no longer stumble over the same pesky problems because we can see where they are and—with God's grace—choose to walk right around them. With the light of the world as the love of our life, we never have to walk in darkness again.

Lord, thank you for rescuing and protecting me. I pray that I never forget all you have done for me and that I can reflect your goodness as I go through everyday life.

WHAT HAS GOD'S LIGHT REVEALED LATELY IN YOUR LIFE? IF THERE'S SOMETHING YOU KEEP STUMBLING OVER, ASK GOD TO CLEARLY SEE A PATH AROUND IT.

MAJESTY

Serve the LORD with fear and rejoice with trembling.
PSALM 2:11 NIV

Do you cringe when you hear someone use the Lord's name in vain? Such a lack of respect shows little fear of the Lord. Sometimes *fear* is translated by us as respect, and that is certainly how we should feel about our Lord. But this verse refers to actual fear and trembling because of who God is and the power he wields. Sometimes it's a *really* good idea to reflect on that aspect of God's being. He wants us to feel safe and loved, but he expects mankind to obey him and, yes, fear him.

Dear God, I do embrace the power you wield, and I pray I'll never take for granted your withholding judgment against me thanks to the sacrifice made by your Son.

CAN YOU PRAY TODAY FOR THOSE WHO ARE IGNORANT OF HIS POWER? ASK FOR THE LORD'S MERCY ON THOSE WHO DO NOT YET FEAR HIM.

MISSION IMPOSSIBLE

Jesus looked at them intently and said,
"Humanly speaking, it is impossible.
But with God everything is possible."
MATTHEW 19:26 NLT

Not all heroes wear capes. Jesus carried a cross. To those who watched him walk the road to Calvary, he must have looked like anything but a hero. Wounded, defeated, deserted by those closest to him, being led to his death…but one thing all true heroes have in common is their willingness to sacrifice, to put the needs of others before their own.

That was Jesus' mission here on earth. He did the impossible, rebuilt the bridge of relationship between God and man by paying for each and every sin that had broken it. He paid with his own body, the fragile, human form he took on as his "cloak of invisibility" while here on earth. His mission was one we could never have done on our own. The impossible was only made possible through the unfathomable love of our almighty God.

Thank you, Lord, for doing the impossible for me. May I never forget the price you paid for my sins. Thank you for loving me so deeply that you were willing to sacrifice so much just to ensure I could spend eternity by your side.

WHEN WAS THE LAST TIME YOU THANKED GOD FOR HIS DEATH ON THE CROSS—NOT JUST REPEATED THOSE WORDS OUT OF HABIT, BUT REALLY THOUGHT ABOUT WHAT THEY MEANT? PERHAPS NOW'S THE TIME TO DO JUST THAT.

OCTOBER

Let everyone give all their praise

and thanks to the Lord!

For here's why—

he's better than anyone could ever imagine.

Yes, he's always so loving and kind,

and it never ends.

PSALM 107: 1 TPT

CHOSEN

You are a people holy to the LORD your God. The LORD your God has chosen you to be a people for his treasured possession, out of all the peoples who are on the face of the earth.

DEUTERONOMY 7:6 ESV

His treasured possession! Imagine the joy experienced by the Israelites upon being pronounced God's chosen people. We're told in the book of Revelation that one day Israel will turn to God's Son and be saved. And God said in Hebrews 9:15 that as believers we are his children, his descendants. What joy we should feel!

Thank you, Lord Jesus, for making it possible for me to be one of your children. I pray for the nation of Israel that they would quickly turn to you. And I ask that you help me to honor my place in your family with my thoughts, behaviors, and how I represent you. Thank you that because of your sacrifice for me, I, too, am one of God's treasured possessions.

DO YOU PRAY FOR THE NATION OF ISRAEL? SPEND SOME TIME TODAY ASKING FOR GOD TO REVEAL HIMSELF TO THOSE WHO ARE HIS TREASURED POSSESSIONS.

THE SWEETEST (AND RIGHT) PATH

Your own ears will hear him. Right behind you a voice will say, "This is the way you should go," whether to the right or to the left.
ISAIAH 30:21 NLT

How many times do we try to do things our own way, only to discover that it doesn't work out quite as we expected? And how many times do we feel as though we know something better than what the ultimate authority—God—has clearly told us? Jesus laid out a very clear plan for our lives, knowing we'd get something stuck in our willful minds that we think we know better.

Dear Jesus, I am eternally grateful that you are right here with me, guiding me down the path you have chosen for me—one that is even sweeter than the taste of the richest premium chocolate.

WHAT ARE THE RESULTS OF GOD'S GOODNESS AFTER YOU HAVE SURRENDERED TO HIM? TRUST THAT HE WILL LEAD YOU INTO ALL THAT HE HAS PLANNED FOR YOU.

UNCHAINED

Remember Jesus Christ, raised from the dead, descended from David. This is my gospel, for which I am suffering even to the point of being chained like a criminal. But God's word is not chained.
    2 TIMOTHY 2:8-9 NIV

The first three words of today's verses tie so beautifully with the last five. No matter what we experience in life, we will persevere and honor God if we remember Jesus Christ—God's Word. We may experience a modern-day version of the chains Paul suffered for his beliefs, but we can take heart that Jesus Christ will never be chained. He is truth, and he is the only freedom that lasts forever.

Dear Jesus, I take such comfort in your absolute power. Anytime I feel socially chained or persecuted for my belief in you and my need for you, please help me to remember you are above being chained down by man. Help me to exhibit graciousness by remembering you, the almighty God, are holding my heart in your hands.

WILL YOU REMEMBER GOD'S POWER WHEN YOUR FAITH IS TESTED? IN THE TIMES YOU FEEL PERSECUTED FOR YOUR BELIEF IN CHRIST, TAKE JOY IN KNOWING THAT YOUR PERSEVERANCE IS A DELIGHT TO HIM.

LAUGH WITH ME

Sarah said, "God has brought me laughter, and everyone who hears about this will laugh with me."
GENESIS 21:6 NIV

There are many times in life when we're disappointed, experience pain, or go through bad circumstances. But God brings us tastes and tidbits of joy, enabling us to be happy and laugh. These times remind us of his presence and enable us to enjoy a little slice of heaven every now and then.

Thank you, Jesus, for bringing us joy in the midst of difficult times. I pray for the patience to deal with bad circumstances and the ability to laugh at all times.

WHAT DOES IT TAKE FOR YOU TO HAVE A GOOD BELLY LAUGH? INCLUDE LAUGHTER IN YOUR EVERYDAY ROUTINE. IT'S GOOD FOR YOU!

INK AND THE SPIRIT

You show that you are a letter from Christ, the result of our ministry, written not with ink but with the Spirit of the living God, not on tablets of stone but on tablets of human hearts.

2 CORINTHIANS 3:3 NIV

What a lovely picture of Christ's gift. In the Old Testament, believers struggled to adhere to the law as it was etched into Moses' stone tablets and written thereafter in ink on the synagogue scrolls. Because we are so far short of God's design, what we all needed was Christ's promise of the Spirit of the living God etched on our hearts. This is what we receive when we accept Christ as our perfect sacrifice.

Thank you, precious Jesus, for being perfect when there was just no way for me to be. Please help me hold dear to my heart the Spirit of the living God and to listen always for your guidance. Please help me to make decisions that honor the sacrifice you made for me.

DO YOU HOLD DEAR TO YOUR HEART THE SPIRIT OF THE LIVING GOD? THANK HIM TODAY FOR HELPING YOU NAVIGATE LIFE IN A GODLY WAY.

ULTIMATE TRANSFORMER

Don't copy the behavior and customs of this world, but let God transform you into a new person by changing the way you think. Then you will learn to know God's will for you, which is good and pleasing and perfect.
ROMANS 12:2 NLT

The world is jam-packed with temptations to conform, and it's difficult to overlook what appears good on the outside to see something that might be wretched on the inside. However, God calls us to keep our thoughts on him and his will, which is the only true goodness we'll ever know. Separating ourselves from the pleasures of the world is never easy. That is why we have to immerse ourselves in God's Word and allow his message to flow in, around, and through us.

Heavenly Father, I thank you for your perfect plan for my life. Embolden me and enable me to see the world's temptations for what they truly are so I can hold onto what is righteous in your eyes.

HAVE YOU EXPERIENCED TRANSFORMATION WHEN YOU RESIST CONFORMING TO THE WAYS OF THE WORLD? IMMERSE YOURSELF IN GOD'S WORD TODAY AND SEE THE DIFFERENCE IT MAKES!

HIS YOKE

"Come to me, all of you who are weary and carry heavy burdens, and I will give you rest. Take my yoke upon you. Let me teach you, because I am humble and gentle at heart, and you will find rest for your souls."
MATTHEW 11:28-29 NLT

The beginning of this verse almost sounds incongruous. If we are weary and burdened, how would yet another yoke give us rest? But Jesus is quick to encourage the weary. We try too hard sometimes. He, the Son of God, promises he is gentle and humble in heart. His yoke is lighter than any other we may choose. He has done *all* the heavy lifting already.

Sometimes, Jesus, I feel so worn out, especially at the end of a long, stressful workday, if someone I love is burdened, or if a problem is unresolved and will await me in the morning. Thank you for this reminder that I can turn my worries over to you, as many times as I need to. Eventually, you will show me it will work out all right.

WHAT YOKE DO YOU WANT TO TRADE FOR THE ONE JESUS OFFERS? HE PROMISES YOU REST AS YOU GIVE YOUR BURDENS TO HIM.

FIRM PROMISE

Let us hold fast the confession of our hope without wavering, for He who promised is faithful.

HEBREWS 10:23 NKJV

So many times we experience broken promises—from our mouths or from others—yet we continue to believe that a promise is someone's word in concrete. The Lord is the only one who remains faithful, no matter what. His promises will never waver or wane. We know we can count on him to come through.

Dear God, I am grateful for hope through your promises. I pray that my heart will continue to be as faithful to you as you are to me.

HAVE YOU EVER HAD SOMEONE BREAK A PROMISE? KNOW TODAY THAT GOD WILL NEVER BREAK HIS PROMISES. HIS WORD IS TRUTH.

EARTHLY FAITH

Faith is the assurance of things hoped for, the conviction of things not seen.
HEBREWS 11:1 ESV

Years ago on the TV show, *Touched by an Angel,* the main character stated that, unlike humans, angels didn't need faith, because they saw God every day. This is a good picture of what our faith represents. While we don't literally see God every day, he does make himself evident all around us: in nature, people, and everyday miracles. We simply need to pay attention.

Heavenly Father, I love the idea that the effort of maintaining our faith is only an earthly enterprise. Thank you so much for your promises and constant fulfillment of them. My faith is fully built on my desire to finally be with you in heaven someday. Please help me always be certain of your love!

ARE YOU CERTAIN OF GOD'S PROMISES FOR YOU? YOU CAN BE. IT JUST TAKES A LITTLE FAITH.

THE CHOSEN

On that day, declares the LORD of hosts, I will take you, O Zerubbabel my servant, the son of Shealtiel, declares the LORD, and make you like a signet ring, for I have chosen you, declares the LORD of hosts."
HAGGAI 2:23 ESV

Have you ever been in a situation that involved someone having to choose you? It could have been for a sports team when you were a child or a promotion at work. It might even have been in a relationship with someone who had to make a decision between you and someone else. It's uncomfortable, isn't it? What is awesome about God is the fact that he has already chosen you. He knew before you were even born that you would be his. How awesome is that!

Lord, thank you for choosing me to be one of your faithful followers. I am immensely honored and know that I will always be in good hands.

HAVE YOU EVER BEEN REJECTED? PUT YOUR HOPE IN GOD WHO WILL NEVER DISAPPOINT YOU OR CHOOSE SOMEONE ELSE OVER YOU.

MORSELS UNWRAPPED

The unfolding of your words gives light;
it gives understanding to the simple.
    PSALM 119:130 NIV

The image of unfolding brings to mind unwrapping a precious gift, and that is what God's Word is for us. Receiving a gift is, in itself, a delight. But as we unwrap each layer and get deeper to the heart of the gift, our delight increases. We don't have to be Harvard graduates to appreciate the wisdom of God's Word.

Lord, thank you for meeting me every day as I consider your Word and unfold the precious gifts you give me within its pages. Thank you for reaching me at every level of my life. Thank you for being as amazing as you are for the well-studied, deeply wise veterans of Bible study and for the immature new believer. You are clearly the light of the entire world.

WHAT REVELATION HAS GOD GIVEN YOU LATELY? SHARE THIS PRECIOUS GIFT WITH OTHERS.

GOD'S CREATION

*God created human beings in his own image. In the
image of God he created them; male and female he
created them.*
GENESIS 1:27 NLT

People were clearly designed to be part of God's kingdom.
After all, we inherited his image merely by being his creations.
Everything else he designed was for his pleasure and for the
pleasure of the people he placed on earth. We can't ask for a
better inheritance than that. God is good!

*Lord, may I be constantly reminded that I was created by
you, in your image. I need to remember to submit to your will
because only then will I be completely fulfilled.*

DO YOU EVER STOP AND THINK ABOUT THE
AWESOMENESS GOD HAS PROVIDED IN YOUR LIFE?
MARVEL ON THAT AS YOU REST IN HIM TODAY.

HIS MYSTERY

Oh, the depth of the riches of the wisdom and knowledge of God! How unsearchable his judgments, and his paths beyond tracing out!
ROMANS 11:33 NIV

Occasionally we might find ourselves wondering why certain things in life happen as they do, especially since we know that God is in control. The old question of unbelievers (and even some believers) is, "How could a loving God allow this to happen?" The truth is, in many instances we simply won't know until we are finally joined with God in heaven. We truly do see through a glass darkly while here on earth. Our place is to accept that one day we will understand—when we see him face-to-face.

Heavenly Father, there are so many things I don't understand about the world we live in and the experiences of people in this world. I pray you will help me to always trust your unfathomable riches of wisdom and knowledge until that glorious day when I will meet you face-to-face.

ARE YOU ABLE TO TRUST HIS UNFATHOMABLE JUDGMENTS? THE DEPTH OF HIS RICHES AND WISDOM CANNOT BE UNDERSTOOD BY OUR HUMAN MINDS, SO WE MUST TRUST IN HIS GOODNESS IN ALL CIRCUMSTANCES.

INNER BEAUTY

Your beauty should not come from outward adornment, such as elaborate hairstyles and the wearing of gold jewelry or fine clothes. Rather, it should be that of your inner self, the unfading beauty of a gentle and quiet spirit, which is of great worth in God's sight.
1 PETER 3:3-4 NIV

Most of us are attracted to someone with outward beauty, but after we get to know the person, we may see something different. The heart of the person will eventually shine through, and no amount of adornment can make someone who is ugly inside look attractive. The reverse is also true: the most beautiful person in our lives may be someone who is lacking in the looks department.

Lord, I know that outer beauty can attract others, but only a gentle spirit will make them want to be around me. I pray that you will remind me to pay more attention to my heart than my outward appearance each day.

HAVE YOU EVER KNOWN SOMEONE WHO BECAME MORE BEAUTIFUL AS YOU GOT TO KNOW HER? YOU ALSO BECOME MORE BEAUTIFUL AS YOU GO DEEPER IN YOUR RELATIONSHIP WITH GOD AND REFLECT HIS LOVE TO OTHERS.

LOOK AND SEE

"Look at my hands. Look at my feet. You can see that it's really me. Touch me and make sure that I am not a ghost, because ghosts don't have bodies, as you see that I do."
  LUKE 24:39 NLT

Even though the disciples knew of the resurrected Jesus appearing to Peter and to the two disciples at Emmaus, when he appeared to them where they gathered, they initially thought he was a ghost. How understanding Jesus was, after all the times he had told them he would rise again. He is equally understanding to us when we falter in embracing the promises he makes to us. If we pay attention, we'll experience many reminders of his love and grace.

Thank you, Jesus, for the sacrifice you made for me on the cross. Thank you for showing us the resurrection and assuring us we would experience the same. Thank you for your patience with the unbelief that sneaks into my everyday decisions, thoughts, and behaviors. Help me to live a life reflective of your undying love.

WILL YOU TAKE COMFORT IN GOD'S PROMISES TODAY? THEY ARE TRUE, AND THEY ARE REAL.

KNOCK KNOCK

"Ask, and it will be given to you; seek, and you will find; knock, and it will be opened to you. For everyone who asks receives, and the one who seeks finds, and to the one who knocks it will be opened."
MATTHEW 7:7-8 ESV

Christ has made himself available to anyone who accepts him as savior. He wants to be part of our lives. It's not difficult. All we have to do is trust him to be who he says he is. He brings us hope through his goodness. He is always there, so let him in.

Thank you, Jesus, for continuing to be at the door, waiting for me with open arms. I pray that I never forget that. Only you bring peace and eternal love.

HAVE YOU EVER WONDERED WHERE GOD WAS DURING A DIFFICULT TIME IN YOUR LIFE? HAVE NO DOUBT; HE WAS RIGHT BESIDE YOU, AND HE WILL NOT LEAVE. ASK HIM TO WRAP YOU IN HIS LOVING EMBRACE IN THOSE TIMES YOU NEED HIM MOST.

CARPE DIEM!

"Look I am about to die," Esau said. "What good is the birthright to me?"
GENESIS 25:32 NIV

Seize the day! We've heard that as the battle cry for enjoying the pleasure of the moment—lest we miss out on life and true happiness. While we should definitely appreciate each day as a gift from God, living fully in that day, some of our worst mistakes are made out of impulsiveness. Esau sold his entire future for a bowl of lentil soup. Before we laugh at his stupidity, we might want to make sure we steer clear of rash decisions of our own.

Thank you, Father, for every day of my life. Sometimes I rush forth, with my decisions, my actions, or my mouth, and really blow it. Please keep your hand on my shoulder, guiding me despite my impulsiveness. Thank you for the times you help me consider more than one aspect of my decisions.

WHAT DECISION REQUIRES YOUR CAREFUL CONSIDERATION TODAY? SPEND SOME TIME SEEKING THE LORD'S WISDOM ABOUT IT. YOU WON'T BE DISAPPOINTED YOU DID.

EXTREME JOY

He will once again fill your mouth with laughter and your lips with shouts of joy.
JOB 8:21 NLT

One of the most pleasant expressions we have is laughter. Unfortunately, most of us don't do it as often as we once did because of all the serious influences that have replaced childhood playtime. Daily life consists of work and family responsibilities that are necessary but not always fun. The Lord has promised us that we will once again find the joy that brings laughter.

Dear Lord, I'm grateful to you for being the source of joy and laughter. As I go through everyday life, may I remember there is happiness tucked somewhere inside. Remind me to stop and enjoy it…to laugh until I cry.

WHEN WAS THE LAST TIME YOU EXPERIENCED REAL LAUGHTER? FIND THE JOY IN YOUR DAY BY NOTICING THINGS THAT ARE HUMOROUS AND DELIGHTFUL.

IN THE BODY

I am torn between the two: I desire to depart and be with Christ, which is better by far; but it is more necessary for you that I remain in the body.
PHILIPPIANS 1:23-24 NIV

For most of us it might sound strange for someone to publically declare they want their earthly life to end. Paul was by no means suicidal or morbid in his statement, and although he certainly suffered greatly, his desire was simply to be with Christ. That part all believers should embrace. When we consider the future, we can also embrace that the Lord wants us here on earth for as long as our work remains undone.

Lord, this verse provides me with comfort when I consider those loved ones who have already passed away. Although I might not be able to understand all of the circumstances, I do understand that you draw us to heaven when our work here is accomplished. I look forward to completing my work someday and meeting you in person.

WHAT DOES GOD ASK OF YOU TODAY? LIVE YOUR LIFE TO THE FULLEST EACH DAY BY DOING THE WORK THAT GOD HAS PREPARED JUST FOR YOU.

RAGS TO RICHES

As for me, I am poor and needy;
please hurry to my aid, O God.
You are my helper and my savior;
O LORD, do not delay.
    PSALM 70:5 NLT

God is generous to all of his children, without fail. He cares for everyone—from the very rich to those who are dirt poor, and everyone in between. Without him, we are all poor and needy in a spiritual sense. With him, we are richly blessed by his goodness.

I am thankful, Lord, for the blessings you have brought to all who are poor and needy in every sense, including physically and spiritually. I pray that I am able to share my blessings to show your goodness to others.

HAVE YOU EVER HAD TO GO WITHOUT SOMETHING YOU NEED OR WANT? THANK GOD FOR ALL OF THE BLESSINGS HE HAS PLACED IN YOUR LIFE. HE IS GOOD.

THE IMPOSSIBLE

Jesus replied: "Love the Lord your God with all your heart and with all your soul and with all your mind. This is the first and greatest commandment."
   MATTHEW 22:37-38 NIV

People of Old Testament times proved what we continue to prove today—no human will ever adequately fulfill the demands of the Ten Commandments. Jesus even boiled them down into two *simple* commands: to love God with everything we have, and to love our neighbors as ourselves. That shouldn't be so hard. But it is. How can anyone doubt we need the gift Jesus offers?

Thank you, Lord Jesus, for forgiving my frail attempts at living a godly life. I will always strive for the perfection you demonstrated, but I thank you that you paid the price for my inevitable failure. Thanks to you, I know that God loves me as if I were perfect.

DO YOU JOYFULLY ACKNOWLEDGE YOUR PLACE AS GOD'S CHILD? LET HIM HELP YOU WITH THE TASK HE HAS REQUIRED; LOVE HIM AND LOVE OTHERS TO THE BEST OF YOUR ABILITY. LET HIM FILL IN WHERE YOU MISS IT.

HIDDEN TREASURES IN SECRET PLACES

I will give you treasures hidden in the darkness--secret riches. I will do this so you may know that I am the LORD, the God of Israel, the one who calls you by name.
ISAIAH 45:3 NLT

It's easy to bask in the joy of life when everything is going well. However, in the darkest moments, when gloom and sadness take over, we might not see God's loving hands. But they are there, ready to embrace and comfort us. His goodness is our treasure, tucked away in places and times when we need him.

Dear Father, I know that you are the strength I need to get through the most difficult times. I come to you for the power and love only you can provide.

HAVE YOU EVER FELT GOD'S HANDS REACHING OUT TO YOU WHEN YOU WERE DOWN? HE IS A GOOD FATHER, AND HE CARES FOR YOU EVERY MOMENT OF EVERY DAY.

LOOK AT ME!

Discretion will protect you,
and understanding will guard you.
PROVERBS 2:11 NIV

People today share private business online that they never would have shared in the past. That's not generally an improvement. Back in the day, blabbing about your business only went so far, traveling from one person to another. But social media is far from discreet, and we never know who will read our posts. Today's verse couldn't be more timely if it had been written an hour ago. Before we post, we should ask if we're comfortable with *everyone* in the world reading it. Because they can.

Lord, it's a different world today, and I ask that you help me protect myself and those I love when I make use of social media. Please bless me with discernment and self-respect about what I post. And help me to never post anything that dishonors you.

DO YOU STRONGLY CONSIDER WHAT YOU POST BEFORE YOU POST IT? USE THE BENEFIT OF SOCIAL MEDIA TO ENCOURAGE AND STRENGTHEN RELATIONSHIPS, AND BE AWARE OF ITS DRAWBACKS.

NO DIMMER SWITCH

This is the message we have heard from him and declare to you: God is light; in him there is no darkness at all.
1 JOHN 1:5

Most of us thread our way through life by weaving in and out of light and darkness with our ever-changing circumstances and moods. However, once we come to Christ, and change our way of thinking, we walk only in light. We recognize that Jesus was a sacrifice for our sin, so we are forgiven and can enjoy his goodness without fear of the dark.

Lord, thank you for the light you have provided in my life by washing away my sin. May I never take your light for granted as it keeps me focused on your truth.

HAVE YOU EVER BEEN AFRAID IN THE DARK? IN GOD THERE IS NO DARKNESS, SO THERE IS NOTHING TO FEAR. STEP INTO THE LIGHT AND BASK IN HIS GOODNESS.

WE SEE HIM

He grew up before him like a young plant, and like a root out of dry ground; he had no form or majesty that we should look at him, and no beauty that we should desire him.

ISAIAH 53:2 ESV

Even today, the powerful and famous often go to great lengths to draw attention to themselves. If *they* aren't flashy, their clothes, cars, or lifestyles are. In Jesus' day, the people awaited a Messiah. They expected him to be regal and extraordinary looking, not someone like Jesus—the simple carpenter. But *we see him*, don't we?

Precious Jesus, I see you. I recognize you in my heart when you awaken me each day and protect me, guide me, and assure me of your existence and love. You are my one true Messiah, and you are both regal and extraordinary. It's still hard to believe you loved me enough to sacrifice the things you did. I can't wait to truly see your face.

HOW DO YOU SEE JESUS? HE IS OUR GLORIOUS AND GRACIOUS KING!

GENEROSITY

The generous will prosper;
those who refresh others will themselves be refreshed.
PROVERBS 11:25 NLT

In his loving nature, God wants us to be generous. After all, he has given us so much that he encourages us to share with others. And then he promises that our generosity will be rewarded with blessings from him.

Dear God, I am grateful for your generosity and goodness that never ends. I pray that I see opportunities to be generous to others—in spirit, in love, and in material things that they may need. And may I do this in the spirit of Christ-like giving.

DO YOU SEE AN OPPORTUNITY TO HELP OTHERS IN NEED? SHOW GOD'S GENEROSITY TODAY.

ESCAPISM

A hard worker has plenty of food
but a person who chases fantasies has no sense
PROVERBS 12:11 NLT

There is nothing wrong about relaxing with entertainment, enjoying good stories in books and films, for example. Creativity is a gift from God, and we are free to enjoy novels and movies just as we enjoy beautiful art and music. But if our minds become so drawn to escapism that we neglect the work the Lord created us to do, we show a lack of sound judgment. God asks that we work at whatever our job is with all our hearts, as if we are working for him.

Thank you so much, Lord, for the creativity with which you've blessed so many people. I appreciate excellent stories and art and music, and I thank you for allowing me some free time to enjoy them. I ask that you help me to always focus the appropriate amount of time to the work you have set out before me. I work to honor you.

ARE YOU ABLE TO PRIORITIZE WORK AND THE ENTERTAINMENT YOU ENJOY? BRING HONOR TO GOD BY MAKING HIS WORK YOUR PRIORITY AND KEEPING YOUR THOUGHTS FOCUSED ON HIM.

BLESSING OF CHILDREN

Behold, children are a heritage from the LORD,
The fruit of the womb is a reward.
   PSALM 127:3 NKJV

Whether we have our own children or have the privilege of enjoying the offspring of others, we are to see them as a blessing—a gift from God. We are to take care of these blessings by tending to their needs and nurturing them as God has nurtured us. We can do this by being loving parents, teachers, or mentors, offering a kind word to a child when they most need it.

Lord, thank you for the blessing of children. I pray that I will be a great mom, aunt, teacher, mentor, or friend to the younger people you have chosen to bring into my life. I want to encourage them and set a good example of someone who loves you.

WHAT CAN YOU DO FOR THE CHILDREN IN YOUR LIFE? BLESS THEM ETERNALLY BY SHOWING THEM GOD'S INCREDIBLE LOVE FOR THEM.

HE'S STILL THERE

Because of your great compassion you did not abandon them in the wilderness. By day the pillar of cloud did not fail to guide them on their path, nor the pillar of fire by night to shine on the way they were to take.
NEHEMIAH 9:19 NIV

Even though the Israelites became stubborn, refused to listen, and forgot about the miracles God worked to release them from slavery, God still provided guidance for them both day and night. When we sin we might feel like we no longer deserve his love or guidance. And we're right. But he provides it anyway. We should keep watching for it!

Dear God, your patience with me is so hard to fathom. I pray I'll never take your forgiveness for granted as I stumble through life! Thank you so much for continuing to put your guiding hand out for me to grasp, no matter how far I fall.

IS THERE A FAILING FROM WHICH YOU NEED TO MOVE ON? GOD WILL CONTINUE TO PROVIDE GUIDANCE FOR YOU EVEN WHEN YOU MAKE MISTAKES. THAT IS HIS GOODNESS SHOWN TO YOU WITHOUT RESTRAINT!

HIS SHEEP

"My sheep listen to my voice; I know them, and they follow me."
JOHN 10:27 NLT

Most of us have people giving us contradictory directions to go first one way and then another, to the point of causing confusion. However, there is one direction that we know is correct, and that is toward God. He knows what is best for us, as the shepherd does for his sheep. We are to rely on him for all of our needs because he will always be good to us.

Heavenly Father, thank you for your voice that rises above the rest in my crazy life. I pray that I continue to have the strength to turn away from anyone who tries to pull me away from you.

HOW DO YOU DEAL WITH ALL THE VOICES AND DISTRACTIONS IN YOUR LIFE, PULLING YOU IN ALL KINDS OF DIRECTIONS? LISTEN TO THE VOICE OF THE ONE WHO WILL NEVER LEAD YOU ASTRAY, AND MOVE TOWARD HIM TODAY.

BE NOT AFRAID

By faith Moses' parents hid him for three months after he was born, because they saw he was no ordinary child, and they were not afraid of the king's edict.
HEBREWS 11:23 NIV

Moses's parents knew that the king's law led to the murders of helpless children. They chose to evade the king's law by hiding their precious son, and their faith in God was lauded years later. While we are to honor our authority figures, we are not to disregard God's law when it is ignored by authority.

Heavenly Father, there are laws today that are heartbreaking. They give liberties to selfish people and lead to the death of the innocent. Please bless our lawmakers to see the wrong in those laws, and please bless believers in their efforts to evade these harsh, wrong, edicts.

WILL YOU PRAY TODAY THAT GOD'S LAWS WILL PREVAIL? KNOW THAT WHEN YOU STAND FOR GOD'S LAW ABOVE THE LAW OF THE LAND, YOU ARE CHOOSING WISELY. YOU WILL BE REWARDED FOR YOUR OBEDIENCE TO GOD'S LAW.

NOVEMBER

Lord, how wonderful you are!

You have stored up so many good things for us,

Like a treasure chest heaped up

And spilling over with blessings—

All for those who honor and worship you!

PSALM 31:19 TPT

LIVING LARGE

*When God gives someone wealth and possessions,
and the ability to enjoy them,
to accept their lot and be happy in their toil—this is a
gift of God.*

    ECCLESIASTES 5:19 NIV

Most people in the U.S. and other civilized countries have more than they need, but not everything they want. On the other hand, there are people whose work will bring them great wealth and everything they could possibly ask for. This is fine as long as they act in a godly manner. However, as soon as they forget where their prosperity comes from, it will become a burden. Boasting and bragging have no place in the kingdom of God, but being humble enhances the sweetness of his goodness.

Father, thank you for the abundance you have provided in my life. I am grateful for all you have delivered for my needs, wants, and pleasure. Don't let me forget that it all comes from you.

HAVE YOU EVER TAKEN YOUR POSSESSIONS FOR GRANTED? SHOW YOUR GRATITUDE TO GOD TODAY FOR ALL THAT YOU HAVE, EVEN IF IT ISN'T ALL THAT YOU WANT.

GOOD SAMARITANS

"He went to him and bound up his wounds, pouring on oil and wine. Then he set him on his own animal and brought him to an inn and took care of him."
LUKE 10:34 ESV

Sometimes on social media, people post clips showing one stranger coming to the aid of another. Those clips usually make most of us tear up. Perhaps part of that emotion comes from seeing innate kindness in another person. Perhaps, also, such a display is emotional because it touches a part of us that will always remain. Unconditional love is a part of eternity, a very important component of our relationship with God. Naturally, it would strike at our core.

Heavenly Father, I thank you for your unconditional love and for the emotions that fill my heart when I think of the sacrifice you and Jesus made for me. Please help me to always have an open heart, one that represents the kindness and love that originated in you.

ARE YOU MOVED BY THE KINDNESS PEOPLE SHOW TO ONE ANOTHER? THINK OF WAYS YOU CAN SHOW GOD'S KINDNESS TO THOSE AROUND YOU.

LOVING HOSPITALITY

When God's people are in need, be ready to help them.
Always be eager to practice hospitality.
ROMANS 12:13 NLT

God is the ultimate example of great hospitality. He has prepared a place for us to live eternally, and he has given us many blessings to enjoy on earth before we go. We need to emulate God's goodness as much as humanly possible by reaching out to others. Perhaps it's a young mother who is frazzled and needs a babysitter so she can have an hour to regroup. Or it might be a person with nowhere to go for the holidays.

Thank you, Lord, for all of the hospitality you have provided with love. Show me how I can provide some of this to others in need.

HOW CAN YOU SHOW LOVING HOSPITALITY TO OTHERS? LOOK AROUND YOU WITH THE INTENTION OF FINDING SOMEONE TO BLESS TODAY!

DAYS OF ELIJAH

"At that time they will see the Son of Man coming in a cloud with power and great glory."

LUKE 21:27 NIV

We've all seen the sky at times when the clouds are doing very strange and beautiful things. Do you ever think about how great it would be if out of such a tableau you saw Jesus coming? It's going to happen at some point—it could just as easily happen during our lifetime, right?

Dear Jesus, I am so eager for that day when you return. I love so much about my life here on earth, because you bless me so richly. But I know what I have here is nothing compared to living face-to-face with you for eternity. I can't wait for you to come riding on the clouds.

DO YOU GET EXCITED AT THE THOUGHT OF JESUS' RETURN? IT WILL BE A GLORIOUS DAY FOR THOSE WHO BELIEVE.

ROYAL MEAL

When I discovered your words, I devoured them. They are my joy and my heart's delight, for I bear your name, O LORD God of Heaven's Armies.
JEREMIAH 15:16 NLT

God has provided the best meal of all: his Word. He wants us to sit down with it, taste it, chew it, savor it, and delight in it. As food sustains life, his Word promises eternal life with him in heaven.

Thank you, God, for providing the sustenance for life with you forever. I fully intend to honor your wishes and read your Word faithfully so that I am nourished with goodness.

HOW HAS GOD'S WORD NOURISHED YOU? THE BIBLE IS LIKE HONEY AND MILK TO YOUR SPIRIT. DRINK IN ITS GOODNESS TODAY AND BE REFRESHED.

GOD'S PERSEVERANCE

Oh, how can I give you up, Israel? How can I let you go? How can I destroy you like Admah or demolish you like Zeboiim? My heart is torn within me, and my compassion overflows.

HOSEA 11:8 NLT

God used the story of Hosea, who worked tirelessly to draw his runaway wife back to him, to represent how he tirelessly draws us to him even when we turn away. Many of us ignored him long before we finally realized our need for him. How blessed are we that his compassion was aroused despite our stubborn ignorance?

Thank you, heavenly Father, for your patience and diligence in drawing me to you. The consequences of my willful choices could have been so much worse, not just here on earth, but eternally. Yet your amazing grace and love persevered. I want to live the rest of my days praising you for your pursuit of my heart.

DO YOU REMEMBER THE DAY YOU REALIZED YOUR NEED FOR GOD? REFLECT ON HOW MUCH YOU STILL NEED HIM TODAY, AND TELL HIM. HE LOVES IT WHEN WE RECOGNIZE THAT.

FOOD THAT NEVER SPOILS

Do not work for the food which perishes, but for the food which endures to eternal life, which the Son of Man will give to you, for on Him the Father, God, has set His seal.

JOHN 6:27 NASB

The food we eat each day keeps our stomachs full and provides the fuel we need to go about our daily business. However, that food will eventually spoil if not eaten. The food that God has provided feeds our spirit, and it never spoils. We have the amazing nourishment for our souls that will live on with us throughout eternity. This is the greatest gift that only God can give.

Lord, thank you for the gift of nourishment that never spoils. I pray that I will take my eyes off the minutiae of everyday life and turn my focus to what you have done for me.

HOW DO YOU PREPARE YOURSELF FOR NOURISHMENT OF THE SOUL? LOOK TO GOD FOR THE FOOD THAT NEVER SPOILS. HIS GOODNESS IS JUST WHAT YOU NEED TODAY.

THE LAST WORD

God's solid foundation stands firm, sealed with this inscription: "The Lord knows those who are his."
2 TIMOTHY 2:19 NIV

God's Word is his solid foundation, and it withstands all of mankind's well-meaning misinterpretations, as well as misinterpretations by those less altruistically motivated. The Lord warned us that there would be false prophets, and we are wise to weigh all teaching against the Scripture. No church should be so wrapped around a particular personality that it cannot function without him. God bless the pastors who encourage us to let God's word be the *last* word.

Thank you, Lord, for godly pastors. May they always turn to your Word before deciding what to teach their congregants. Please bless them with humility and wisdom as they represent you and draw seekers to your loving arms.

ARE YOU CAREFUL TO MAKE GOD'S WORD (AND HIS WORD ALONE) YOUR GUIDE? IT IS REALLY THE ONLY SOLID FOUNDATION TO BUILD YOUR LIFE ON.

ENOUGH TO GO AROUND

This is a trustworthy saying, and everyone should accept it: "Christ Jesus came into the world to save sinners"— and I am the worst of them all.
    1 TIMOTHY 1:15 NLT

Everyone needs Jesus in their lives. No matter how good we think we are, we are still sinners, and the only way to eternal life with him is through Christ. We are blessed that in God's goodness, he chose to sacrifice his Son so we could enjoy eternity with him.

Lord, I am humbled by your grace and mercy—that you would make such a humongous sacrifice for me. I know that I don't deserve what you have done, and I pray that I never forget to thank you each and every day.

HOW HAVE YOU EXPERIENCED GOD'S GOODNESS? THANK HIM FOR HIS SACRIFICE AND YOUR OPPORTUNITY FOR RELATIONSHIP WITH HIM TODAY.

WAITING FOR STRENGTH

Those who wait on the LORD
Shall renew their strength;
They shall mount up with wings like eagles,
They shall run and not be weary,
They shall walk and not faint.
    ISAIAH 40:31 NKJV

It's interesting that the verses just before those above talk about how weary the young can become, eventually stumbling badly in their fatigue. There's clearly something to be said for those who become mature as they wait on and hope in the Lord. If we lean purely on our own efforts to get through life's plans and challenges, we'll feel as if we're spinning our wheels. But leaning on God's plans and solutions will carry us above our earthly struggles in ways we could never have imagined.

Heavenly Father, thank you for being there for me. My life seems so busy at times—so overwhelming. But you offer a renewed strength and endurance to those who lean on you. Please help me remember to do that, even before I start to grow faint!

OVER WHAT CHALLENGE WOULD YOU LIKE GOD TO HELP YOU SOAR? PUT YOUR HOPE IN HIM AND WATCH IT HAPPEN.

DOUBLE BLESSING OF FORGIVENESS

Make allowance for each other's faults, and forgive anyone who offends you. Remember, the Lord forgave you, so you must forgive others.

COLOSSIANS 3:13 NLT

What a blessing God gave us when he chose to forgive us for all of our sins. And now he gives us the opportunity to forgive others and show his loving nature as we do so. We need to look past our pride and see it as another part of the blessing we have received. Forgiving others is not only his desire, it will clear the way for you to move forward in the life he has blessed you with.

Dear God, I know that my pride stands in the way of forgiving others, but that is not what you want from me. Thank you for your compassion. Give me the desire to extend forgiveness to others.

WHAT IS STANDING IN YOUR WAY AND PREVENTING YOU FROM FORGIVING OTHERS? TAKE A MOMENT TO REFLECT ON GOD'S FORGIVENESS OF YOU, AND THEN BE READY TO OFFER THAT TO THOSE WHO HAVE WRONGED YOU.

FULL DISCLOSURE

There is nothing hidden that will not be disclosed, and nothing concealed that will not be known or brought out into the open.
LUKE 8:17 NIV

No matter how hard we study God's Word, there are so many things about God and heaven and life that we just won't understand until God's chosen time for us. At several points in the Bible, God discusses this. Everything that is hidden will be brought to light. So there is no secret sin, and there is no enlightenment that God plans to withhold from us forever. Two things worth considering daily!

Lord God, I'm sorry for anything I've done that I foolishly think I'm carrying in secret. I thank you that you've already forgiven me for such things. I'm especially thankful for your promise to help me someday to understand those aspects of life, eternity, and your will with which I struggle today. Please help me wait faithfully for that day!

WHAT ARE YOU EAGER TO SEE UNCOVERED? LET GO OF NEEDING ALL THE ANSWERS AND TRUST IN GOD'S GOODNESS.

HE'S GOT YOUR BACK

No man shall be able to stand before you all the days of your life. Just as I was with Moses, so I will be with you. I will not leave you or forsake you.
  JOSHUA 1:5 ESV

Are you a worrier? Do you ever lie in bed at night, staring up at the ceiling, agonizing about something someone said or something you should do? Through this verse, the Lord promises you that he will be with you every step of the way. He knows what you have to deal with, and he is right there by your side.

Thank you, Jesus, for having my back. May I be reminded of the fact that you always know what I need, and you are with me every step of the way.

DO YOU EVER WORRY? ALLEVIATE YOUR WORRIES BY HANDING THEM OVER TO GOD.

TIPPING POINT

*A word fitly spoken is like apples of gold
in a setting of silver.*
  PROVERBS 25:11 ESV

We've all been there—we're tired, frustrated, stressed, or hungry, and we allow something to tip us over the edge. Out pops a comment clearly *not* like an apple of gold in a setting of silver. It's more like a dirt clod in a setting of slime. And there it sits. We can't take it back. God forgives us and loves us anyway, but before we get to that point, let's try to turn to him for endurance or peace—whatever it takes to represent him in a lovely way.

Heavenly Father, I'm so sorry for the way I allow ugly words to fly out of my mouth when I should have sought your peace. Please help me to recognize when I'm approaching my melt-down temperature and give me the presence of mind to know I need a boost from the Holy Spirit.

WILL YOU TRY TO RECOGNIZE WHEN YOU'RE FEELING A MELT-DOWN APPROACHING? HEAD OFF THE UGLY COMMENTS BY ASKING FOR GOD'S PEACE TO FLOOD YOUR HEART AND MIND IN THAT MOMENT.

ULTIMATE COMFORTER

Praise be to the God and Father of our Lord Jesus Christ, the Father of compassion and the God of all comfort, Who comforts us in all our troubles, so that we can comfort those in any trouble with the comfort we ourselves receive from God.

2 CORINTHIANS 1:3-4 NIV

Most of us have days when we feel like giving up. Loved ones pass away. We get sick. Money doesn't stretch as far as it needs to. Our kids misbehave. Life is so stressful at times that without God, we'd be hopeless. On the flip side, when we have God, we have hope.

Dear God, thank you for being my comforter every single day of my life. Teach me to accept your comforting love graciously and without hesitation. I pray that you'll enable me to share your comfort with others who might need it.

WHAT BRINGS YOU COMFORT DURING DIFFICULT TIMES? WHEN YOU FEEL LIKE GIVING UP, SPEND SOME EXTRA TIME WITH THE LORD AND ASK HIM FOR HIS SUPERNATURAL STRENGTH.

HEALING THE "SICK"

Jesus said, "It is not the healthy who need a doctor, but the sick."

MATTHEW 9:12 NIV

We are certainly not as morally strong as Jesus is, so we do need to take care where we go in life. We have freedom, but we don't want to tread where we might be tempted to sin. Still, we never want to adopt the attitude of the Pharisees, considering certain people too sinful to be reached by Jesus. And sometimes we're the only representative of Jesus people will ever see.

Help me, Lord Jesus, to represent you kindly, in order to show your acceptance of people who may be searching or who may search in the future. Help them remember me as a nonjudgmental Christian. And bless them with an openness to your gift of salvation.

ARE YOU ABLE TO SEE PEOPLE THROUGH GOD'S EYES? ASK GOD TO HELP YOU BE CAREFUL TO WALK IN PURITY AROUND THEM, BUT TO ALSO BE ACCEPTING AND KIND.

TREASURE CHEST

Wherever your treasure is, there the desires of your heart will also be.
  MATTHEW 6:21 NLT

There are so many worldly things that most of us value. We place a tremendous amount of importance on our homes, our cars, our wardrobes, our shoes, and our fancy appliances. Although we need food, shelter, and clothing, we sometimes put more stock in those things than our relationship with the Lord. It's time to rearrange our priorities and put the value back where it belongs.

Jesus, thank you for the many blessings you have provided for my family and me. I pray that you'll enable me to place the proper value on everything and constantly remind me to put you first.

HAVE YOU ALLOWED EARTHLY POSSESSIONS TO BECOME YOUR MAIN TREASURES? CHANGE YOUR ATTITUDE ABOUT EARTH'S TREASURES TODAY AND SEEK OUT THE TREASURES THAT LAST INTO ETERNITY.

REDEMPTION IS NEAR

When these things begin to take place, straighten up and lift up your heads, because your redemption is drawing near.

LUKE 21:28 NASB

These things, referenced by Jesus, are not good—nation against nation, earthquakes, famines, and fearful events. But this is an exciting verse for believers, because Jesus tells us that when they occur, redemption is drawing near. These events have been occurring more and more during our lives. We can take joy and comfort in knowing he is drawing near!

Dear Jesus, I know time as we know it isn't the same as you know it. But when I helplessly watch the news and see what's going on in this sinful world, I do take such comfort in knowing you knew this would be the world's path. You foretold it all, and you assured us that redemption would be near. Come, Lord Jesus!

DOES IT COMFORT YOU, KNOWING THE WORLD'S PATH IS NO SURPRISE TO GOD? LET THE PROMISE OF HIS RETURN BE YOUR JOY TODAY.

THANKS FOR EVERYTHING

Be thankful in all circumstances, for this is God's will for you who belong to Christ Jesus.
1 THESSALONIANS 5:18 NLT

All sorts of things happen to us in our lives, and some of it we don't want to be thankful for because it isn't all good. However, God calls us to give thanks in *all* circumstances, not just those that we are happy about. Gratitude opens our hearts to him, while anger and frustration close us off. Think about this: you need God during those troubling times, and an open, grateful heart is more malleable than one that is closed and hardened. His ultimate goodness is greater than any hardships we will ever face.

Lord, I give thanks to you for everything, even the troubling times that make me cry. May I continue to be grateful to you in all circumstances as I live according to your will.

HAVE YOU EVER FOUND IT DIFFICULT TO BE THANKFUL? GOD IS WITH YOU IN ALL OF YOUR STRUGGLES. THANK HIM FOR HIS PRESENCE AND PEACE DURING YOUR TIME OF TROUBLE.

IT WILL TAKE

"If you hold to my teaching, you are really my disciples. Then you will know the truth, and the truth will set you free."

JOHN 8:31-32 NIV

Some people dabble in faith and then walk away, saying it didn't take. But if their hearts were in the right place—fully open and submissive to accepting Jesus's sacrificial gift—something permanent would happen. The true believers know in their hearts they aren't going to walk away—and God is here to stay.

Thank you, Jesus, for that moment when it all came together for me—my heart, my need, my willingness, and, of course, your constant availability. I pray for that blessing and life-saving moment for everyone on this planet. Please draw all mankind to you so everyone will know that only you can set them free.

WHOSE SALVATION WILL YOU PRAY FOR TODAY? ASK THE HOLY SPIRIT TO PUT SOMEONE ON YOUR HEART AND PRAY FOR THEM TO COME TO THE TRUE KNOWLEDGE OF CHRIST AND HIS WORK ON THE CROSS.

PRUNING YOUR TREE

He cuts off every branch of mine that doesn't produce fruit, and he prunes the branches that do bear fruit so they will produce even more.
JOHN 15:2 NLT

This verse talks about cutting branches that are dead or simply not productive so that all the tree's energy can be put into the branches that bear fruit. There are times in our lives when we need to cut something off because we know it isn't pleasing to God. It may be something that distracts us from worshiping him, or it might be a person who constantly questions our faith. Doing this is rarely easy, but we are rewarded by a more fruitful faith.

Lord Jesus, I have the desire to walk with you every day of my life. No matter how difficult it is, I pray that you will give me the strength to prune the dead branches that pull me away from you.

ARE THERE SOME DEAD BRANCHES THAT YOU NEED TO PRUNE? ASK GOD TO SHOW YOU THE AREAS IN YOUR LIFE THAT HE WANTS YOU TO PUT YOUR ENERGY INTO.

EAGER HANDS

She selects wool and flax and works with eager hands.
PROVERBS 31:13 NIV

We've all heard of the impossibility of being a Proverbs 31 woman, and no one should discourage anyone's efforts to be a Godly woman. But the interesting thing about this verse is the *eager hands* part. How often do our hands clench against the work that lies before us in a day? God asks us to look forward to what we can do for him.

Dear God, I definitely have times when I would just as soon not take on the responsibilities of my day. Those are the times I need special encouragement about the fact that my work is done for you before it is done for anyone else, including me. Thank you for the ability you've given me to do what I do each day.

WILL YOU COMMIT TODAY'S EFFORTS TO GOD? WHEN YOU DO, YOU WILL FIND IT ALL THE MORE FULFILLING. YOU MIGHT EVEN ACTUALLY ENJOY IT.

GOD'S PROVISIONS

Then God opened her eyes and she saw a well of water.
And she went and filled the skin with water and gave
the boy a drink.
    GENESIS 21:19 ESV

God takes care of his followers. His well of mercy and comfort
is always there, waiting for us to drink, but until we see him
as our Father, we are unaware of its presence. As soon as we
accept him, he opens our eyes, bringing the joy of knowing
we have the hope of eternal life with him.

Lord Jesus, thank you so much for opening my eyes to the
well of grace when I was thirsty. May I continue to praise your
goodness that surrounds me every second of my life.

IS THERE SOMEONE IN YOUR LIFE WHO IS THIRSTY FOR
GOD'S GRACE? LEAD THEM TO THE WELL THAT YOU
DRAW FROM EVERY DAY.

THE PRAYERS OF THE RIGHTEOUS

The eyes of the LORD watch over those who do right;
his ears are open to their cries for help.
   PSALM 34:15 NLT

As believers, we are not guaranteed an easier life than anyone else. But if we focus on God's tenets and try to live righteously, making decisions based on his will, we can be guaranteed that he will be more attentive to our prayers for deliverance, healing, and help. The answer to our prayers won't necessarily be what we want, but they will be the result of the Lord's special attention to our needs.

Heavenly Father, I put my life and the lives of my loved ones in your hands. You know my needs and their needs. Help me, please, to walk a righteous path. Thank you that you listen attentively when I pray, and especially so when I am living within your will.

DO YOU EXAMINE YOUR LIFE BEFORE CRYING OUT TO GOD FOR HELP? KNOW THAT HE HEARS YOU NO MATTER WHAT STATE YOU ARE IN, BUT HIS EAR IS ATTENTIVE TO YOUR CRY WHEN YOU ARE WALKING CLOSELY WITH HIM.

GOD'S PLEASURE

He does not delight in the strength of the horse;
He takes no pleasure in the legs of a man.
The LORD takes pleasure in those who fear Him,
In those who hope in His mercy.

    PSALM 147:10-11 NKJV

We don't have to be the strongest or the best at anything to earn God's love. All he asks of us is to respect him, have faith in him, and turn all of our hope toward him. He lets us know each and every day that he loves us, even if we're not the best at our worldly endeavors.

Lord, you are good and mighty. I love you, trust you, and put all of my hope in you. I pray that I continue to delight you each and every day. I know that your love will never fail me.

HAVE YOU EVER TRIED AND FAILED AT SOMETHING?
PUT YOUR HOPE IN GOD AND HE WILL SHOW YOU HIS
DELIGHT IN YOU REGARDLESS OF YOUR FAILURES.

GIVING PROPER THANKS

Let us be grateful for receiving a kingdom that cannot be shaken, and thus let us offer to God acceptable worship, with reverence and awe.

HEBREWS 12:28 ESV

Our taking special time to thank God for our many blessings in life might cause us to reflect on hardships he brought us through. Or needs he satisfied. We know from experience that everything we have can be shaken at any moment, so we are grateful for his goodness and protection. One thing that will never be shaken, though, is the kingdom God has preserved for us. For *that* our thanks should be full of reverence and awe.

Dear God, your goodness and greatness are so hard to fathom. I am in awe of your power and unfailing kindness. Thank you for giving me a place in your unshakeable kingdom. I join my loved ones in thanking you for our earthly and spiritual blessings. May I always appreciate the life you have given me, today and for eternity.

WHAT ARE YOU THANKFUL FOR TODAY?
POUR OUT YOUR THANKSGIVING BEFORE
THE LORD. HE LOVES A GRATEFUL HEART.

COMPLETE

All of you together are Christ's body, and each of you is a part of it.

1 CORINTHIANS 12:27 NLT

Every part of our body is useful and makes us complete. God made us that way, just as he created each of us to be part of the body of Christ. We are not meant to go it alone. As we worship, praise, and honor him, we each have a part in his kingdom.

Heavenly Father, I know that you made me in your likeness, just as you created me to be part of your church. Lead me to what you want me to do in your kingdom here on earth as well as in heaven.

WHAT PART DO YOU PLAY IN THE BODY OF CHRIST? RECOGNIZE TODAY THAT YOU ARE SPECIAL, AND YOU ARE NEEDED!

EVERYTHING WE NEED

His divine power has given us everything we need for life and godliness through our knowledge of him who called us by his own glory and goodness.

2 PETER 1:3 NIV

Peter's book was addressed to believers who were starting to look for more than what they had from the gift of salvation. False prophets were rising up and leading them astray. Peter tells us that all we need for godliness is Christ's divine power, demonstrated by the resurrection. From there we can simply grow to be stronger followers of Christ. No man or woman will add to our spirituality by teaching us from anything that strays from God's Word.

Dear Jesus, thank you for the completeness of your gift of salvation. As I seek to grow as your follower, please give me discernment about my teachers. Help me to compare everything with your Word, to be certain I never stray from what you want me to know.

DOES THE GUIDANCE YOU'RE GETTING SQUARE WITH GOD'S WORD? REMEMBER THAT GOD HAS EVERYTHING YOU NEED TO LIVE A LIFE THAT IS PLEASING BEFORE HIM.

ALL INCLUSIVE

*Everyone who calls on the name of the Lord
will be saved.*

ACTS 2:21 NIV

Can you imagine hopping up every time someone called your name? That's exactly what Jesus does, and he doesn't want to leave anyone out. He is there every moment of every day, listening for us to call him by name. There is always room in Jesus' heart for anyone who has faith in him. He never puts up a *No Vacancy* sign, and he always listens to whatever we need to tell him.

Thank you, Lord Jesus, for opening your heart to me. As I call your name, I know that I am accepted into your mighty kingdom to live with you forever.

WHEN WAS THE LAST TIME YOU CALLED OUT FOR JESUS? SPEND SOME TIME WITH HIM TODAY, THANKING HIM FOR ALWAYS BEING READY TO LISTEN TO YOU.

COMPASSION AGAIN

He will again have compassion on us,
And will subdue our iniquities.
You will cast all our sins
Into the depths of the sea.
MICAH 7:19 NKJV

This verse comes near the end of the Old Testament, and one of the most interesting word choices is the use of *again*. The prophet knew that God's people sin again and again, and he forgives them again and again. The beauty for a believer is in knowing that Jesus' act of salvation did, in fact, hurl our sins to the depths of the sea.

Thank you, Lord Jesus, for cleaning my image with God. As people throughout time have proven, we sin again and again no matter how hard we try to live righteously. Without your final sacrifice on my behalf, there would be no hope for me. I love you.

WILL YOU CONSIDER HIS CONSTANT FORGIVENESS AS YOU START YOUR DAY? HE HAS COMPASSION ON YOU AGAIN AND AGAIN.

DECEMBER

I'll keep coming closer and closer to you,

Lord Yahweh,

For your name is good to me.

I'll keep telling the world of

Your awesome works,

my faithful and glorious God!

PSALM 73:28 TPT

PRICELESS

How priceless is your unfailing love, O God!
People take refuge in the shadows of your wings.
PSALM 36:7 NIV

Everything in this world has a price. The one thing that has already been paid for—one that we don't have to worry about—is the love of God. The most amazing thing is that his love is the most valuable thing we can possess. He is beyond good. He has blessed us and freed us from our sin.

Lord, thank you for your immense goodness. Your gift is immeasurable and beyond anything I can ever comprehend. Your blessings are priceless.

WHAT IS THE MOST VALUABLE GIFT YOU'VE EVER RECEIVED? KNOW THAT NOTHING YOU'VE BEEN GIVEN COMPARES TO THE GIFT OF GOD'S LOVE.

THE MOST IMPORTANT EVENT

*On the day I called, You answered me; You made me
bold with strength in my soul.*
PSALM 138:3 NASB

Depending upon our age, we may or may not remember
when major world events happened: the moon landing, the
fall of the Berlin wall, the attacks on the twin towers, the
election of America's first African-American President. But
assuredly we each remember that moment we called out to
Jesus and he promptly answered us. That event surpasses all
others in our lives. We should feel bold and strong knowing he
resides within us and always will.

*Precious Jesus, thank you for answering my call the moment I
realized I needed you. I ask that you remind me you are with
me whenever I falter and I need your strength and boldness to
follow your will.*

DOES JESUS MAKE YOU FEEL BOLD AND STRONG IN YOUR
SPIRIT TODAY? ASK HIM FOR CONFIDENCE TODAY AND BE
ASSURED THAT HE WILL ANSWER.

BEST PRESENT EVER

When the set time had fully come, God sent his Son, born of a woman, born under law, to redeem those under the law, that we might receive adoption to sonship.

GALATIANS 4:4-5 NIV

God knew that no matter what we did we would always fall short of perfection. In spite of our efforts that could never match up, all we would experience in vying for faultlessness was frustration. So he took it upon himself to show his love by sending his Son who made everyone who had faith in him righteous in his eyes.

God, you and you alone are good. Your gift of love shows us that we have the best Father ever. Never let me forget how awesome your mercy is.

DO YOU TRY YOUR BEST TO LIVE UP TO PERFECTION AND GET FRUSTRATED WHEN YOU FAIL? THERE IS NOTHING YOU CAN DO TO MAKE YOURSELF WORTHY OF GOD'S BLESSING. SO DON'T TRY. JUST THANK HIM FOR HIS GOODNESS AND ACCEPT HIS GIFT OF LOVE.

FROM THE WOMB

You brought me safely from my mother's womb
and led me to trust you at my mother's breast.
I was thrust into your arms at my birth.
You have been my God from the moment I was born.
  PSALM 22:9-10 NLT

The day when he brought us out of the womb was a bit longer ago for some than for others. Whenever each of us was born, God was already working on us, blessing us with innocent trust, caring for us, and drawing us to a loving relationship with him. Some grew up learning about him, and some didn't know about him or seek him for quite some time. Praise God for his patience with each of us!

Heavenly Father, I know you have been my God even during the days when I was ignorant of that fact. Thank you so much for waiting for me to understand my need for you. Thank you for protecting me for so long, while I stumbled through a sinful life and finally fell at your feet.

WHEN DID YOU REALIZE GOD WAS YOUR GOD? THANK HIM TODAY FOR HIS PATIENCE WITH YOU.

HUMBLE BEGINNINGS

While they were there, the time came for the baby to be born, and she gave birth to her firstborn, a son. She wrapped him in cloths and placed him in a manger, because there was no guest room available for them.
LUKE 2:6-7 NIV

God could have sent his Son to live in a castle on earth, but he didn't. He chose a much more humble beginning—something that made Jesus more relatable to the people he came to save. He promises that the joys of his kingdom will come later to those who believe.

Thank you, Lord, for presenting us with a Savior who lived on earth as a humble servant. I pray that I will replicate his humble goodness in my own life.

HOW CAN YOU BE A HUMBLE SERVANT TO OTHERS? BE WILLING TO SET ASIDE SOME OF THE MORE LAVISH BLESSINGS TO BE HIS SERVANT TODAY, AND YOU WILL BENEFIT GREATLY LATER ON.

INVITATION TO A CELEBRATION

"The wedding feast is ready, but those invited were not worthy. Go therefore to the main roads and invite to the wedding feast as many as you find."
MATTHEW 22:8-9 ESV

In this parable, Jesus describes those who rejected his invitation and those who are invited instead. Most consider the original invitees as the Jewish people who rejected him as Messiah. Many consider the alternate guests to be the Gentiles who accept him, and some consider the alternate guests to be those who will come to Christ during the tribulation. Regardless, we're all blessed to receive an invitation!

Dear Jesus, thank you for inviting me to the banquet. And thank you that you will welcome any guests who join me at your celebration. We humbly accept!

IS THERE SOMEONE YOU WANT TO INVITE TO CHRIST'S BANQUET? ASK THE LORD TO MAKE THEIR HEARTS READY FOR THE INVITATION.

INDESCRIBABLE GIFT

They will pray for you with deep affection because of the overflowing grace God has given to you. Thank God for this gift too wonderful for words!
2 CORINTHIANS 9:14-15 NLT

God's generosity is not only indescribable; it is abundant and everlasting. He calls us to be generous givers who are never reluctant to help provide for the needs of others. The amazing thing is we don't have to have much as long as we give in the spirit of Christ. We should never aim to bring glory to ourselves but to God. After all, he is the ultimate provider of all that is good.

I am grateful, God, for your indescribable gift of eternal life with you. I pray that you will guide me to have mercy and grace on others, and that I have the opportunity to give when needed.

WHAT DO YOU HAVE TO GIVE? BE GENEROUS IN YOUR GIVING AS YOU ARE REMINDED OF ALL GOD HAS BLESSED YOU WITH.

BURSTING INTO SONG

Sing for joy, O heavens! Rejoice, O earth! Burst into song, O mountains! For the LORD has comforted his people and will have compassion on them in their suffering.
ISAIAH 49:13 NLT

The affliction mentioned here could apply to so many people from the persecuted Israelites to those who suffer from physical or mental affliction today. It could even apply to those who haven't yet discovered Jesus' offer of salvation. We are all afflicted to some degree, but God's promises and compassion will eventually lead all of his people to shout for joy, rejoice, and burst into song. Sounds like heaven, doesn't it?

Dear God, I know many people who struggle with affliction in their lives. I pray you will show them your compassion now and bring them joy and rejoicing in this life. And if your will is to bring them that comfort in heaven, I humbly look forward to that day.

IS THERE SOMEONE YOU WANT TO PRAY FOR TODAY? ASK GOD TO BLESS AND FILL THEM WITH THE JOY OF HEAVEN. SING A NEW SONG TO THE LORD AS YOU REMEMBER HIS COMFORT AND COMPASSION.

HEAVENLY GIFTS

"A man can receive nothing unless it has been given to him from heaven."

JOHN 3:27 NKJV

Everything we have—from our job skills to the people in our lives—comes from God. He is the one who has blessed us with everything good. And the biggest and most impressive gift of all was his Son who laid his life down so we could live forever with him. This is why we should never forget him and always be generous with our efforts, our time, and our wealth.

Thank you, God, for your heavenly gifts. I pray that you will remind me that everything I have comes from you. Never let me hold onto my blessings so tightly that I seem selfish. I pray that I'll use everything you given me to glorify you.

WHAT ARE SOME OF THE BIGGEST BLESSINGS GOD HAS PROVIDED YOU? SPEND SOME TIME THANKING HIM FOR THOSE BLESSINGS NOW.

BIBLICAL DOCTRINE

Watch your life and doctrine closely.
Persevere in them, because if you do,
you will save both yourself and your hearers.
1 TIMOTHY 4:16 NIV

People who know exactly where they stand on issues always gain more followers than those who waffle. That's one reason why it's a good idea for us to see what God's Word has to say about concerns of the day. When asked what we think about a particular social, political, or ethical problem, we have an opportunity to not only please the Lord with our answer, we have an opportunity to draw someone closer to him.

Dear God, please help me learn how the Bible addresses issues of the day. Help me to recognize points that are backed up by your Word. If there's a way my stance can reflect your will and can make a seeker want you more, I want to be open to your guidance.

ARE YOU ABLE TO SEE BIBLICAL ARGUMENTS FOR TODAY'S ISSUES? WHEN YOU FEEL STRONGLY ABOUT SOMETHING, LOOK FOR YOUR SUPPORT IN GOD'S WORD.

GOOD DEEDS

What good is it, dear brothers and sisters, if you say you have faith but don't show it by your actions? Can that kind of faith save anyone?

JAMES 2:14 NLT

We know that all that is required to be a Christian is the simple act of believing that Christ is our savior. That's the only way we are assured a place in heaven. The Book of James makes the point that our faith comes alive when we live according to God's wishes. That includes doing the right thing and honoring our Father through our good deeds. God's goodness is so great, why wouldn't we want to show our faith through our works?

Lord, I am honored that you have given so much to me. Although I know that I can't earn my way to heaven, I pray that I am able to show my love for you through the deeds I do every day.

WHAT TYPE OF SPIRIT DO YOU HAVE WHEN YOU DO GOOD DEEDS? MAKE IT YOUR GOAL TO BRING HONOR TO THE LORD IN ALL THAT YOU DO.

MAKING BEAUTIFUL MUSIC

*Addressing one another in psalms and hymns and
spiritual songs, singing and making melody to the Lord
with your heart, giving thanks always and for everything
to God the Father in the name of our Lord Jesus Christ.*
EPHESIANS 5:19-20 ESV

Attitudes are infectious. So if we snipe about life, about
fellow Christians, or about our church services or worship
music, how might that infect the experience and growth of
the body? If we keep ourselves open to the uplifting grace
of the Holy Spirit and allow him to sing life's praises through
us, we can be a part of the blessings of God on others. Paul
encouraged us to have this attitude. It's a good one to strive
for and return to over and over again.

*Lord God, please help me to keep my heart open to the Holy
Spirit's grace so that there is music in my heart about you and
your many blessings in my life. I pray that my attitude will
never turn anyone away from you or the joy available through
your love.*

IS YOUR HEART SINGING ABOUT GOD? KEEP IT OPEN TO
HIS GRACE AND LET THE SONG OF JOY WASH OVER YOU.

IT'S ALL GOOD

I know what it is to be in need, and I know what it is to have plenty. I have learned the secret of being content in any and every situation, whether well fed or hungry, whether living in plenty or in want. I can do all this through him who gives me strength.

PHILIPPIANS 4:12-13 NIV

So many people think that being well-to-do is the key to their happiness, but that type of happiness is short-lived. We might enjoy sitting down in front of a five-course meal or buying a designer outfit that costs more than the rest of our entire wardrobe. Then as soon as something else comes along, or we see that someone else has something we want, the joy fades. However, if we find our pleasure in the Lord, our contentment will last. He is the only way to lasting joy.

Thank you, Lord, for giving me the strength to get through whatever circumstances come my way. May I continue to find contentment through your Word and knowing that you are steadfast in your love.

WHAT MAKES YOU HAPPY? FIND YOUR LASTING CONTENTMENT IN GOD TODAY. HIS GOODNESS FAR EXCEEDS ANYTHING MONEY CAN BUY.

THE SHEPHERD

When he saw the crowds, he had compassion on them,
because they were harassed and helpless like sheep
without a shepherd.
MATTHEW 9:36 NIV

Jesus is the shepherd, so if we're feeling lost, confused, or helpless, prayer and his Word are definitely where we'll find direction and power. We can further shore up that direction and power when we associate with a sound church body and a Bible-grounded pastor. When the numbers are committed to following the Lord, there is strength. A loving, friendly church family is a gift from God.

Thank you, Lord Jesus, for being my one true shepherd. You are my source of direction and strength, and I am never alone thanks to you. Thank you, also, for my church family. They are a good source of accountability and love.

DO YOU HAVE A CHURCH FAMILY THAT EDIFIES YOU? MAKE YOURSELF ACCOUNTABLE TO SOMEONE YOU CAN TRUST. IT'S GOOD TO HAVE SOMEONE YOU CAN GO TO FOR PRAYER AND SOUND ADVICE.

KNOWING YOU

*I knew you before I formed you in your mother's womb.
Before you were born I set you apart and appointed you
as my prophet to the nations.*

JEREMIAH 1:5 NLT

No one has known us as long as or as well as God. He
created each of us with a purpose, and he loves his creation.
Based on this, our relationship with God should be close and
intimate, and we should know that he loves us without fail.

*Lord, thank you for having a plan for my life—one that is solely
for me. I am grateful that you chose me. I pray that I never
forget this and that I always keep you in the forefront of my
mind and heart as I go about each day.*

DO YOU EVER FEEL UNQUALIFIED FOR SOMETHING GOD
HAS CALLED YOU TO? IF IT'S HIS PLAN AND PURPOSE
FOR YOU, YOU CAN BE CERTAIN THAT HE WILL GIVE YOU
EVERYTHING YOU NEED TO CARRY IT OUT.

EARTHLY DWELLING

Will God really dwell on earth? The heavens, even the highest heaven, cannot contain you. How much less this temple I have built!
1 KINGS 8:27 NIV

This verse has a lovely, prophetic feel to it. Solomon continued to be amazed at the idea that God could be contained anywhere on earth. And when he asked if God would really dwell on earth, our first thoughts may be of Jesus and how God took human form to dwell on earth with us. How grateful we should be for that!

Thank you, Jesus, for humbling yourself by taking on human form and dwelling on earth to reach us. I can't imagine how wonderful it must have been living here on earth when you walked with men and women. I'm so excited to see you face-to-face.

CAN YOU PICTURE WALKING SIDE-BY-SIDE WITH JESUS? IMAGINE THAT!

DELIGHT AND REJOICE

The LORD your God is with you,
the Mighty Warrior who saves.
He will take great delight in you;
In his love he will no longer rebuke you,
but will rejoice over you with singing.
    ZEPHANIAH 3:17 NIV

This is the ultimate praise verse as it shows his feeling for us. Out of love for us, God is delighted and shows his heart through song. His goodness comes through in his feeling for his creation in us.

Dear Lord, thank you for the mighty praises and the ability to worship you through song that touches the heart and soul of my being. I pray that I will always delight in you as you do me.

HAVE YOU EVER BEEN DEEPLY MOVED BY A SONG? SING PRAISE TO THE GOD WHO IS ALWAYS WITH YOU AND DELIGHTS IN BEING CLOSE TO YOU.

ON ALL OCCASIONS

Pray in the Spirit on all occasions with all kinds of prayers and request. With this in mind, be alert and always keep on praying for all the saints.
EPHESIANS 6:18 NIV

Some of us might think of saints as those *special* believers—the ones who were martyred for their faith, for example. But Paul is exhorting us to pray for each other here. *We* believers are the saints: God's people. All saved through his sacrifice. And we are not given a specific time or reason to pray. God wants us praying about everything, in all circumstances. We are blessed to have a Father who wants constant communication with us.

Dear God, thank you for caring so much about me that you sent your only Son to die for me. If you would do such a thing, it shouldn't surprise me that you care enough to want to hear from me, whether I'm praising you or making requests. It does surprise me, though. Your love and attention are simply unfathomable!

DO YOU SPEAK WITH GOD ALL THROUGH YOUR DAY? HE WANTS TO BE ON YOUR MIND AND IN YOUR HEART IN EVERY MOMENT. THANK HIM FOR HIS GIFT OF RELATIONSHIP.

BEYOND DELIGHTFUL

As it is written, "What no eye has seen, nor ear heard, nor the heart of man imagined, what God has prepared for those who love him."

1 CORINTHIANS 2:9 ESV

As believers, we're promised eternal life with God, but it's difficult to imagine how wonderful it will be. Envision the prettiest garden of flowers and magnify that to an infinite number. Take the feeling you get when you are with your favorite people and intensify the sensations by numbers with more zeroes than you can count. God's goodness on earth is delightful, but what he has waiting for us in heaven is beyond anything we can imagine.

I thank you, Lord, for all the pleasures you have provided for me on earth. I look forward to the day when you call me home to live in the palace that you have prepared for those who love you.

HOW WOULD YOU DESCRIBE YOUR VISION OF HEAVEN? IF NO MIND HAS CONCEIVED IT, IT MUST BE PRETTY IMPRESSIVE!

HIS LIGHT

There will be no night there--no need for lamps or sun-- for the Lord God will shine on them. And they will reign forever and ever.

REVELATION 22:5 NLT

It can be hard to imagine an absence of darkness, an absence of night. We're so used to the bodies we have, needing hours of darkness and sleep on a daily basis, that it might not even sound like a great idea! But that simply shows how little we know about our glorified bodies and the plans God has for eternity. The idea that God, himself, will emanate all the light we need, and that he will be that close to us always, certainly *does* sound like the best idea ever. And ever!

Lord God, I can't imagine and I can't wait for heaven. Thank you that you are so brilliant and will be so present as to provide all the light any of us will need. I love my life here on earth, Lord, but the wonders of eternity with you assure all of us that this life is sorely lacking in comparison. Come soon, Lord Jesus!

HOW DO YOU IMAGINE ETERNAL LIGHT FROM GOD? THERE IS SO MUCH TO PONDER WHEN IT COMES TO OUR ETERNAL DESTINATION. MOST OF ALL, LET IT FILL YOUR HEART WITH LOVE AND HOPE TODAY.

PARENTAL PRIDE

I have no greater joy than to hear that my children are walking in the truth.

3 JOHN 1:4 NIV

Some of the greatest sources of pride that parents have are their children. We often praise their tiniest accomplishments beyond what they deserve, but we are sometimes so proud of them we can't help ourselves. God's joy in us is much deeper than that. He revels in our delight in him and our desire to walk in his truth.

Dear God, thank you for reminding me that I am your child. I want to continue to bring joy to you by staying in your Word, and walking in your truth.

HOW DO YOU FEEL KNOWING THAT YOU BRING JOY TO GOD? LET THAT THOUGHT BRING A SMILE TO YOUR FACE TODAY.

CALL HIM IMMANUEL

*All right then, the Lord himself will give you the sign.
Look! The virgin will conceive a child! She will give birth
to a son and will call him Immanuel (which means 'God
is with us').*

ISAIAH 7:14 NLT

The prophet Isaiah predicted Jesus's birth 700 years in
advance. Among many other names—Resurrection, Life, Lamb
of God, Lord of Lords, Savior, Messiah—Jesus was called
Immanuel which means "God with us." When you consider
the meaning of that name on a personal level, consider that
Immanuel—Jesus—is God with *you*. He chose you and is with
you right now.

*Precious Immanuel, I will never be able to thank you enough
for the sacrifices you made for me. Thank you for humbling
yourself, for coming to us as a perfect child and a living
sacrifice. Thank you for showing me that you are, and always
will be, with me.*

WHAT DO YOU WANT TO SAY TO JESUS—GOD WITH
YOU—TODAY? TELL HIM NOW.

GOD WITH US

"Behold, the virgin shall be with child, and bear a Son, and they shall call His name Immanuel," which is translated, "God with us."
MATTHEW 1:23 NKJV

This verse is a Christmastime favorite for a good reason. It sums up what we know of God sending his Son to earth for us. What a wonderful thing God did! He knows that we are incapable of perfection after the fall of Adam and Eve, and out of his goodness, he has provided our path to heaven.

Oh, Lord, thank you so much for the birth, life, and death of your Son who will forever live with me in my heart. I know that I'll never be alone. I pray that I'll take every opportunity possible to share this love with others.

HOW CAN YOU SHOW YOUR GRATITUDE FOR WHAT GOD HAS DONE FOR YOU? THANK HIM FOR ALWAYS BEING WITH YOU.

HER TREASURE AND OURS

Mary kept all these things in her heart and thought about them often.
LUKE 2:19 NLT

Can we just stop for a moment and consider what life must have been like for Jesus' mother, Mary? Everything about the conception and birth of her Son was out of the ordinary. And although the shepherds marveled at her child, she was soon plunged into confusion about him, and years later she suffered his horrific death. His coming to earth is our celebration, but the cost of our salvation was great for Mary, too. God saw a special woman in her.

Dear Jesus, I can never repay the sacrifice you made for me, and I will thank you for the rest of my life. I thank God for choosing such a strong woman to raise you and to release you to God's will. I have such admiration for the strength with which God blessed your mother. I am so glad she's with you again in heaven.

ARE YOU ABLE TO FATHOM MARY'S SACRIFICE AS JESUS'S MOTHER? GOD WILL ALWAYS GIVE US THE AMOUNT OF GRACE WE NEED IN EACH SITUATION. ALL WE HAVE TO DO IS ASK FOR IT.

BEST CHRISTMAS EVER

After Jesus was born in Bethlehem in Judea, during the time of King Herod, Magi from the east came to Jerusalem and asked, "Where is the one who has been born king of the Jews? We saw his star when it rose and have come to worship him."
MATTHEW 2:1-2 NIV

The magi had to put quite a bit of effort into visiting Jesus. They walked a long way, and they brought gifts to celebrate his birth. This is an example of the effort we should make to show our love to Christ. In God's goodness, he made the ultimate sacrifice that requires nothing from us but faith in him. And we are blessed to be able to celebrate that relationship.

Dear Lord, thank you for the gift of Jesus and the sacrifice you made for me. I pray that I can turn my thoughts away from the external trappings of Christmas and toward the true gift of all: your Son.

HAVE YOU EVER MADE A SACRIFICE SO SOMEONE ELSE COULD HAVE WHAT THEY NEEDED? YOUR GIFT TO OTHERS DOES NOT GO UNNOTICED BY GOD. HE LOVES IT WHEN WE CHOOSE TO HELP OTHERS WITH THE GIFTS HE HAS GIVEN US.

A LITTLE BIT MORE?

Don't wear yourself out trying to get rich.
Be wise enough to know when to quit.
PROVERBS 23:4 NLT

When wealthy American industrialist John D. Rockefeller was asked, "How much money is enough money?" he answered, "Just a little bit more." To his credit, he was a philanthropist, but his example is the exact opposite of what today's verse counsels. There is nothing wrong with being a good steward of our finances; in fact, God commends that. But our spiritual future and those of others are far more enduring and important.

Heavenly Father, I thank you for all of my blessings, including my financial blessings, whatever they may be. Please help me to show wisdom in both my financial stewardship and my sense of priorities. I never want to be in love with money. Rather I want to reserve my love for you, my family, my friends, and those I might draw to you.

ARE YOU ABLE TO TRUST GOD WITH YOUR FINANCES? ASK HIM FOR WISDOM TO STEWARD ALL HE HAS GIVEN YOU WELL.

FOREVER KIND OF LOVE

Praise the LORD!
Oh, give thanks to the LORD, for He is good!
For His mercy endures forever.
  PSALM 106:1 NKJV

Life is filled with all kinds of trouble, pain, and sorrow, but one thing we can all count on is the love of God. Out of his goodness, we can turn to him for comfort, regardless of where we are emotionally, mentally, or physically. Whether we have managed to amass riches or find ourselves dirt poor, he loves us forever.

Heavenly Father, I know you are always good. Although I might not always understand my circumstances, you know what I need, and you provide. May I learn to accept your goodness as you see fit.

HAVE YOU EVER LOOKED BACK ON CIRCUMSTANCES THAT SEEMED DIRE AT THE TIME BUT ULTIMATELY REALIZED GOD'S GOODNESS WAS THERE ALL THE TIME? YOU CAN RELY ON THAT GOODNESS. IT WILL NEVER FAIL.

MORE THAN WORDS

The Samaritan woman said to him, "You are a Jew and I am a Samaritan woman. How can you ask me for a drink?" (For Jews do not associate with Samaritans.)
   JOHN 4:9

Sometimes an unbeliever will recognize a Christian because the Christian makes a point of passing judgment. Or maybe the Christian offers unsolicited prayer or spiritual wisdom. We might mean well, and we may witness sin from which we want to publicly distance ourselves. But the best way to achieve recognition as a Christian is by behaving as Jesus would. An unbeliever might be surprised by, and drawn to, Jesus if our behavior is influenced by him.

Heavenly Father, please guide me to watch my words and let my actions speak more loudly than anything I can say. I pray your love and acceptance will shine through me when I interact with people who don't yet know you.

DO YOU KNOW HOW YOU WOULD DEMONSTRATE CHRIST'S LOVE, RATHER THAN TALKING ABOUT IT? SHOW YOUR LOVE TO OTHERS TODAY, AND IN DOING SO, DRAW THEM TO JESUS!

I LACK NOTHING

Surely your goodness and unfailing love will pursue me all the days of my life, and I will live in the house of the LORD forever.
PSALM 23:6 NLT

One of the most well-known verses in the Bible is the twenty-third psalm, starting with, "The Lord is my shepherd…" There's a very good reason for that. This verse about God's immeasurable goodness is what gives us hope as we travel through life's rugged terrain. No matter how difficult times are, he will lead us down the path that eventually takes us to heaven to live with him forever.

Dear God, I am grateful for your goodness and love that stay with me from the moment I call you my Father, until the day I die, and throughout eternity. Keep me centered on you and give me the power to never stray.

DO YOU FEEL GOD'S HAND IN LEADING YOU TO LIVE WITH HIM? REST IN HIS OVERWHELMING GOODNESS FOR YOU TODAY.

VALUE THE AGED

Stand up in the presence of the aged, show respect for the elderly and revere your God. I am the LORD.
LEVITICUS 19:32 NIV

It is a sad fact about most Western countries—versus those of the East—that we tend to dismiss the value of the elderly, rather than holding them in reverence. If we are blessed to still have our parents and other elders alive, we should make the effort of showing them special love and respect in their later years of life. They often have wisdom to share, but even if their minds falter, the Lord commands that we hold them in esteem.

Lord, thank you for my elders and what they have contributed to my life. Please help me to remember to stay in touch with them, to visit them as often as possible, and always to show respect for them. Please bless my elders, Lord, with good health and a sense of peace through faith in you.

IF YOUR PARENTS ARE ALIVE, DO YOU CALL THEM REGULARLY? MAKE A POINT TO REACH OUT TO YOUR ELDERS TODAY. BLESS THEM AND THANK THEM FOR THEIR ROLE IN YOUR LIFE.

GOD'S GRACE

He has said to me, "My grace is sufficient for you, for power is perfected in weakness." Most gladly, therefore, I will rather boast about my weaknesses, so that the power of Christ may dwell in me.

2 CORINTHIANS 12:9 NASB

God's grace gives us strength through his power to overcome whatever problems we have. Whether the issues are concrete or stress-based, he wants us to rely on his power. Things that we can't control happen in this unsteady, unsure world we live in. However, he is always there for us, so we can put all of our trust in him.

Your grace is the one thing I can count on, oh Lord, and I thank you for that. May I learn to turn to you for comfort in your goodness.

WHAT DO YOU DO WHEN YOU ARE AT YOUR WEAKEST? GOD'S GRACE IS SUFFICIENT FOR EVERY SITUATION YOU FIND YOURSELF IN. CALL OUT TO HIM IN YOUR WEAKNESS AND WATCH HIM MOVE.